CAN I BRING MY PET MONKEY TO WORK?

ANSWERS TO 45 OF THE WILDEST WORKPLACE LAW QUESTIONS

CHARLES T. PASSAGLIA

Can I Bring My Pet Monkey to Work?: Answers to 45 of the Wildest Workplace Law Questions
Published by Employment Law Solutions, Inc.
Litttleton, Colorado

Names: Passaglia, Charles T., author.
Title: Can I bring my pet monkey to work? : answers to 45 of the wildest workplace law questions. / by Charles T. Passaglia.
Description: First trade paperback original edition. | Littleton [Colorado] : Employment Law Solutions, Inc., 2020. | Also published as an ebook. | Appendix included.
Identifiers: ISBN 978-0-578-79106-7
Subjects: LCSH: Labor laws and legislation—United States—Popular works.
BISAC: LAW / Labor & Employment.
Classification: LCC KF3455.Z9 | DDC 344.7301–dc22

Cover and interior design by Victoria Wolf, Wolf Design and Marketing

EMPLOYMENT
LAW SOLUTIONS, INC.

For Sarah, Rachel, Rita and Lucy

CONTENTS

FOREWORD

IF YOU'D ASKED ME for my impression of employment law at the start of my business career, right after I'd completed an MBA, I'd have told you, "dull and bureaucratic – employment law is basically about administering impractical employee manuals and enforcing questionable employment contracts."

Now, well into my business life and as the host of an award-winning podcast through which I've interviewed more than 100 world-class CEOs about their businesses, the words I'd use to describe employment law are "complex, nuanced, and scary."

It's clear to me that every good business leader, and wise employees, should know enough about employment law to be able to stay out of trouble. Following a misguided employee policy, deciding in favor of one employee over another for the wrong reason, perhaps even choosing the wrong words when trying to do the right thing, and even as I learned in this book, telling an employee he or she can't bring a monkey to work, could result in massive distractions and productivity disruptions, the business being blasted in social media or pilloried on Glassdoor, and countless sad hours in lawyers' offices or courtrooms.

It's a fact: Employment law is fraught with danger. Right

and wrong are no longer "common sense." It's not enough to be well-intentioned as even nice people overlook legal complexities, misjudge a workplace scenario, or inadvertently use words that offend.

That's why you should read *Can I Bring my Pet Monkey to Work?*

With entertaining, and what seem at first to be crazy examples to explore each learning topic, *Can I Bring my Pet Monkey to Work?* conditions the reader to think about the context, nuance, and what ifs of work. As a podcast host, it's my job to entertain an audience so that they'll listen and learn. You'll find that Chuck Passaglia has done that for you here.

Dave Tabor
Host, PROCO360

INTRODUCTION

Work is great, except for all the people ...

The exasperated manager looked at me as if he'd just taken a bullet. We were in the middle of a contentious employment dispute that had recently escalated to a full-blown lawsuit. He sighed, looking at me hopelessly, and said, "Work is great, except for all the people."

Many of us feel the same way: love work, hate dealing with the people. And it's often true. People can be the hardest part of work. In 1948, shortly after the launch of the United States' post-war economic juggernaut, Article 23 of the Universal Declaration of Human Rights was adopted by the United Nations General Assembly, declaring that "[e]veryone has the right to work, to free choice of employment, to just and favourable conditions of work." Work was declared a universal human right. However, the Universal Declaration of Human Rights never once mentions the word "happiness."

The pursuit of happiness is an American right. As our Declaration of Independence puts it, an "unalienable Right." No one, not even your boss, can take it away from you. However, pursuing *your* happiness—whatever happiness means to you—can conflict with *others* at work and the objectives of an organization.

This book addresses some of the struggles between management, employees, and co-workers. What can a manager legally do when others fail to meet performance or behavioral expectations, such as disrupting the workplace? Do employees have rights at work of which they may not be aware, even if their behavior is a bit strange, unconventional, or disruptive? What happens when an employer's expectations and an employee's rights conflict?

As examples of conflicts that can arise today, ask yourself, which of these are okay to say or do in the workplace?

Shari says she was fired for voting for her candidate in the last election.

Mary can't afford childcare, so she insists on bringing her children to work.

That's nothing, Bob brings his pet monkey to work.

Andy constantly uses annoying expressions like "damn skippy" and "putting lipstick on a pig." Surely, there must be some place in Hell waiting for him.

Speaking of Hell, Alice complains she is required to pray with her boss every morning.

Damien, on the other hand, casts evil spells on his co-workers.

Bob reeks of horrible body odor which casts an even greater spell over his co-workers.

Even worse, Stan brings bad-smelling food to work and leaves it in the fridge for days.

Tina is sad all the time, which is sad.

Martin is happy all the time, which is annoying.

People are great . . . except when they are not. The vast majority of people don't harass a co-worker or discriminate on the basis of race, religion, sex, or sexual orientation, but some do. People are usually reasonable but at times can be emotional, messy, and extremely unpredictable. Some are terribly unhappy. Others can be too damned happy, and still others are barely tolerable. Some people thrive on chaos and drama. Others are company men and women toiling in blissful anonymity as proverbial cogs in the machine. Some people don't like you, don't trust you, or are at odds with you for seemingly no reason at all. Like cats.

This book is about employment law. But it's really about people . . . and the protections they have (or don't have) at work. At least until computers, robots and artificial intelligence take all our jobs. How far away is that, exactly? Far enough, for most of us. In the meantime, we still work. So let's make the most of it!

I hope this book offers a different perspective about work, because most of us spend more waking hours at work than any other place. Work can make you feel great about yourself and your accomplishments, or it can literally snuff the life out of you. At the end of this book, you may even realize that you don't have it so bad or, better yet, you may discover a renewed passion to make work better for yourself and others.

Can I Bring my Pet Monkey to Work? is intended to make

you a little smarter and help you navigate workplace craziness—all in less than the time it takes to fly from New York to L.A. I've filled this book with cases from the trenches. As a workplace lawyer for what seems like 300 years, I've represented dozens of clients, delivered educational seminars to hundreds of employees, and answered thousands of questions. Just when you think you've seen it all, though, you realize you can't possibly have seen it all. But I have, in fact, seen a great deal in more than 25 years.

You should read this book if you, too, have ever seen, heard, asked, or been asked about something weird at work and wondered what is the legal answer. We might agree that the best way to learn is by correcting our own mistakes. But the second-best way to learn may just be to laugh at other people's mistakes and learn from them.

This book is intended to help you learn comfortably how work really works.

The situations described in this book reflect the difficult, and often confusing, people issues in the workplace and work law, which is a witch's brew of complex federal, state, and local laws, slathered with a generous helping of employer-sponsored rules, policies, and procedures, all roiling over a fire stoked by business's seemingly unbridled quest for "results," or a "bigger bottom line," whatever the costs.

To borrow from William Shakespeare, when all is said and done, we are all just "warriors for the working day." Interestingly, the term "warrior" is derived from an Old French word, werre, meaning "confusion." And that sums up much of our experience at work today! This book is for you: the workplace warriors, cubicle commandos, and corporate cannon fodder, who have engaged in battles with the forces of darkness at work—discrimination, harassment, and jerks.

So grab your copy of this book, take it to work, and even read it out loud to educate and entertain your co-workers.

DISCLAIMER

This book does not, and is not intended to, constitute legal advice. And monkeys can be dangerous. All content is for informational purposes only and may not be the most up-to-date legal information, or may be overturned by a subsequent legal development, especially if the book sits on your shelf for a few years or you drop your e-reader in a lake. Contact an attorney to obtain advice with respect to a particular legal matter. Do not rely on the information in this book without first seeking legal advice from an attorney in the jurisdiction where you live or work. Finally, I am not your attorney and this book is not engaging in the practice of law. The receipt of, or reliance on, the information in this book, or laughing while reading it, does not establish an attorney-client relationship between the reader and me.

PART I

EEO: IT'S THE LAW

1

ARE BLONDES A PROTECTED CLASS?

The Scope of Anti-Discrimination Laws

A Russian, an American, and a blonde were talking one day. The Russian said, "We were the first in space!" The American said, "We were the first on the moon!" The blonde said, "So what? We're going to be the first on the sun!" The Russian and the American looked at each other and shook their heads. "You can't land on the sun, you idiot! You'll burn up!" said the Russian. To which the blonde replied, "We're not stupid, you know. We're going at night!"

"DUMB BLONDE" IS A UNIQUELY American expression. The war on blondes may have started in 1925, with the publication of Anita Loos's bestselling comic novel *Gentlemen Prefer Blondes: The Intimate Diary of a Professional Lady*, which popularized the notion that attractive blondes needed little else to turn men into silly putty. Marilyn Monroe, who was neither dumb nor truly blonde, capitalized on the stereotype to attain career success in the film adaptation of *Gentlemen Prefer Blondes* and, again, in *How to Marry a Millionaire* and *Some Like it Hot*. The stereotype has since spawned countless "dumb blonde" jokes and, while women more often bear the brunt of these particular jokes, blonde men are frequently included in similar negative stereotyping of "dumb jocks" and "surfer dudes."

Despite the negative characterization of blondes, having golden hair is not likely protected at work. However, the law in this area is evolving rapidly.

To be protected under U.S. civil rights laws, an individual must be a member of a "protected class" carved out by federal, state, or local law. Following the passage of the Civil Rights Act of 1964 (Title VII), the recognition of protected groups in the workplace has been an ever-expanding universe. Federal and most states' laws define those protected classes based on race, color, religion, national origin or ethnicity, gender, age if 40 or older, Reserve and Guard status, physical and mental disability, veteran status, and genetic information (including family health history). In addition, sexual orientation, gender identity and expression, and marital status are included under many state and local laws.

Hair color, alone, is not protected at work. Brigitte Shramban identified herself as a "blond, white, Jewish female from [the former Soviet republic of] Moldavia." I know, it already sounds like this story could go in several different directions. She complained, among other things, that her supervisor harassed her with discriminatory comments about being blond and openly shared his opinions about the "only way to tell a natural blond" and what "other people say" about blondes. Weeks later, Shramban's employer, Aetna, Inc., transferred her to another position in a different facility but at the same pay. She considered her involuntary transfer a demotion, so Shramban brought a lawsuit, alleging unlawful harassment in violation of Title VII.

Shramban complained that her supervisor's inane comments about her hair color were both sexist, meaning biased towards women, and sexual, such as prurient statements about his ability to discern a blonde's "natural" hair color. In a lengthy opinion, a federal trial court in Pennsylvania made short work of Shramban's claim. A boss's jerk-like behavior is not enough to constitute harassment. Among the many elements necessary to establish a claim of sexual harassment is proof of mistreatment *because* of one's membership in a protected group. The court rejected her claim with a single sentence: "We also note that being blonde is not a protected group under Title VII." Furthermore, although the supervisor's comments were boorish and unprofessional, "simple teasing" and isolated "offhand comments" were not sufficiently severe or pervasive to alter the conditions of a person's job and create a hostile or abusive work environment. The decision in favor of the employer was upheld on appeal.

Being blonde, though, might possibly be protected under a different factual scenario.

How? If an employer has a stated preference for hiring only blonde applicants, then the employer may intentionally prevent the employment opportunities of applicants who are not blonde. Many racial and ethnic groups have disproportionately fewer members with blonde hair, such as Blacks, Asians, and Hispanics/Latinx. Therefore, the failure to hire any dark-haired persons could result in a viable "disparate impact" (or "adverse impact") discrimination claim based on an applicant's race or ethnicity. Adverse impact is a theory of discrimination in which members of a protected group show that an apparently neutral employment practice or policy—in this case, "blondes only"—has a disproportionately negative *effect* on members of one protected class, e.g., Asians, as compared with those who are not members of that class, e.g., Caucasians.

Professor D. Wendy Greene, a law professor at Drexel University's Kline School of Law, is among the growing group of legal scholars who have lamented that workplace protections have not gone far enough to link a person's hair color (and certain other variable conditions) with racial and ethnic identity. In her article, "Title VII: What's Hair (And Other Race-Based Characteristics) Got To Do With It?" published in the *University of Colorado Law Review*, Professor Greene argued that courts should abandon the traditional legal syllogism necessary for workplace protection: U.S. civil rights laws protect only "immutable" characteristics, such as race, skin color, national origin, and gender; hair color is not an immutable characteristic but, rather, is quite changeable; therefore, hair color is not protected under Title VII.

Professor Greene takes another view. Hair color, clothing styles, and language patterns are inextricably intertwined with a person's race and ethnicity. Therefore, the courts' blanket approval of employers' restrictive dress codes and appearance standards stigmatize applicants and employees based on race and ethnicity by prohibiting or otherwise limiting their hair styles, hair length, and hair color, even though those characteristics may otherwise be mutable.

More recently, in her 2011 article, "Black Women Can't Have Blonde Hair . . . in the Workplace," published in the *Journal of Gender, Race and Justice*, Professor Greene focused specifically on the few cases involving adverse treatment of Black women who had blonde hair. She argues that arbitrary appearance standards at work, which hold a Black woman's unnatural blonde hair color against her, are the perpetuation of an "invisible norm of white womanhood and beauty." Black women, suggests Greene, must suffer the consequences when they tread into "visibly white" territory by wearing blonde hair. Conversely, employers have been permitted to prohibit natural hairstyles which are deemed "visibly Black," such as braids, twists, and dreadlocks.

Professor Greene pointed to the case of Andrea Santee. Santee, who is Black, applied for a job as a housekeeper at Windsor Court Hotel in New Orleans. She dyed her hair blonde, which became the key issue in her prospective hire. In her interview, Santee was informed by the executive house-keeper that the hotel's grooming policy prohibited "extremes" in hair color. Asked whether she would be willing to change her hair color if she was offered a job, Santee said no and, as a result, was not offered the job.

Santee filed a complaint in the federal district court in New Orleans, alleging that the Windsor Court Hotel engaged in racial discrimination when it refused to hire a Black applicant because of her blonde hair color. The court rejected her claim. According to the court, hair color was not an immutable condi-tion. Therefore, Santee was not protected on the basis of her blonde hair color. The hotel had informed her of its policy (no "extremes" in appearance) during the hiring process. Although limiting "extremes" in appearance is a subjective assessment, observed the court, employers can set unique standards of appearance for their business. The court was also influenced, no doubt, by the fact that every housekeeper hired by the hotel during the relevant time period was Black. This reinforced the court's view that Santee's hair color, rather than her race, was the determinative factor in the refusal to hire her.

This result doesn't mean one's hair is not protected at work.

In perhaps the fastest-moving employment protection of the recent past, New York City amended its Human Rights Law in February 2019 specifically to protect the right of residents to maintain natural hair or hairstyles that are closely associated with their racial, ethnic, or cultural identities. In July 2019, the "Create a Respectful and Open World for Natural Hair," or CROWN Act, was signed into California law and became effective January 1, 2020. The CROWN Act specifically protects hair texture, hair type, and hairstyles commonly or historically associated with race, such as braids, dreadlocks, twists, tight coils or curls, cornrows, Bantu knots, Afros, and headwraps. New York and New Jersey also passed the CROWN Act in 2019. The impetus for New Jersey's passage of the law may have been a humiliating December 2018 incident in which a 16-year-old high school wrestler's dreadlocks were forcibly cut before he was allowed to wrestle his opponent. In 2020, Virginia, Colorado, and Washington enacted the CROWN Act, and 20 more states were considering the legislation. A federal CROWN Act has been introduced which would make the protection federal law.

If you still think it's safe to tell dumb blonde jokes, or to otherwise engage in similar stupid behaviors at work, then consider the novel legal theory underlying the decision of the Washington Court of Appeals in *Strong v. Terrell*. Humiliating anyone, for any reason, can lead to serious legal problems. Gina Strong, a school district employee in Washington, complained that her supervisor, James Terrell, verbally abused her daily by screaming at her and criticizing her work in a sarcastic, unprofessional manner. He pointedly told "blonde jokes" and made fun of Strong by ridiculing her about her personal life. Terrell disparaged the house she purchased and her husband's job. He said to her that her son was going to find out she was a "bum" mother because she placed him in therapy. The verbal abuse caused Strong to vomit frequently and suffer anxiety attacks and heart palpitations. She filed a complaint of "harassment" against Terrell in 2002. Under the weight of an investigation into his behavior, Terrell resigned in April 2004, an event which might have afforded Strong some relief. Nonetheless, Strong quit her job in August 2004 and brought a lawsuit against her employer and former supervisor.

Strong never alleged her supervisor sexually harassed her or his conduct created a hostile work environment based on her gender. Instead, she brought state tort claims for "intentional infliction of emotional distress," also known as "outrage" under Washington state law, and "negligent infliction of emotional distress." After the trial court dismissed her claims, Strong appealed to the Washington Court of Appeals. The appeals court issued its decision in 2008.

Proving outrage is a lofty legal standard: A victim must show behavior "so outrageous in character, and so extreme in degree, as to go beyond all possible bounds of decency, and to be regarded as atrocious, and utterly intolerable in a civilized community." The appellate court concluded the verbal insults, including the dumb blonde jokes, did not exceed "all possible bounds of decency," therefore agreeing with the lower court and rejecting the claim of *intentional* infliction of emotional distress.

However, *negligent* infliction of emotional distress is a different legal claim that is allowed in many states, and the burden of proof is much lower. For this claim, an alleged victim like Strong need only show the existence of a duty of care, a breach of the reasonable standard of such care, misconduct that proximately caused her injury, and that damages occurred. Personality disputes at work are usually not enough to constitute a violation of the standard of care. Here, though, among the many offenses directed her way, Strong alleged that Terrell continuously made demeaning comments and jokes about her blonde hair color until she dyed it brown. The Washington appeals court reversed the trial court's dismissal of this claim and remanded the claim to the trial court for a jury to consider the merits of a claim of negligent infliction of emotional distress claim.

While harassing blondes is not right, and could be unlawful in some situations, one thing remains certain: Lawyers are not protected under any law.

A blonde traveler was sitting next to a lawyer on an airplane flight. The lawyer kept bugging the blonde with his demands they play a game testing their intelligence. Finally, the lawyer offers the blonde an incredible bet to get the blonde to play: Every time the blonde can't answer one of his questions, the blonde would owe him $5.00; however, every time he can't answer one of the blonde's questions, he would pay her $50.00. The lawyer figured he couldn't lose, and the blonde reluctantly accepted the bet.

The lawyer first asked, "What is the distance between the Earth and the nearest star?"

Without saying a word, the blonde handed him $5.00.

The blonde than asked, "What goes up a hill with three legs and comes back down the hill with four legs?"

The lawyer was puzzled. He took the remainder of the flight looking up everything he could on his laptop and even placing numerous air-to-ground phone calls to his staff trying to find the answer. Finally, angry and frustrated, he gave up and paid the blonde $50.00.

The blonde accepted the $50.00 without comment, but the lawyer insisted, "What is the answer to your question?"

Without saying a word, the blonde handed him $5.00.

2

IS BEING UGLY PROTECTED AT WORK?

Appearance Discrimination

IN HER FASCINATING BOOK, *Survival of the Prettiest: The Science of Beauty* (Anchor 2000), Harvard Medical School professor Nancy Etcoff argues convincingly that appreciation of physical beauty is the biological product of natural selection and has been prized in nearly every civilization. For Professor Etcoff, wearing high heels is not only a modern fashion statement, but it also plucks a biological chord in many men by accentuating a woman's breasts and buttocks and thereby signaling her fertility. Even babies have been shown to gaze much longer upon the symmetrical beauty of an attractive person's face. As a matter of biology, and not just cultural preferences, she reasons, good-looking people may be better equipped to survive, find advantageous partners for themselves, and propagate the species.

Today, surveys consistently show that "beautiful people" also rule the world of work. Attractive men and women are more likely to be hired, less likely to be fired, and are often paid significantly more than their less attractive co-workers. Tall, handsome men, in particular, are most likely to earn more than all of their male or female counterparts.

Appearance discrimination is the legal term commonly used to describe bias in favor or against a person's physical appearance. Some also rely on the expressions "beauty bias" or "lookism," particularly to highlight discrimination against unattractive persons. Psychologists have even identified a fear of ugliness, known as cacophobia.

Civil rights laws protect applicants and employees based on certain "immutable," meaning unchanging or fixed, characteristics. Title VII protects a person's race, color, national origin, religion, and sex. The Age Discrimination in Employment Act of 1967 added one's age, when 40 or older, to employment protections. The Americans with Disabilities Act of 1990 protects qualified individuals with a disability.

Even though beauty is often described as timeless and, frequently, "ugly goes clean to the bone," physical appearance, or the lack of an attractive physical appearance, is not specifically protected under federal law. Therefore, technically, an individual's appearance can be held for or against them. This is why the attractive members of the Kardashian family—who are "famous for being famous" and little else—have amassed a lucrative global entertainment, clothing, and beauty products empire and, on the other end of the spectrum, people who look like I do have to be funny!

Beauty bias, though, can still create problems for employers. In fact, some lawsuits have flirted with the question of whether appearance is protected at work. Most of these cases are "traditional" discrimination claims in which aspects of a worker's physical looks were the basis for a claim of race, gender, religious, or disability discrimination.

In 2003, for example, a librarian sued her employer, Harvard University, claiming she'd been passed over sixteen times for promotion because she was Black, just a "pretty girl," and wore attire too "sexy" for work, such as low-cut blouses and tight pants. In August 2005, a federal court concluded she had not experienced any unlawful discrimination based on her race or gender.

In another well-publicized case, *Yanowitz v. L'Oreal USA, Inc.*, Elysa Yanowitz refused to follow her male supervisor's repeated orders to fire a female sales associate because she was not sexually attractive, or "hot" enough, to sell the company's products. Yanowitz claimed she was retaliated against and forced to resign for not firing her "unattractive" co-worker. In 2005, the California Supreme Court held that Yanowitz could have reasonably believed that the order was unlawful sex discrimination since the manager held women to a different appearance standard than men in the company. The Court allowed the case to go to trial.

In 2010, the U.S. Court of Appeals ruled that a "tomboy" with an "Ellen Degeneres kind of look" who was denied a front desk position at an Iowa hotel solely because she wasn't "pretty" and lacked the "Midwestern girl look" met the burden for bringing a gender discrimination claim against her former employer.

On the other hand, an employee could be fired for being too attractive. Melissa Nelson, a dental assistant, was fired by her employer, Dr. James Knight, for being "too beautiful and irresistible." Nelson and Knight worked together for more than a decade and had established a personal friendship, at least until Dr. Knight's wife saw some of the texts between Nelson and Knight. Knight's wife demanded he fire Nelson immediately because she was a "big threat" to their marriage. Dr. Knight complied and, with his pastor present, fired Nelson while reading from a prepared statement that their relationship had become a detriment to Dr. Knight's family (as in, "my wife is really pissed off"). Nelson brought a gender discrimination claim against Dr. Knight, alleging that she was fired only because she was female, and he never would have treated a male employee the same way. Nelson lost. In 2013, the Iowa Supreme Court ruled that Nelson wasn't fired because of her gender or her attractiveness. She was fired because Knight's wife was jealous and demanded Nelson be fired to preserve their marriage. Although it may not have been fair to fire Nelson because she was an attractive distraction, it was not illegal. Had Mrs. Knight demanded that Dr. Knight not hire or fire all female employees, it might have been easier to show gender was a motivating factor in Dr. Knight's decision-making.

By far, though, Abercrombie & Fitch, the trendy youth clothing retailer, has faced almost every style of appearance discrimination claim. It's not hard to see why: Appearance matters at Abercrombie. The company maintains a formal "Look Policy" which details what employees can, and cannot, wear to work. The policy has been challenged, and amended, frequently. In 2004, the company paid $40 million to settle a class action lawsuit claiming that it discriminated in favor of hiring mostly white male—or, in A&F parlance, "All-American"—applicants for its sales positions to the exclusion of Blacks, Hispanics/Latinx, and Asians. In 2015, Abercrombie & Fitch was rocked by the U.S. Supreme Court ruling that the company may have violated Title VII when it refused to hire a job applicant because she wore a hijab, the traditional head scarf worn by Muslim women, to her interview. Abercrombie had been sued previously, and settled similar religious claims, yet pressed forward to the Supreme Court. A month after its loss, the company settled the case by paying $25,670 in damages to Samantha Elauf. Also in 2015, a California court certified a class action lawsuit brought by 62,000 current and former Abercrombie employees alleging that the Look Policy, which required employees to wear Abercrombie's clothes, without reimbursement, violated state labor standards for paying the costs of uniforms. In 2018, Abercrombie settled the case with a $25 million payment, including $7.5 million in plaintiffs' attorneys' fees.

So, can an employer just hire the better-looking candidate, whether male, female, white, Black, Asian, Hispanic/Latinx, Greek, Christian, Muslim, Buddhist, Hasidic Jew, gay, or straight? Yikes, let's slow down! Remember the employee who wasn't selected for a position because she looked more like comedian and talk show host Ellen Degeneres than a "pretty Midwestern girl?" A decisionmaker who relies on an idealized positive or negative stereotype for determining physical beauty may unwittingly step into unlawful racial, gender, ethnic, religious, or disability discrimination. Preferring blondes over brunettes, or both over redheads, may not itself be unlawful discrimination. But refusing to hire a woman with very short hair, like Ellen Degeneres, because you believe that she looks too "masculine," could create a claim of unlawful gender stereotyping. The same goes for associating ideals of beauty with a particular race or ethnicity and making employment decisions that reinforce this conscious, or even unconscious, bias. Or refusing to consider an otherwise qualified applicant wearing religious garb or with a disfiguring facial scar following surgery to remove a cancerous tumor—a potential disability—because the employer believes it is unpresentable to customers or clients.

Also, there are a few jurisdictions that protect applicants and employees from appearance discrimination. Most notably, the State of Michigan, the District of Columbia, and the City of San Francisco, California, specifically prohibit employment discrimination based on height or weight.

Looks can and do matter in business, and the law recognizes reasonable business judgment in this area. For example, employers can establish reasonable dress codes and professional appearance standards. In very narrow circumstances, a certain "look" can even be a bona fide occupational qualification (BFOQ) for the job. The "breastaurant" chain Hooters, which features only scantily clad women as servers, has insisted for decades, and defended itself vigorously and successfully, that it is primarily selling "feminine sex appeal" to its diners, not burgers and beers. However, the exact same argument failed earlier when a struggling new airline, Southwest Airlines, tried to sell a sexy "love" image to its predominately male passengers by insisting all of its flight attendants be young, attractive women. The court ruled that flight attendants are hosts and safety managers in flight; being female, young, and attractive to male passengers are not essential for the position. In the end, all that matters is whether the employee can do the job well and further the legitimate interests of an employer without relying on unlawful stereotypes.

3

WHY CAN BLACK EMPLOYEES USE THE N-WORD BUT WHITE EMPLOYEES CAN'T?

Racial Discrimination

THESE ARE STRANGE DAYS, indeed, but one thing is certain for anyone who goes to work: Using offensive racial epithets can get you fired immediately.

On May 29, 2018, ABC Entertainment canceled the hit television program "Roseanne"—effectively firing the entire cast and crew—after the show's star, Roseanne Barr, tweeted on her personal Twitter account that Valerie Jarrett, a Black former senior advisor to President Barack Obama, was from the "Planet of the Apes." The U.S. Equal Employment Opportunity Commission (EEOC) has long held the position that a degrading comparison of a person to an animal—such as comparing a Black person to a monkey—can be sufficiently severe to constitute unlawful racial harassment.

More than a decade earlier, on April 12, 2007, after a speedy trial and summary execution of his reputation by the national media, legendary "shock jock" Don Imus was fired by his employer, CBS Radio, for being insensitive. Imus had made a long career of saying insensitive things on the radio and was, in his view, being himself when he referred to members of the Rutgers University women's basketball team as "nappy-headed hos" on his nationally syndicated talk radio program the day after the Rutgers women lost the NCAA basketball championship game. All the starting players on the team were Black; Imus is white. Imus's remark, and subsequent termination, were tabloid and talk radio fodder for months. Noted civil rights leaders, including Al Sharpton and Jesse Jackson, demanded Imus's termination. Then-Senator Barack Obama, who at the time was a mere presidential hopeful, called for Imus's immediate ouster. Senator Obama previously had been a guest on Imus's radio program without apparent objection to the format of the show or his insensitive yakking on the airwaves. To their credit, Imus later said publicly he regretted making the remarks, and the Rutgers University women's basketball team publicly forgave Imus. Rutgers head coach C. Vivian Stringer even offered public condolences to his family upon Imus's death in 2019.

I am asked this question frequently: Does the law treat whites and Blacks differently when it comes to the n-word?

A few months after Don Imus's famous career meltdown, Tom Burlington sought an answer to this question . . . the hard way. Like Imus, Burlington is white. Also, like Imus, Burlington was a media personality, but on a much smaller scale. He was a news anchor and reporter at WTXF Fox 29 television station in Philadelphia, Pennsylvania. On June 23, 2007, in an editorial meeting, during which the news team was discussing a story about a local branch of the NAACP holding a symbolic mock burial for the n-word, Burlington asked, "Does this mean we can finally say the word 'nigger?'" Three of the nine persons in the meeting were Black, including Nicole Wolfe, who responded, "I can't believe you just said that!" No one who attended the meeting complained that Burlington had used the word in a pejorative or malicious sense. Burlington later apologized to everyone who attended the meeting. However, Joyce Evans, Burlington's co-anchor, who is Black and did not attend the meeting (but apparently heard about it later), allegedly confronted Burlington by saying, "Because you're white, you can never understand what it's like to be called a nigger, and you cannot use the word 'nigger.'"

Burlington was suspended two days later, after he allegedly continued to use the n-word in subsequent meetings in which he was asked to explain what happened in the first meeting. Burlington was fired less than two weeks later—despite already having gotten a final warning for the incident—after the matter was leaked to the local media and a number of media outlets ran negative stories about Burlington's behavior.

Burlington fought back. In May 2009, he brought a "reverse" race discrimination claim against his former employer. He alleged that a racial double-standard existed at his television station, claiming he was fired for conduct for which Black employees would not be fired. Burlington specifically cited the station manager's failure to fire a Black employee who repeatedly used the n-word in e-mails to management describing Burlington's actions. Burlington also alleged that his co-worker, Joyce Evans, influenced the decision to terminate him when she telephoned the station's head of Human Resources days before his firing to express her "concern" that "people on the street" were offended by Burlington's behavior.

Acknowledging that this issue had not been decided by the federal courts, the trial court proposed the question for its consideration as follows: "Can an employer be held liable under Title VII for enforcing or condoning the social norm that it is acceptable for African Americans to say 'nigger' but not whites?" In late 2010, the court ruled in favor of Burlington, denying his employer's motion for summary judgment, and allowed his claim against the television station to advance to a jury trial. In 2015, when the case finally went to trial, however, it took only three hours for the jury to determine that Burlington was not a victim of race discrimination when it ruled in favor of the television station.

Very few people took interest, but a year after Imus's and Burlington's high-profile terminations, WAAY-TV, in Huntsville, Alabama, fired veteran TV news anchor Michael Scott after he referred to his producer, Jabaree Prewitt, as a n-word during a commercial break on the news set. Mr. Prewitt is Black. However, Mr. Scott, the offending party, is also Black. No one criticized Mr. Scott's termination for his single, apparently isolated, use of the n-word.

The reality is that anyone—regardless of race— can be fired for using the n-word at work.

Interestingly, in July 2008, movie star and television personality Whoopi Goldberg explained to a national television audience on the program she moderated at the time, *The View*, that Black people should be able to say the n-word, but white people should not. Ms. Goldberg was defending Reverend Jesse Jackson, who had recently used the term while describing then-presidential candidate Barack Obama's propensity to "talk down" to persons of color. Reverend Jackson previously had encouraged the firing of Imus for his use of the n-word and his general insensitivity towards persons of color. Goldberg's support for the use of the n-word by Black persons prompted not only disagreement, but even tears, from her co-host, Elizabeth Hasselbeck. Hasselbeck is white. Hasselbeck believed the n-word should never be used.

These and other examples prompt endless questions: Should a white employee be fired for using the n-word at work? Should the white employee be fired when Black employees can use the same word? What if the employee used the n-word only one time and promised to refrain from using it in the future? Is it really different, as Whoopi Goldberg suggested, when a Black employee uses the n-word? Is it ever okay for anyone to use the n-word at work?

Goldberg raised some points worthy of discussion in the public domain: Is there a place for the n-word and, if so, is it only Black persons who should be able to use it?

Any person who has an interest in learning about race relations in America, would do well to read *Nigger: The Strange Career of a Troublesome Word* by Harvard Law School professor Randall Kennedy. In the first paragraph of his book, Professor Kennedy raises the same questions in the workplace context: "Should Blacks be able to use 'nigger' in ways forbidden to others?" and "Under what circumstances, if any, should a person be ousted from his or her job for saying 'nigger'?"

Without specifically answering these questions, Professor Kennedy takes a fascinating and sober look at the historical use of the n-word in our society. Professor Kennedy raises some thought-provoking notions. The term has a long history of denoting denigrated status—what Professor Kennedy refers to as the "paradigmatic racial slur" in the English language. The word has migrated to other racial group members, such as use of the offensive terms "sand-nigger" or "nigger-lover."

Professor Kennedy also raises the point that scores of prominent whites have used the n-word in casual speech yet, at the same time, were the leading civil rights advocates of their day.

He cites Abraham Lincoln, Harry S. Truman, and Lyndon Johnson as examples of men who used the n-word but who also greatly advanced the rights of Blacks in America.

Interestingly, Professor Kennedy distinguishes the n-word from what he calls "nigger-as-insult," that is, the vile racial epithet. The use of the n-word by whites and other non-Blacks is often a form of insult or psychological warfare against Blacks or, in its adapted form, members of other racial groups.

Professor Kennedy contrasts the myriad other uses of the term from his perspective as a Black man. According to Professor Kennedy, the n-word is used by Blacks as a "rhetorical boomerang" against racism—as a form of comic relief or social commentary among Black entertainers to describe their social condition, as an expression of affinity among Blacks, and even as a racial dividing line among Blacks who purposely use the n-word to set themselves against Blacks who refuse to use the term. In other words, among Blacks, the n-word is used to separate the more "authentic" representatives of the group.

Given the many meanings of the term, some of which are contradictory, consideration of the word's use nearly always requires interpretation. Even among Blacks, use of the n-word must be taken in context.

Professor Kennedy's thesis may resonate with many Americans. My father is the son of Italian immigrants to America. In my father's own life experience, if a person who was not an Italian American referred to him as a "dago," "guinea," or "wop," he was quick to take offense. If a fellow Italian American said to him, "we wops have to stick together," however, their brotherhood would have been sealed and "wop" worn as a "badge of honor." Same word, different context.

Let me give you another real example. If a male employee refers to his female co-worker as a "bitch," most women at work would take offense (and it is possible the male employee could lose his job). At the same, a woman who uses the word "bitch" to describe other women, including complete strangers, may not raise any objection. While "bitch" is a tremendously uncomfortable word to hear, it is less common for women to object to another woman's use of the term to describe another woman. Why? Again, context matters.

Clearly, use of the n-word or, in Imus's case, "nappy headed hos," can constitute evidence of racial bias under Title VII. The fact that one Black employee refers to another Black employee by the n-word does not necessarily insulate the speaker from being challenged by an offended co-worker. There is no "it's-part-of-my-culture" defense to claims of unlawful harassment.

Context is critical in assessing offensive behavior at work. In particular, the U.S. Supreme Court has emphasized the importance of understanding and evaluating context in discrimination cases.

Every employee might be best to heed the lesson of *Ash v. Tyson Foods Inc.*, a brief, otherwise unremarkable 2006 Supreme Court decision. The Supreme Court considered the straightforward case of two African American employees who alleged racial discrimination after they were passed over for promotions at a Tyson Foods poultry plant in Gadsden, Alabama, in favor of arguably lesser-qualified white co-workers. This case is also about the use of offensive words.

Ash is rich with irony. Gadsden, Alabama, home of the Tyson plant, is nestled on the Coosa River, a tributary of the Alabama River, in the northeastern corner of the state. The settlement was an industrial center and big company town since the first steamboat arrived in 1845. The city was named after James Gadsden. He was a fierce proponent of slavery and Southern nationalism, even encouraging South Carolina's secession from the Union as early as 1850 when California was admitted to the United States as a free state. He considered slavery a "social blessing" and abolitionists the "greatest curse of the nation." He died in 1858, less than two years before South Carolina became the first state to secede from the Union. He would not live to see the attack on Fort Sumter and the country's descent into civil war.

You can imagine Colonel Gadsden rolling over in his grave nearly 150 years after his death when Anthony Ash and John Hithon, two Black employees at the Tyson plant in Gadsden, had the "audacity" to apply for management positions. A white employee selected for one promotion had worked at the plant less than three years. Despite a stated preference for promoting from within the plant, the other successful white candidate was selected from another Tyson facility.

Ash and Hithon brought a race discrimination lawsuit in federal court in Alabama, alleging that they were not selected due to their race. As part of the evidence presented at their trial, Ash and Hithon testified that the white plant manager, who made the disputed decision, occasionally referred to Black employees by the term "boy." The Black employees argued that use of the term "boy" in this context was evidence of the manager's racial bias against them. The jury agreed, siding with the employees, to the tune of $1.75 million in compensatory and punitive damages each.

Nonetheless, the trial judge set aside the jury verdict and found for Tyson Foods as a matter of law. One of the most interesting parts of the case is that, on appeal, the U.S. Court of Appeals for the Eleventh Circuit affirmed the trial judge's decision finding the use of the term "boy" (alone and without any modifiers such as "white" or "Black") could not constitute evidence of racial bias *as a matter of law*.

A unanimous Supreme Court—a rarity in these contentious times—made short work of rejecting the lower courts' reasoning. Ruling in favor of the Black employees, the Supreme Court concluded that, as proof of job bias, a "speaker's meaning may depend on various factors including *context, inflection, tone of voice, local custom and historical usage.*" Words, then, may harbor offense simply by their historical use.

In other words, context matters in determining what is offensive at work. Given the historical use of the term during slavery, "boy," when directed at Black men by whites, reinforces stereotypes of Blacks as racially subordinate to whites or serves to marginalize, intimidate, and put Blacks "in their place." One is reminded of Dr. King's compelling "Letter from Birmingham Jail," in which he wrote, in 1963, that "when your first name becomes "nigger," your middle name becomes "boy" (however old you are) and your last name becomes "John,"... then you will understand why we find it difficult to wait."

Many rely on the expression, "context is everything." Well, not quite, in employment law anyway. The occasional stray remark, such as an off-hand reference to "the good old boys club" or "OK boomer," is unlikely to be enough to support a claim of unlawful discrimination. Typically, for a "hostile" work environment, work must be permeated with offensive language, ridicule, insult, and intimidation that is sufficiently severe or pervasive enough to alter a person's employment and create an abusive work environment.

In closing, the n-word has no place at work . . . any workplace. We should put aside any defense of the term, or who can say what in our society, or contrariwise, any belief that a double standard exists. Since context matters, it's often the person on the other end of the conversation at work who determines what is unwelcome, not you. White and Black and Asian employees have been fired and they or their employers have been sued (or both) for using the n-word toward a co-worker. There is only one standard: **Don't say offensive things to people at work.**

4

DOES HAVING A "COOL" NAME HELP YOU GET A JOB?

The Broad Scope of Discrimination

Lady in Car:	*What are you gonna name it?*
Alison Bradbury:	*What?*
Lady in Car:	*The baby.*
Alison Bradbury:	*[realizing she's faking being pregnant] Oh, the baby. Well, if it's a girl, Cynthia, and if it's a boy, Elliot.*
Lady in Car:	*Those are lovely names.*
Walter (Gib) Gibson:	*Elliot? You're gonna name the kid Elliot? No, you can't name the kid Elliot. Elliot is a fat kid with glasses who eats paste. You're not gonna name the kid Elliot. You gotta give him a real name. Give him a name. Like Nick.*
Alison Bradbury:	*Nick?*
Walter (Gib) Gibson:	*Yeah, Nick. Nick's a real name. Nick's your buddy. Nick's the kind of guy you can trust, the kind of guy you can drink*

a beer with, the kind of guy who doesn't
mind if you puke in his car, Nick!
[Alison looks disgusted]

Walter (Gib) Gibson: *[to Lady in Car] Oh, vomit. I'm sorry.*
Vomit.

—*The Sure Thing* (1985)

THERE'S SOMETHING ABOUT MARY . . . and Michael. For generations, Michael and Mary were among the most popular baby names in the United States. While Michael is still hanging in there, Mary has free-fallen from the list of the most popular baby names in the United States. Sophia, for the ninth consecutive year, was the most popular baby girl name in 2018. Three in a million babies born in 2008 were named "Palin," but, in 2009, the number of baby Palins surged to 20 Palins per million. Was this some recognition of the popularity of vice-presidential candidate Sarah Palin? It does make you wonder how many babies were named Hubert in 1965 or Spiro in 1969. The Israeli newspaper, Haaretz, ran an article in May 2011 about an Israeli couple, apparently inspired by Facebook, who named their newborn daughter "Like." It would be hard not to like Like. The couple's other children are Dvash ("Honey" in Hebrew) and Pie. It's even harder not to like Pie. How many babies in the United States have been named Honey Boo Boo or Katniss? After the coronavirus pandemic of 2020, how many babies will be named Corona, Pandemonia, or Covid (like Ovid, but more contagious)?

There's certainly something about a name. Without being too risqué, ask yourself which is more memorable, the movie exploits of James Bond or the sexually suggestive names of the

"Bond Girls," such as "Plenty O'Toole," "Xenia Onatopp," "Holly Goodhead," and the all-time classic, "Pussy Galore?" At the other end of the movie spectrum, even the family friendly Walt Disney Company has not avoided controversy surrounding the naming of its film characters. When Disney released *The Princess and the Frog* in 2009, the first animated full-length film featuring an African American heroine, Disney executives decided to use the name, "Tiana," for the main character instead of "Maddy," the name used in the original screenplay. "Maddy," it seems, drew fire for sounding too much like the negative racial caricature "mammy."

Having a cool name may not help you get ahead at work, but experts say your name could hurt you. Discrimination based on names exists. At least one significant study has shown job applicants with "white names" are more likely to get an interview than applicants with "African American names." Between July 2001 and May 2002, two economics professors conducted a novel social sciences experiment in Chicago and Boston. They looked for the existence of race-based hiring by sending identical fictitious resumes of prospective job candidates to employers in response to actual employment ads. Half of the resumes bore traditionally "African American" names (Lakisha Washington and Jamal Jones) and the other half had traditionally "white" names (Emily Walsh and Greg Baker).

In total, the researchers responded to more than 1,300 employment ads in sales, administrative support, clerical, and customer services job categories (sending out almost 5,000 resumes). Even the choosing of the fake applicants' names was methodical, relying on name frequency data from birth certificates for all babies born in Massachusetts between 1974 and 1979. They cross-checked the distinctiveness of the names they selected for the experiment by conducting a survey in various public areas in Chicago, asking respondents to assess a resume, with a given name, for the race of the named person. Aside from the names and fake addresses, the resumes were identical.

The findings, with the catchy title, "Are Emily and Greg More Employable than Lakisha and Jamal? A Field Experiment on Labor Market Discrimination," were published in the *American Economic Review* in September 2004. The results were alarming: Researchers found that—regardless of industry or occupation—there was significant discrimination against "African American" names. "White" names received 50 percent more callbacks for interviews. Ironically, employers who specifically identified themselves as "Equal Opportunity Employers" in their ads were just as likely to discriminate based on name as other employers. Also, regardless of having a racially distinct name, applicants with fake addresses from neighborhoods in the community that were characterized as both wealthier and predominantly comprised of white residents were more likely to receive a callback than those from neighborhoods that were characterized as both less wealthy and predominantly comprised of Black residents.

Of course, the study had its limitations. Given the fictitious nature of the applicants, the researchers could only measure callbacks for interviews and not whether an applicant was hired. Also, the study only examined responses to newspaper ads rather than other methods for seeking employment, such as Internet ads. Finally, some later studies have had differing results, which suggest some forward progress in this area. And since the study was released, a man with a very African-sounding name, Barack Obama, was elected and re-elected President of the United States.

May an applicant or employee establish liability against an employer for name discrimination? Ironically, well before the landmark study, the U.S. Equal Employment Opportunity Commission (EEOC) attempted to employ actual (not fictitious) "testers" to challenge racially discriminatory hiring practices. Testers are people who apply for jobs solely for the purpose of testing for discriminatory hiring practices, even though they have no intention of accepting such employment. As early as 1990, the EEOC took the legal position that testers could challenge "any discrimination to which they were subjected." According to the EEOC, people simply testing the waters of employment discrimination, without any intention of getting into the labor pool, nevertheless suffered harm and could file suit. In 1998, however, a federal district court in Chicago struck down the employment testing program on the grounds that persons who have no intention of taking a job have not been harmed and, therefore, have no standing to sue an employer under Title VII. Shortly thereafter, the EEOC shelved its employment testing program.

So what can be done about name discrimination? Applicants should know it exists and be cognizant of potential bias in hiring. In response, some applicants have been known to alter their resume or application to change or remove racial or gender identifiers, for example, "Alexandra" applies for a job as "Alex." Employers also should recognize that the problem exists and that, unlike individual applicants, they are in a position to root it out. Many organizations are addressing the problem by making efforts to raise awareness of our unconscious biases and how they can adversely influence decisions at work. However, some argue that unconscious bias training is not effective and, if done poorly, can even exacerbate the problem. Therefore, employers have adopted "name-blind" hiring procedures, removing the names and gender from applications, before they are reviewed by the hiring decisionmakers in order to neutralize potentially unlawful bias toward applicants.

5

CAN WICCANS LOSE THEIR JOB FOR REFUSING TO CUT THEIR HAIR?

Religious Discrimination

I say, 'Hey, Lama, hey, how about a little something,
you know, for the effort, you know.' And he says,
'Oh, uh, there won't be any money, but when you die,
on your deathbed, you will receive total consciousness.'
So I got that goin' for me, which is nice.

—Carl Spackler, *Caddyshack* (1980)

YEARS AGO, one of my business clients adopted a new dress code requiring all men to wear close-cropped, well-groomed hair. The company sold a luxury product and wanted all of its salespersons to have the "look" of clean-cut, wholesome users of their product. The only problem was their best salesperson, someone we will call Yanni. That's not his real name, but he bore a striking resemblance to the popular, new-age musical performer with the same name: stunningly handsome, with dark, shoulder-length hair that appeared to flow like a lion's mane. The manager elaborated, "After prodding him for months, Yanni just wouldn't cut his hair. Finally, I sat him down in my office and ordered him to cut his hair." Yanni looked at the manager, sincerely, and said, "I can't cut my hair." The manager then said, "Why the hell not?" And Yanni replied, "I am a practitioner of the ancient Wiccan arts. I worship the Earth Mother Gaia. My hair is a source of my spiritual strength. I cannot cut my hair." That's when I got the call from the manager.

I don't know what Gaia has in store for any of us, but you should never mess with Mother Nature. A Wiccan employee is protected under Title VII and most states' and many local governments' EEO laws.

Title VII, which applies to most employers, protects religious rights in the workplace. The law states: "It shall be an unlawful employment practice for an employer . . . to discriminate against any individual . . . because of such individual's . . . religion." Employers have a duty to attempt to reasonably accommodate the religious practices of an employee or applicant, unless doing so would cause undue hardship for the employer's business. Failure to accommodate is a separate claim which can be brought in addition to a claim of religious discrimination.

Where work and the law collide, it is always important to be precise. Does the hair policy demand that the Wiccan employee cut his hair or does the policy specify that hair must be worn short, that is, above the collar of a shirt? Therefore, can the employee wear his hair like Princess Leia in *Star Wars: Episode IV – A New Hope* (the memorable enormous cinnamon bun twists) and still comply with the dress code?

Hair length and style have historically been associated with many religions, not just Wicca. Hair is often associated with piety or special powers. In the Bible, Samson gained strength from his hair and lost it when Delilah cut it. Mary Magdalene washed Jesus's feet and dried them with her hair, a humble act of devotion. In the Sikh religion, men do not cut their hair to demonstrate a lack of vanity. Buddhist monks do the same by shaving their heads.

Dress codes and appearance standards are lawful. Nonetheless, employers may have to accommodate exceptions to a dress code based on religious beliefs and practices.

Wicca (which is often compared to witchcraft) is recognized as a protected religion in the United States. Therefore, absent some undue hardship on an employer, Wiccan practices must be accommodated in the workplace. For example, in 2005, a hospital worker brought a claim of religious discrimination against her employer, Mercy Medical Center, a Catholic hospital in Sioux City, Iowa. The worker alleged she was fired for being a Wiccan. The court never addressed the religious discrimination claim because the case was dismissed based on an exemption from liability for religious organizations. Religious organizations, such as Catholic hospitals, can prefer members of their own religion over other religions. In 2007, a Starbucks barista sued Starbucks in Oregon claiming she was fired for wearing a Wiccan "pentacle" to work. A federal court allowed the barista's claims of religious discrimination and retaliation to proceed to trial.

The Wiccan cases are a reminder that religion is defined broadly in the United States. For purposes of Title VII, religion is defined to include "all aspects of religious observance and practice, as well as belief." The EEOC further defines "religious practices" to include "moral and ethical beliefs as to what is right and wrong which are sincerely held with the strength of traditional religious views."

As a result, even "non-traditional" beliefs can constitute

a protected religion under Title VII. Persons old enough to have walked through an airport in the 1970s and 1980s will likely easily remember Hare Krishnas singing their mantra in public and selling books written by Bhaktivedanta Swami. Krishna Consciousness is a religion. Some other instances of lesser known belief systems that have been recognized by courts and the EEOC as a religion may startle employers:

In 2016, a New York federal court held that "Onionhead," or "Harnessing Happiness," a system of beliefs imposed on employees at a healthcare company constituted a religion under Title VII because it relied on religious imagery, chanting and ritualistic cleansing practices to help persons strive for more positive emotions and unity.

In 2012, an Ohio federal court refused to dismiss a case brought by a hospital worker who was fired after she refused to get a mandatory flu vaccination because she is vegan and refuses to ingest or use animals or their by-products. For most flu vaccines, the vaccine virus is grown in chicken eggs.

In 2005, Red Robin Gourmet Burgers paid $150,000 to settle a religious discrimination claim brought by the EEOC for its refusal to accommodate the "Kemetic beliefs"—an ancient Egyptian religion—of an employee. Red Robin fired him for his refusal to cover Kemetic tattoos.

In 2002, a Wisconsin federal court found that an employee who professed to be a member of the "World Church of the Creator," the fundamental tenet of which is white supremacy, was in a protected religion.

In July 2000, the EEOC ruled that patent examiner Paul LaViolette's unorthodox scientific beliefs could fall within the protections of Title VII. Mr. LaViolette believed in cold fusion—that energy can be generated inexpensively at low temperatures through fusion of hydrogen or deuterium nuclei—and that he was receiving alien radio communications from space. Mr. LaViolette alleged his views caused his discharge from the U.S. Patent and Trademark Office.

The EEOC sued a Chi-Chi's Restaurant in Maryland in June 1996 on behalf of a Jehovah's Witness who alleged she was fired from her job as a waitress for refusing to sing the restaurant's 90-second "birthday song" to customers. Jehovah's Witnesses believe personal birthdays are pagan celebrations contrary to their religion. The restaurant allegedly refused to accommodate the employee's beliefs and fired her for failing to sing the birthday song.

Given these cases, the dumbest thing a supervisor can ever say to an employee at work is, "that's not a religion," because . . . it may well be treated as a religion under U.S. law.

So . . . Are there any limits on employee protections from religious discrimination?

Yes, not every belief or practice is protected. First, personal preferences are not necessarily religious beliefs. In 1977, a Florida district court ruled that an employee's desire to eat Kozy Kitten Cat Food to improve work performance was beyond the concept of a religion.

Similarly, one's personal taste in music is probably not protected as a religion. In June 2000, a federal district court rejected a Cub Foods employee's claim that his supervisor's playing of "Satanic death metal" music over the store's loudspeakers constituted a religiously hostile work environment. The employee, a Lutheran, asserted that the Satanic music offended his religious beliefs at work. The court found that death metal music was not inherently "religious." Also, the employee never complained that the supervisor's conduct offended his religious beliefs.

Political, cultural, or social beliefs, such as membership in the Ku Klux Klan, likewise are not considered to be religions for purposes of Title VII. The Church of Marijuana—devoted solely to growing, possessing, distributing and, sometimes, praying to marijuana—was found to be secular and not a protected religion. The worship of a college or professional sports team—however zealous or offensive to others—is probably not a protected religion (although there are plenty of people, especially in Alabama or Texas, who would argue otherwise).

Finally, people have the right to be left alone from other people's religion at work. In most workplaces, excessive religious preaching, or proselytizing, will eventually offend someone. Religious harassment is a form of unlawful religious discrimination . . . and it can ruin your work and personal life. In 1996, the U.S. Court of Appeals for the Fourth Circuit affirmed the dismissal of a religious discrimination claim brought by Charita Chalmers. Chalmers, an evangelical Christian, believed she should share the Gospel and eagerly looked for opportunities to do so at work. Believing her manager was lying to customers, Chalmers wrote him a letter addressed to his home telling him, "The Lord wants you to . . . get your life right with him. You are doing some things in your life that God is not pleased with and He wants you to stop." Unfortunately, the supervisor's wife opened the letter and mistakenly believed the letter suggested the husband was having an affair. The wife called Chalmers in tears, claiming the letter had retraumatized her due to her husband's infidelity years earlier. The wife then accused her husband of infidelity based on the letter. To say that the supervisor became upset, given his past, would be stating it lightly.

But there's more . . . .

While investigating the first letter, the company discovered Chalmers had written a letter to another employee, who had a baby out of wedlock, informing her, "You need the Lord Jesus in your life right now. One thing about God, He doesn't like when people commit adultery. You know what you did was wrong." She further stated, "God can put a sickness on [people who sin]." The company fired Chalmers for the two letters claiming she had irreparably damaged her work relationships with her co-workers. Chalmers alleged religious discrimination because her religion motivated her to write the letters and her employer failed to accommodate her conduct.

The court decided that Chalmers failed to show her religion compelled her to send "personal, disturbing letters" to her co-workers. She never asked for any religious accommodation which could have avoided the religious harassment of her co-workers. Finally, the court didn't buy Chalmers's clever argument that a warning—some forgiveness instead of firing—would have been the most reasonable religious accommodation of her beliefs. Title VII does not require employers to give "lesser punishments to employees who claim, after they violate company rules (or at the same time), that their religion caused them to transgress the rules."

Allowing employees to force their religious beliefs on coworkers may generate a discrimination or harassment claim against the employer. In September 1998, the EEOC sued—and later settled with—a veterinary hospital for pressuring six employees to follow the teachings of the Church of Scientology. The hospital had required employees to participate in religious training and study programs in order to keep their jobs and receive employment benefits. But those veterinary employees did not need religious training and study to do their jobs.

What's the best advice about religion at work?

The United States is the most religiously-diverse country in the world. An organization and its employees must be flexible and open-minded. Each situation should be examined on its own facts and circumstances. A prudent supervisor does not challenge the sincerity of an employee's beliefs because that could sound to the employee a lot like religious harassment or discrimination.

Also, employers must always consider religious accommodations, as opposed to a flat rejection, since ultimately the employer gets to decide what accommodation is reasonable under the law. The most common accommodations for religion are allowing time off to attend religious services or providing a private location to pray while on breaks, allowing employees to swap duties to avoid interference with religious beliefs, and making exceptions to dress codes or grooming standards for religious reasons.

Religious harassment is a form of religious discrimination. Therefore, unwelcome religious proselytizing or jokes and teasing a person based on their beliefs are not acceptable.

Finally, employers must avoid using religion as a motivating factor in any employment decision. An employer cannot refuse to hire persons of a certain religion, impose different standards or work requirements on an employee because of the employee's religious beliefs or practices, give a preference to employees of one religion over employees of another religion, or refuse to consider a request for religious accommodation. Usually, what an employer does for employees of one religion creates a reasonable expectation and precedent for employees of differing beliefs. For example, if employees are permitted to wear the Christian Cross or Ichthys (Jesus Fish) openly at work, then employees would have a commensurate right to wear the Jewish Star of David, Crescent Moon of Islam, or Wiccan Pentacle.

6

CAN AN EMPLOYEE REFUSE TO USE BIOMETRIC SCANNERS OR GIVE A SOCIAL SECURITY NUMBER BECAUSE THEY ARE THE "MARK OF THE BEAST?"

More Religious Discrimination

Raymond Stantz:	*Fire and brimstone coming down from the skies! Rivers and seas boiling!*
Egon Spengler:	*Forty years of darkness! Earthquakes, volcanoes...*
Winston Zeddmore:	*The dead rising from the grave!*
Peter Venkman:	*Human sacrifice, dogs and cats living together... mass hysteria!*

—*Ghostbusters* (1984)

THE BIBLE IS THE STARTING POINT for this question. The Book of Revelation, also known as the Revelation of John, is the last book of the New Testament. For seemingly as long as Revelation has existed, its significance in Christian eschatology has been heavily debated. Eschatology is the aspect of theology which studies, literally, the "last things." In Christian theology, the discussion tends to focus on mankind's destiny—or "End of Days"—as foretold by the Bible. Some Christians—in particular, evangelical Protestant Christians—consider Revelation and its prophesies to be of central importance to their faith and a guidepost for future events.

Revelation is not for the faint of heart. Its imagery brings the reader up close and personal with Satan. The book foretells (in disturbing detail) Armageddon, the second coming of the Messiah, the imprisonment and rebellion of Satan, Judgment Day (which does not bode well for non-believers), the dawn of new heavens and a new earth . . . and the "Mark of the Beast."

The thirteenth chapter of Revelation describes two beasts—one from the sea and one from the land—the latter of which "causeth all, both small and great, rich and poor, free and bond, to receive a mark in their right hand, or in their foreheads: And that no man might buy or sell, save he that had the mark, or the name of the beast, or the number of his name. Here is wisdom. Let him that hath understanding count the number of the beast: for it is the number of a man; and his number is Six hundred threescore and six." 666. Those who accept the Mark of the Beast will not survive Judgment Day.

For some true believers, the Mark of the Beast is seemingly everywhere: UPC and other bar codes, radio frequency identification (RFID) tags, biometric devices, microchip implants, Social Security numbers, and a proposed national identification card. Some say that it's all a part of world's most well-known secret conspiracy, The New World Order, the culmination of the Biblical end times prophesy, where vast forces of darkness (including, depending on whom you ask, the United Nations, the Bilderberg Group, the Trilateral Commission, Freemasons, the Federal Reserve System, Wall Street, the Council on Foreign Relations, the Rockefellers, the Bush family, the Clintons, Barack Obama, the Roman Catholic Church, the Pope, the Society of Jesus, and even Justin Bieber) conspire to create one world government for the benefit of the Antichrist. Justin Bieber? It makes sense! Justin (6 letters), Bieber (6 letters), whose favorite number may be "6," adds up to the Mark or Number of the Beast, which is 666!

It might surprise you, but a sincere belief in the Mark of the Beast is protected at work. And, in some cases, the belief may have to be accommodated.

In 2017, in *EEOC v. Consol Energy, Inc.*, an appellate court affirmed a trial court judgment in favor of Beverly Butcher in the amount of $150,000 in compensatory damages and $436,860.74 in front and back pay and lost benefits. Butcher, a coal miner for 37 years, claimed he was forced to retire because he refused to use a new biometric hand scanner system installed at his mine. The system monitored work hours and attendance. Employees were required to scan their right hand which was then linked to a unique personnel number that identified each employee. Butcher, a life-long evangelical Christian and the associate pastor of his church, objected to the use of the scanner on religious grounds: The scanner would assign him the "Mark of the Beast" referenced in the Bible. Even though the scanner did not imprint any "mark" on the hand, Butcher believed the scanning procedure could mark him for the Antichrist.

In response to Butcher's objections, the mine superintendent gave Butcher a letter written by the scanner's manufacturer, offering assurances that the scanner cannot detect or place a mark—including the Mark of the Beast—on the body of a person. Offering its own interpretation of "[t]he Scriptures, the letter explained that because the Mark of the Beast is associated only with the right hand or the forehead, use of the left hand in the scanner would be sufficient to obviate any religious concerns regarding the system." Still conflicted, Butcher refused to scan either hand.

At the same time, though, the mine was accommodating two workers with injured hands, allowing them to opt out of the scanner system and to use a keypad to enter their employee identification number. Still, the employer insisted Butcher use his left hand in the scanner. He offered to write down his hours and turn them in, but the mine refused. Butcher retired in protest and brought his claim of religious discrimination, including the failure to accommodate his religious beliefs.

The appellate court found that Butcher sincerely believed his participation in the scanning system—whether it left a literal mark or not—was showing allegiance to the Antichrist and, therefore, conflicted with his religious convictions. The court made it clear that it is not an employer's place "to question the correctness or even the plausibility of [an employee's] religious understandings." Finally, allowing Butcher to bypass the scanner would have imposed no additional burden or cost as the employer had accommodated other employees for non-religious reasons. Therefore, the court agreed with the jury that the mine had failed to accommodate the employee's religion.

Refusing to give your Social Security number for religious reasons is treated differently.

Under federal law, employees are required to submit a valid Social Security number to the Internal Revenue Service (IRS) for wage reporting purposes after hire. There is no mechanism under federal law for an employee to revoke, or give up, a Social Security number once issued. Employees have devised clever arguments to circumvent the requirement to produce a Social Security number. For example, in *Cassano v. Carb*, the U.S. Court of Appeals for the Second Circuit rejected a claim by an employee that she could not divulge her Social Security number because she was in dire fear of identity theft.

Many employees have raised religious objections to producing a Social Security number. Unlike *Consol Energy*, where a court weighed a religious challenge to the use of biometric devices, courts have soundly rejected the argument that sincerely held religious beliefs excuse an employee from obtaining or divulging a Social Security number, because a Social Security number is required by law. For example, in *EEOC v. Allendale Nursing Centre*, an employee raised the objection that the Social Security Administration (SSA) engages in the "unbiblical" practice of taking money from people with jobs and distributing it to people who do not work. The employee believed it was the job of one's family and church to care for persons unable to work. In her view, the government was stealing, which the employee viewed as a sin. Dismissing the employee's religious discrimination lawsuit, the court concluded the employee's dispute should more properly be with the IRS or SSA, challenging the constitutionality of the wage reporting requirement and not the employer for following the law.

Many (usually former) employees have argued that the Social Security number is the "Mark of the Beast," claiming that they should not have to provide their Social Security numbers to an employer. Courts have routinely rejected these arguments. For example, in 1996, Don M. Weber II applied for a job as a truck driver for Leaseway Dedicated Logistics in Kansas. The employment application used by Leaseway at the time required all applicants to disclose their Social Security number as part of the hiring process. This was not uncommon at the time—before we truly understood the risks of identity theft—in order to conduct a background check, including a motor vehicle record check, on a prospective driver.

Weber refused. He wrote in the blank space on his application form, "none for religious reasons." Instead, Weber gave his prospective employer a copy of his birth certificate and his commercial driver's license, which was also a requirement for the job, on the day he applied. A U.S. birth certificate is not only proof of citizenship (all persons born in the United States are citizens according to the Fourteenth Amendment to the U.S. Constitution) but, combined with valid photo identification (such as a driver's license), is proof of authorization to work in the United States. Weber gave what he needed to gain employment with Leaseway.

Nonetheless, Leaseway would not hire Weber. Leaseway decided Weber failed to complete the application in full and refused to hire him. Leaseway never asked Weber why he refused to give his Social Security number or inquired into the nature of the "religious reasons" that influenced Weber's decision. Leaseway never explored whether it could accommodate Weber's lack of a Social Security number when it already had proof of his authorization to work.

Weber insisted that he would never obtain a Social Security number. Yet he admitted he had a Social Security number at one time and conceded that he had used it for 30 years. However, he claimed that in 1995, the year before he applied for the job at Leaseway, he "surrendered" his Social Security number because it is a "reflection of the mark of the beast as described in the Book of Revelations" and, therefore, providing a Social Security number would have doomed him to eternal life . . . in Hell.

Weber sued for religious discrimination under Title VII. Leaseway argued that Weber was required by the government, not Leaseway, to have a Social Security number. An employer and employee may be penalized for failing to report the employee's wages to the IRS. Moreover, Weber wanted to be a commercial vehicle driver. By regulation, the federal Department of Transportation (DOT) requires every applicant for a commercial motor vehicle driver position to include their Social Security number. An employer can be penalized if it fails to meet the DOT requirement. The court ruled in favor of Leaseway, finding that Leaseway did not discriminate against Weber on the basis of religion by requiring a Social Security number as a condition of hire.

Courts agree that an employer need not violate the law as an accommodation of one's religious beliefs. Breaking the law, facing possible penalties as a result, or even having to take the time to apply for a waiver of the Social Security requirement, simply are not reasonable accommodations of an employee's religious convictions but, instead, would create an undue hardship for an employer.

The lesson of these cases is that Butcher and Weber are not alone. Rejection of the Mark of the Beast is a movement. In early 2013, Walter Slonopas opened his annual W-2 Wage and Tax Statement from his employer, Contech Casting, in Clarksville, Tennessee, only to discover it was marked with the number "666." To the payroll company issuing the forms, it was just a control number. To Slonopas, it was the "Number of the Beast." Therefore, he quit his job rather than "accept the devil." At last word, Slonopas rejected his employer's offer of a new W-2 and his job back.

In 2017, a Pennsylvania resident, James Schlosser, was

convicted of tax evasion in a federal court in Allentown, Pennsylvania. He didn't file taxes from 1994 to 2014 and failed to report nearly $2.3 million in income as a medical equipment salesman. Schlosser claimed he didn't file taxes for twenty years because using his Social Security number constituted using the Mark of the Beast. Instead, he hid his money in foreign business trusts and Nevada shell corporations, and bought and sold gold for cash.

Although times have changed, the duty to accommodate religious beliefs in the workplace has not. Religion is defined broadly to include traditional and non-traditional beliefs. An employer has a duty to accommodate an applicant or employee's sincerely held religious beliefs and practices. The duty to accommodate ends, though, at undue hardship on the operation of an employer's business. Therefore, employers should consider all options for accommodating employees' religious beliefs and practices before resorting to termination or some other adverse employment action.

7

CAN AN EMPLOYEE BE REQUIRED TO GET A FLU SHOT?

The Duty to Accommodate Religion or a Disability

AS I ANSWER THIS QUESTION, in the midst of a deadly pandemic, scientists are working hard to develop a coronavirus vaccine in the hope of preventing illness and saving lives. Despite these efforts, many Americans will refuse the vaccine, including my neighbor. He says "they" are going to put a microchip in the vaccine that will be used to track people. I'm a good neighbor: I reassured him "they" are already tracking his cell phone. I haven't seen him in a while.

Many people don't like getting injections. Some people are hesitant or outright refuse to receive vaccinations. But, if you are going to get any vaccination, you might want to consider getting a flu shot. In his 2005 book, *The Great Influenza: The Story of the Deadliest Pandemic in History*, John M. Barry gives a terrifying account of the Spanish Flu pandemic that broke out during World War I. Few people alive today can even comprehend that, in a little over one year (1918-1919), the greatest "medical holocaust" in history killed more than 50 million people (and by some estimates, as many as 100 million) worldwide! It may also be hard for people today to grasp that this global flu pandemic ravaged the healthiest segment of the population—killing mostly young adults, with more than half of the deaths occurring in persons 20 to 40 years of age. The pandemic created a culture of fear that threatened to destroy entire communities.

In the early days of immunology, medical researchers risked their own lives to find a vaccine that would stem the spread of this "new" disease. As a result, the flu vaccine is widely available today. Ironically, many people refuse the flu vaccine (and other vaccinations) even though we remain as vulnerable to deadly new strains of the flu as we did in the early 1900s.

In defense of all employees, employers should be aware that resistance to compulsory vaccination is as old as the vaccines themselves. Maybe it's just the rebellious teenager in all of us, or we have issues with authority, or, in the case of vaccines, we have serious concerns about the side effects of vaccines or sincere religious objections to being vaccinated.

For example, in December 2012, Joyce Gingerich, a nurse who had direct care of cancer patients and clearly understood that some of her patients had weakened immune systems, refused to get a required flu shot. She said her refusal was mostly "a personal thing." She had no objection to other vaccinations but felt it should be her choice whether she received the flu vaccine. Asked why, she simply said she was opposed to "the injustice of being forced to put something in [her] body."

That's a straightforward, and sympathetic, position. It does make one wonder, though, whether she'd feel the same way if she was forced to eat a Krispy Kreme doughnut?

Gingerich and seven other like-minded medical professionals

were fired for refusing to get the flu shot. Gingerich had been employed for twenty-five years. Her employer, Indiana University Health Goshen Hospital, took the legal position that their nurses' personal freedom and sense of justice were subordinate to the care of immunocompromised patients. The firings made national news. The former employees made the media rounds, but Gingerich didn't sue her former employer. Perhaps she understood that the hospital's legitimate interest in protecting immunocompromised cancer patients constituted a reasonable basis for requiring a health care provider to get a flu shot.

Although some states have protective laws barring mandatory vaccinations, employers in most states *usually* can legally require employees to get a flu shot for a business-related reason. In particular, hospitals and other care facilities have the greatest interest in ensuring that patients and other vulnerable persons are not exposed to the flu and other infectious diseases.

But, since nothing about work (or workplace law) is ever easy, some may say that the exceptions may have overtaken the rule. Firing an employee who refuses to get a flu shot brings with it some significant legal risks for employers.

Some employees may have a disability that prevents them from getting a flu vaccine. For example, a person with a severe allergy to eggs might suffer an adverse reaction to the flu vaccine since most forms of the vaccine are cultured using eggs. According to the U.S. Equal Employment Opportunity Commission (EEOC), employers must consider a reasonable accommodation, such as wearing a surgical mask during flu season, or a temporary transfer, instead of requiring the flu vaccine.

Some employees have raised religious objections to the flu vaccine. For example, Sakile Chenzira was a customer service representative at the Cincinnati Children's Hospital Medical Center for more than a decade. She was fired by the hospital in

December 2010 after refusing to get a flu shot. Before firing her, the hospital had excused Chenzira's failure to get a flu shot for years (in effect, condoning her behavior), yet later cited "patient safety" as the basis for her termination.

Chenzira brought a federal lawsuit, alleging that she was fired in violation of her religious beliefs: She is a vegan. Vegans do not eat any animals or use any animal by-products. The flu vaccine contains eggs, an animal by-product. The trial court rejected the hospital's attempt to dismiss the case. The hospital argued that veganism is not a religion but merely a social philosophy or a dietary preference. Instead, relying on the broad definition of a "religion" under federal law—a set of moral or ethical beliefs of right and wrong that are sincerely held with the strength of traditional religious views—the trial court allowed Chenzira's claim of religious discrimination to proceed. Therefore, she could argue in court that her employer should have attempted to accommodate her refusal of the vaccine on religious grounds. Ultimately, as often happens, the case settled in October 2013 with no disclosure of any settlement amount.

Religious objections to getting a flu shot are likely to continue. Employers must entertain all requests for accommodation of religious beliefs, but they also have the right to obtain a clear understanding of the basis for objection. In 2017, a federal appeals court rejected a health care worker's claim that he was unlawfully fired for refusing to get the flu vaccine. The twenty-year employee sincerely believed the vaccine might do more harm than good to his body. The court ruled that medical qualms about the health effects of the flu vaccine—for an employee with no affiliation with any religious group—do not necessarily amount to a religious objection.

Employees who belong to a union may pose objections to a mandatory vaccine policy. Under the federal National Labor

Relations Act, a policy mandating a flu shot for all employees is likely to be the subject of mandatory collective bargaining. In other words, a unionized hospital would have to give notice to the union of the intended policy and bargain over the implementation of the policy.

The more direct contact an employee has with a vulnerable individual, such as a patient or an elderly person, the more an employer can likely compel the employee to get the vaccine. However, employers must consider refusals to get the vaccine on an individual case-by-case basis to determine whether a reasonable accommodation is necessary and available. For instance, allowing an employee to refuse the vaccination but requiring the employee to wear a surgical mask to prevent the spread of disease seems to be a reasonable response to a sincere refusal. In the end, rather than force flu shots on reluctant employees, employers may want to encourage rather than require employees to get flu shots.

8

ARE YOUNG PEOPLE PROTECTED?

Age Discrimination

So far, this is the oldest I've been.

—George Carlin

SINCE TIME IMMEMORIAL, the younger generation has gotten a bad rap from their elders. The current crop of youngsters is no different. A Time Magazine cover from May 2013 famously described "Millennials"—persons born between 1980 and 2000—as the "Me Me Me Generation." Stereotypically narcissistic, lazy, self-important, armed with a selfie stick in one hand and a pile of participation ribbons in the other, Millennials are reputedly difficult to employ.

Then again, Millennials shall also inherit the workplace. In 2018, they constituted approximately 35% (56 million workers) of the U.S. labor force, surpassing Generation Xers (53 million workers), and making them the largest generation at work. At least for a few more years until they are protected by federal, state, and local laws prohibiting age discrimination, Millennials are also the last unprotected minority in the United States.

At the same time, America has become an "old" country. According to the U.S. Census Bureau, in 1900, the median age in the U.S. was just 22.9 years of age! The median age rose to just over 30 by 1950. Thanks to the Baby Boom following World War II, the median age dropped back into the twenties in the 1950s and 1960s. By 2000, however, the median age shot up to a record high 35.2 years of age. In the 2000 census, nearly half of U.S. workers were age 40 and older. Today, most of the U.S. labor force is over age 40.

40 is truly a magic number. Once applicants or employees are age 40 or older, they are protected from age discrimination in employment under federal law. In other words, it's generally lawful to discriminate against young people but not older people. Want to pass over the 29-year-old know-it-all, who also happens to be the best qualified person in the department? No problem . . . except that some states do protect younger workers. For example, the Minnesota Human Rights Act protects persons from age discrimination in employment once an applicant or employee reaches age 18.

But why do you have to be 40 to be protected under federal law? Shouldn't the law, like Minnesota's statute, protect any person whose age is held against them?

Looking at the law itself, it doesn't even make sense to exclude persons under age 40. Congress passed the Age Discrimination in Employment Act (ADEA) in 1967 in the wake of the Civil Rights Act of 1964 (Title VII). Title VII was specifically enacted to prevent all discrimination based on race, skin color, religion, gender, and national origin. Therefore, the scope of the protections under Title VII was made purposely broad in order to be inclusive.

The ADEA was modeled partly on Title VII and contains a

similarly sweeping prohibition against all discrimination based on an "individual's age." Age. Period. Not a particular age. It is only later in the ADEA, almost as an afterthought, that the protections were limited to "individuals who are at least 40 years of age." Again, this begs the question, why 40? Why not 65? Or 21?

The U.S. Supreme Court and the U.S. Equal Employment Opportunity Commission (EEOC) have addressed this question. Congress only intended to protect older workers, not younger workers, even though both might be treated less favorably at work. Congress didn't want claims to be brought by young people who were mistreated to eclipse the claims by older people who were mistreated. This hardly seems fair.

Congress was certainly aware that age discrimination existed prior to the passage of Title VII. In fact, Congress considered adding age to the protections sought in 1964 but ultimately chose not to. Unlike the other protections, there are times when age-related decisions are appropriate for work; for example, the age when one can perform certain safety-sensitive positions (such as airline pilot, firefighter, or police officer) or sell liquor. In typical Congressional fashion, though, they called for a "study" of the issue by the U.S. Secretary of Labor.

That report, published in 1965, concluded that there was widespread discrimination against "older" workers to the advantage of younger workers and recommended a legislative fix. Still, there was wrangling over the age threshold for protection of "older" workers. The Secretary of Labor's report and subsequent Congressional hearings zeroed in on ages 45 and 55.

When the ADEA passed in 1967, Congress settled on age 40 based on testimony presented during its hearings. The 40-year-old threshold was a compromise, since objections were raised that discrimination against "older" people begins at an even younger age. For example, at the time, female flight attendants were often disqualified (or fired) much younger than age 40. But Congress specifically rejected calls to include coverage under the ADEA for ages younger than 40. Without much objective data, the experts suggested 40 is the age at which age discrimination in employment becomes "evident." Fifty-three years later, we often struggle with what this means, especially when "50 is the new 40."

When interpreting this limitation, the Supreme Court remarked that, "If Congress had been worrying about protecting the younger against the older, it would not likely have ignored everyone under age 40." Therefore, younger workers were intentionally left out of the ADEA's protections.

Over the ensuing five decades, the ADEA has become an enormously powerful workplace law. The most common claims remain: failure to hire or promote persons over age 40; terminating older workers—often as part of layoffs or business restructuring; or the denial of benefits to older workers. Proof of violations is shown by direct evidence of age discrimination, such as age-related offensive remarks, or indirect evidence of bias in hiring, such as an advertisement for "young" and "energetic" workers, or rejecting a candidate as "overqualified" (often code for "you've been on the planet a long time to have done so many things"). Statistics can also be used to show evidence of age bias in employment decisions.

Interestingly, the law originally protected workers only between 40 and 65. This was later raised to age 70. In 1986, President Reagan (who was 75 at the time) signed legislation eliminating the cap on protection, thereby protecting an employee to Methuselah's age (969!). Therefore, mandatory retirement—that is, forcing an employee to retire at a certain age—is unlawful except in limited circumstances, such as certain highly-compensated executives and public safety personnel, such as airline pilots, police, and firefighters.

Unlike Title VII, the ADEA carries enhanced penalties for violations, including "liquidated damages" for willful violations of the law. Further, courts now permit "disparate impact" (also known as "adverse impact") claims against employers. Under an adverse impact theory, an applicant or employee can challenge a seemingly neutral rule or policy that disproportionately "impacts" a protected group. No intent to discriminate is required to be shown. Instead, qualifications or requirements for employment that "screen out" older workers are subject to challenge. Therefore, weight standards and speed, fitness, and physical agility tests—all of which might be impacted as one grows older—may draw scrutiny if a disproportionate number of older workers are treated adversely as a result of the requirements. Business necessity is a defense to an adverse impact claim. For example, law enforcement employees may be held to higher physical fitness standards, regardless of their age, in order to be able to pursue criminal suspects on foot, subdue them, and make arrests, and to back up fellow officers who are in harm's way.

Finally, older workers have another protection based solely on their age. In many instances, applicants and employees can voluntarily waive their potential claims against employers—giving up the right to sue their employer—if they receive payment, such as severance or other consideration. Age discrimination is different. To waive a claim of age discrimination, a worker must be afforded additional protections, including extra time to consider and even revoke any waiver of rights, under the Older Workers Benefit Protection Act of 1990 (OWBPA). This law, which amends the ADEA, was intended to ensure that older workers are not pressured to waive their rights under the ADEA, particularly during layoffs when employees are financially vulnerable (and just might be willing to sign anything to obtain severance benefits for short-term survival or to transition to other work).

9

ARE SINGLE PEOPLE PROTECTED?

Marital Status Discrimination

All my friends are getting married. I guess I'm just
at that age where people give up.

—Amy Schumer

SHE WAS OBVIOUSLY UPSET and needed to vent. So she launched, saying, "I'm the only single person in my entire office! I always get extra work piled on me because my boss just assumes I can work late. My married co-workers and co-workers with kids need only a snotty-nosed child, a T-ball game, or a birthday party at the House of Bounce to miss work for 'family' reasons. It's not fair!"

Indeed, it is not fair. Yet unfortunately, being single is not a protected status under the law. No great consolation, but I was single into my thirties, and I could only offer my friend a small bit of non-legal advice: If you can't beat 'em, you *might* join 'em! Perhaps find a soulmate: No more sitting at the singles' table at weddings; more tax breaks; and far fewer probing questions from family and friends, like "Why is a person like you single?" or the annoyingly blunt "What happened?"

In all seriousness, though, surveys consistently show that unmarried employees are often paid less, especially in benefits, than married employees who have the same job title and do the same work. Across the board, single people face higher insurance costs than married people. A married person's Social Security benefits are paid to the spouse upon that person's death. Similarly-situated single people without children are often shocked to learn that they can work a lifetime, paying Social Security and Medicare taxes the entire time, but when they die, their Social Security benefits don't get paid to their next of kin but instead go back into the large governmental trust fund from which others are then paid. And, if the anecdotal evidence is true, single people are discriminated against in employment for being single. For example, employers often assume a single person is more available to travel for work, will work more, or will be more willing or able to work undesirable shifts or assignments.

Single people are also a large group, and their ranks continue to grow steadily. Far fewer Americans are marrying today. According to the U.S. Census Bureau, 99.6 million Americans age 18 or older (43.6% of all adult U.S. residents) were unmarried in 2010, up from 28.3% in 1970.

Nonetheless, there may be little strength in numbers when popular culture continues to reinforce misplaced stereotypes about single people: From the lovelorn, overworked cartoon character "Cathy," to the stealth-working serial womanizer "Barney Stinson" on the long-running CBS television comedy, "*How I Met Your Mother*," single people can never win at work. They are either assumed to "have no life" or "have no family" . . . and negative treatment at work can flow from either stereotype.

Despite the growth in the number of singles and evidence of some mistreatment of single people at work, the federal government does not protect a person's marital status, whether single, married, widowed, or divorced. Over the last 50 years, U.S. anti-discrimination laws have carved out certain "immutable" characteristics that may not be used to make employment decisions. Some are a product of one's birth, such as race, sex, national origin, or age. Others are viewed as so fundamental to a person's self-identity as to be unchangeable or not readily changeable, such as religion, citizenship status, or disabling conditions acquired during a person's lifetime.

To the surprise of many employees, those with certain arguably "immutable" characteristics are not specifically protected by federal law, including parental status, political party affiliation, criminal history and, generally, physical beauty or appearance, and marital status.

According to the Sloan Work and Family Research Network, only the Civil Service Reform Act of 1978 (CSRA) protects employees from marital status discrimination so long as they are federal employees. Other federal laws do not protect employees from discrimination based on their marital status. However, twenty-one states and the District of Columbia offer some protection against discrimination in employment based on marital status; that is, whether a person is single, married, divorced, separated, remarried, or widowed. Four of the five most populous states—California, New York, Florida, and Illinois—protect employees based on their marital status. Therefore, it depends on where someone lives and works as to whether they are protected from discrimination for being single.

In conclusion, we should recognize that "singleism"— stereotyping and discrimination against people who are single— commonly occurs at work and in society in general. Therefore, employers are reminded, and single workers should kindly assert, that all employees have lives, regardless of their marital status. Treating people differently based on stereotypical notions of how a married, single, or divorced person should act at work not only leads to avoidable misunderstandings but some employees' increased dissatisfaction and eventual departure.

Finally, misplaced stereotypes and discrimination based on marital status will invariably catch up with an employer. Keep in mind that mistreating any employee, single or married, *who has additional family responsibilities,* can lead to claims of family responsibilities discrimination (FRD). FRD is a broad term used to describe employment discrimination against caregivers. FRD includes holding a single parent to more exacting standards than childless workers or treating employees adversely because they have the responsibility to care for an aged parent or a family member with a disability. There is no federal law that expressly prohibits FRD, but FRD can easily give rise to other civil rights claims. A single mother who is treated worse than childless men at work may claim gender discrimination under Title VII. An employee responsible for the care of a disabled parent who is discriminated against or denied leave based on their association with a disabled person may claim discrimination under the Americans with Disabilities Act (ADA) or the Family and Medical Leave Act (FMLA). And state laws may afford even greater protection for caregivers.

10

DO BLACK PEOPLE HAVE THE RIGHT TO MISS WORK ON MARTIN LUTHER KING'S BIRTHDAY?

Unlawful Discrimination and the Right to Time Off

HE WAS ADAMANT, telling me, "I am Black, and my company knows this time is very important to me." The employee went on to explain that he had always participated in community events, including walking in a "marade," a parade to celebrate the life of Rev. Dr. Martin Luther King, Jr. This year, though, when he asked his boss for Martin Luther King's Birthday off, the boss replied, "Sorry, no time off is authorized this month." The employee was flaming mad and wanted to sue his employer for racial discrimination . . . that day.

I asked only one question: "Can anyone else take time off?" He answered, "No." I learned the company was in a peak production period and no vacation time was authorized for any employee. The only reasonable excuse for time off during the period was for medical reasons.

Title VII of the Civil Rights Act prohibits unlawful discrimination based on race, color, religion, national origin, and sex.

Under Title VII, employers must treat employees equally, not better than other employees. Also, unlike an employee's religious beliefs or having a disabling condition, employers have no duty to accommodate a person's race, color, national origin, or gender. An employer is simply required to treat employees the same. Therefore, if the employer insists no one can take time off due to legitimate business needs and has treated other employees similarly, then there is no right for any employee (regardless of race) to take Martin Luther King's Birthday off.

Now, if the employer had allowed employees to take time off for other racial or cultural celebrations, such as St. Patrick's Day, Columbus Day, or Cinco de Mayo, then an employee would have good reason to question whether they were being treated differently . . . and unlawfully.

The answer in this case might also be different if the employee asked for a day off for religious reasons, instead of a day off for a cultural or community event. For example, if the employee had said he was attending a devotional service at his place of worship on Martin Luther King's Birthday, then the employer would have to consider time off for religious reasons under its duty to accommodate an applicant or employee's sincerely held religious beliefs and practices.

However, even if a request for time off was for religious reasons, an employer could still weigh whether the requested time off would cause an undue hardship on the operation of the business. In this particular case, it sounded like it was a busy week at work and no other employee was permitted time off.

As my boss used to snicker when I started working in employment law, employees have the right to equal treatment under the law: equally good or equally bad. Here, it was equally bad that no one was allowed to leave work.

In the end, while the employer wasn't required to grant an

employee's request for a day off for racial or cultural reasons, a great employer would still have tried its best to permit the time off work for an employee who was passionate about honoring an important person and even more important legacy in his life. As Martin Luther King, Jr. said, "The time is always right to do what is right."

PART II

SEX & SENSIBILITY

11

ARE WOMEN WHO CAN'T GET PREGNANT PROTECTED FROM PREGNANCY DISCRIMINATION?

The Pregnancy Discrimination Act

Me: What is the most common pregnancy craving?
My wife: For men to be the ones who get pregnant.

MY WIFE LOOKED AT ME, calmly, almost dismissively, like a kindergarten teacher schooling a young student, and said, "Sarah was 90 when she had a baby!"

Foolishly, I'd been bemoaning the fact that we'd recently become parents again at the age of 37 which, at the time, seemed old to me. My wife was attempting to assuage my concerns about being an older parent by recalling the Biblical account, in the Book of Genesis, of Sarah, the wife of Abraham, giving birth to their baby, Isaac, when she and Abraham were both in their 90s.

It didn't help. I replied, "Yeah, maybe. But could she even pick up the baby after he was born?" This is why it's hard to be married to an employment lawyer.

The story of Sarah in the Bible is also an age-old reminder of the difficult experience of infertility. Today, in the era of *in vitro* fertilization (IVF) and other procedures, women who were previously unable to conceive naturally can bear children well into their 50s. In fact, the oldest person recorded to give birth was a 74-year-old Indian woman who had twin daughters in 2019.

Today, an employee who is infertile has a potential bundle of legal recourse on their hands. Three federal laws, along with possible state law counterparts, immediately come to bear: the Americans with Disabilities Act (the ADA), the Pregnancy Discrimination Act (PDA), and the Family and Medical Leave Act (FMLA).

Infertility may be a disability protected under the ADA. In 1998, the U.S. Supreme Court decided *Bragdon v. Abbott*. The case is compelling and a good reminder that interesting facts often make new law. The case involved Sidney Abbott who went to her dentist and discovered she needed to have a cavity filled. She disclosed on the medical registration form at the dentist's office that she was HIV positive.

Abbott's dentist refused to fill the cavity unless he could use the "extra safety precautions" of a hospital facility and only if Abbott was willing to pay for the cost of hospitalization. Of course, the dentist never indicated to Abbott what "extra precautions" might be necessary or whether he had admitting privileges at any hospital (which is extremely rare for a dentist). Moreover, getting a room at a hospital and using its surgical suite is not like checking into a Marriott or getting a day pass at a spa. The cost alone is probably more than most people make in a year.

Abbott sued her dentist under the provision of the ADA that requires places of "public accommodation," like doctors' and dentists' offices, to provide services to the disabled. Ultimately, the Supreme Court concluded that being infected with HIV is a disability under the ADA because having HIV substantially limits the major life activity of reproduction. The possibility that a child could acquire HIV from a pregnant mother brings elevated risk to the child and substantially limits a person's inclination to reproduce. Therefore, the inability to reproduce—infertility—is a disability under the ADA.

The ADA was amended by the ADA Amendments Act of 2008 (ADAAA). Under the new law, the definition of a "disability" was significantly broadened. Infertility, which could be viewed as an impairment of the reproductive system, could be substantially limiting on the major life activity of reproduction. Therefore, an employer may not discriminate against an infertile worker and may have to consider time off for medical treatments as a reasonable accommodation.

Alternatively, an infertile couple could conceivably take time off work for infertility treatments under the federal Family and Medical Leave Act (FMLA). Eligible employees are entitled to up to twelve weeks of leave, with their jobs guaranteed, for a "serious health condition." Leave can be taken intermittently (a day here, a week there, a month off, or more) for the treatment of a serious health condition. The FMLA and its regulations do not specifically mention whether infertility or IVF treatments are serious health conditions. However, what constitutes a "serious" health condition has been interpreted broadly under the FMLA.

At least one court has addressed the question of time off under the FMLA for IVF. The case is not entirely helpful for those seeking time off for infertility. Kimberly Culpepper requested FMLA leave from her employer, Blue Cross Blue Shield of Tennessee, for two separate three-day periods (six days in total) of intermittent leave for IVF treatment. The separate treatment periods were for egg retrieval and transplantation through outpatient surgical procedures. However,

Culpepper missed two full weeks and claimed she was physically unable to work because she "was sore from the surgery." The employer granted Culpepper the six days of FMLA leave she requested for IVF treatments but fired her for five unexcused work absences. Rejecting Culpepper's FMLA claim, the court concluded Culpepper never provided any medical evidence that she could not work on the five days she took off outside of the IVF treatments. Therefore, the case focused on an employer's right to discipline and fire an employee for her unexcused absences, rather than any right to time off that the employer provided for IVF treatments.

Perhaps the best protection for a working woman who is presently unable but nevertheless desires to become pregnant is the Pregnancy Discrimination Act of 1978 (PDA). The PDA amended Title VII of the Civil Rights Act of 1964, reinforcing protections based on one's biological sex by making it unlawful to discriminate based on "pregnancy, childbirth, or related medical conditions." In other words, the PDA governs the entire child-bearing process, including the *desire* to become pregnant and, therefore, time off for infertility treatments. Under sweeping PDA guidance issued in June 2015, the Equal Employment Opportunity Commission (EEOC) echoed the ruling of a federal court that "discrimination against an employee because she intends to, is trying to, or simply has the potential to become pregnant is . . . illegal discrimination." The EEOC specifically addressed time off for IVF treatments, stating:

> Because surgical impregnation is intrinsically tied to a woman's childbearing capacity, an inference of unlawful sex discrimination may be raised if, for example, an employee is penalized for taking time off from work to undergo such a procedure.

Therefore, an employer who refuses to grant time off for infertility treatments, when it grants time off for other medical reasons, could face a strong claim of gender discrimination. Women usually need time off for IVF treatments, while men usually do not. Men "participate" in IVF by providing necessary "material" but don't suffer negative work consequences for their role. Therefore, taking adverse action against a woman in such a situation is likely to show disparate treatment of men and women.

Finally, employers and their employees need to check state law. There is a movement across the country to extend to pregnant workers and persons desiring to have children the same reasonable accommodation efforts required for disabled workers. Recently, several states adopted "pregnancy accommodation" laws requiring employers to accommodate applicants' and employees' pregnancy-related health conditions. Some of these new state laws require employers to provide leave to an employee or otherwise accommodate an employee undergoing treatment for infertility.

12

CAN MEN BE REQUIRED TO WEAR SHORT HAIR?

Grooming Standards and the Law

IMAGINE A SITUATION in which an employer adopts a new appearance standard and orders all male employees to wear short hair—cutting their hair if need be—or be fired but permits all female employees to wear their hair any length they desire. Ask yourself: Surely, this different treatment of men must be unlawful discrimination based on sex?

Maybe, but maybe not. In some circumstances, employers legally may treat men and women differently . . . so long as it's "reasonable."

In fact, men have brought many cases challenging the hair length policies of their employers. Men have argued that restricting their hair length, while permitting women to wear long hair, is illegal discrimination based on their sex. Courts have overwhelmingly denied such claims for three reasons: (1) hair length, unlike one's race, skin color, or gender, is not immutable but can easily be changed, so those with short or long hair are not protected at work; (2) the wearing of one's hair at a certain length is not considered a fundamental right, such as the freedom of religion or due process of law; and (3) hair length has very little impact on an individual's employment opportunities. Accordingly, hair length is considered a minor difference in personal appearance and is not protected at work.

For example, in *Willingham v. Macon Telegraph Publishing Co.*, decided in 1975, the U.S. Court of Appeals for the Fifth Circuit upheld an employer's grooming policy that required male and female employees who met the public to be neatly attired and "groomed in accordance with the standards customarily accepted in the business community." The employer interpreted its own rule to mean that male employees could not wear long hair. As a result, Willingham, a 22-year-old male applicant with long hair, was not hired.

Willingham filed a lawsuit, alleging that he was discriminated against because his employer allowed women to wear their hair long. The appellate court upheld dismissal of the case. The Fifth Circuit concluded that, since women were also subject to dress and grooming standards, the employer could regulate the length of male employees' hair.

This theory, permitting sex-differentiated grooming standards, is often referred to as separate but equal. The court found as follows:

> Distinctions in employment practices between men and women on the basis of something other than immutable or protected characteristics do not inhibit employment opportunity in violation of [the law]. Congress sought only to give all persons equal access to the job market, not to limit an employer's right to exercise his informed judgment as to how best to run his shop.

The Fifth Circuit also observed that "an employer cannot have one hiring policy for men and another for women if the distinction is based on some fundamental right," such as having children or getting married. Therefore, it would violate Title VII, which protects all people on the basis of sex, to hire only married men, and to refuse to hire married women. Wearing long hair, on the other hand, is not a fundamental right.

More than three decades after *Willingham*, in *Jespersen v. Harrah's Operating Company*, the more liberal U.S. Court of Appeals for the Ninth Circuit reached the same result, endorsing a decision by Harrah's, a casino in Reno, Nevada, to fire bartender Darlene Jespersen for refusing to wear makeup on the job. Harrah's had recently adopted a comprehensive grooming policy requiring all bartenders to wear the same uniform. It added that women must wear makeup, while men were prohibited from doing so; and men must wear their hair above the collar, while women were allowed to have long hair. Jespersen was a twenty-year employee and a fantastic bartender, but she objected strongly to the requirement to wear makeup as degrading and demeaning, and that it took away her credibility as an individual. So she quit and filed a lawsuit alleging gender discrimination.

Jespersen claimed the appearance policy perpetuated unlawful gender stereotyping. In other words, she maintained that her employer had required women to conform to more burdensome appearance standards—wearing makeup is an attempt to "sell" women's appearance—as a condition of employment. The court concluded that Jespersen failed to show that the policy was motivated by the sexual stereotyping of female bartenders and upheld the dismissal of her case. There was no evidence that the makeup requirement was created to be sexually provocative or to treat women as sex objects. Here, both men and women were subjected to the policy. According to the appeals court, "[g]rooming standards that *appropriately* differentiate between the genders are not facially discriminatory." Only policies that "unreasonably burden" one gender violate Title VII. Unfortunately for Jespersen, the court's majority refused to consider her clever argument that it costs far more time and money for a woman to comply with a daily makeup requirement than for a man to keep his hair short.

A dissenting opinion in Jespersen's case provided perhaps the best advice for employers:

> I note with dismay the employer's decision to let go a valued, experienced employee who had gained accolades from her customers, over what, in the end, is a trivial matter. Quality employees are difficult to find in any industry and I would think an employer would long hesitate before forcing a loyal, long-time employee to quit over an honest and heartfelt difference of opinion about a matter of personal significance to her. Having won the legal battle, I hope that Harrah's will now do the generous and decent thing by offering Jespersen her job back and letting her give it her personal best—without the makeup.

There is no indication that Darlene Jespersen ever returned to Harrah's. You can be a good bartender in a lot of drinking establishments that don't require makeup. In fact, in most of the bars I've frequented, I wouldn't have known whether anyone was wearing makeup unless it was David Bowie on his Aladdin Sane tour in the 70s.

Employees should know that employers may adopt reasonable appearance standards and dress codes, particularly requirements that are related to the employer's business interests. For example, a hot dog vendor could require you to wear a wiener in some way, shape, or form. A workplace policy that treats men and women differently in grooming requirements is not necessarily unlawful so long as the policy imposes equal burdens on both men and women. For example, allowing only women to wear facial jewelry, or requiring only men to wear ties, yet requiring both men and women to look and dress professionally, likely would be lawful. (This is not intended to suggest that a lawful policy is the most contemporary, appealing, or inclusive appearance standard.) On the other hand, an unreasonable standard for one sex likely would violate the law against sex discrimination. For example, requiring only women to wear a uniform—or a miniskirt—to work is likely to be unreasonable, demeaning, and unlawful.

13

IS A TSA PAT-DOWN A FORM OF SEXUAL HARASSMENT?

The Scope of Sexual Harassment

Flying? No, I'm just here for the pat-down.

THE MOST-FEARED WORDS in America today may be: "You have been selected to participate in TSA's enhanced pat-down procedures." Selected to participate used to mean congratulations were in order, as if "you've won." Enhanced was also usually a good thing, like you've gained superpowers. Times have changed, starting with enhanced interrogation techniques and now, enhanced pat-downs.

For many air passengers, a pat-down by the Transportation Security Administration (TSA) is synonymous with unwelcome sexual assault. For others, the procedure is the tolerable price we pay to feel safer on an aircraft in a post 9/11 world. As actor Ben Affleck famously commented in 2012, "So they grab your dick a little bit, it's not the end of the world." This comment only makes regular air travelers worry even more about Hollywood, or whether Mr. Affleck ever flies on commercial aircraft with the rest of us.

Of course, 9/11 changed everything about air travel. Just two months after the attacks, Congress authorized the creation of the TSA, and President Bush established it. For the price of security, according to critics, TSA has managed to take the often unpleasant experience of flying and make it even worse. In its defense, TSA has a herculean task, screening over 700 million travelers each year at U.S. airports across the country.

The job can also be dangerous. In 2019 alone, TSA discovered more than 4,432 firearms on passengers or in carry-on luggage at its security checkpoints, almost 90% of which were loaded. About a third of the guns had a round in the chamber. In 2013, Officer Gerardo Hernandez was the first TSA agent killed in the line of duty when he and two other officers, who were wounded, were attacked at the Los Angeles International Airport.

In 2010, TSA adopted "enhanced" security screening measures. Those measures routinely involve touching the breasts, buttocks, and genital area of the traveler. TSA amended its "universal pat-down" procedures in 2017.

"Universal" pat-down certainly sounds intrusive, and the parade of anecdotal abuses by TSA is endless. TSA agents have been accused of being overly intrusive, embarrassing passengers, and, in some instances, even physically assaulting men, women, and young children. Some of these incidents have generated lawsuits and led to the termination of TSA gropers. A TSA pat-down could amount to criminal sexual contact or assault, particularly if the contact is toward the most intimate parts of a human being. However, in 2018, a federal appeals court ruled that TSA screeners are not liable for alleged assaults on passengers under the governmental immunity provisions of the Federal Tort Claims Act.

And (sorry Ben Affleck) from a legal perspective, grabbing your dick a little bit and other unwelcome physical contact of a sexual nature falls squarely within the definition of sexual harassment under the U.S. Equal Employment Opportunity Commission's (EEOC) regulations. Individuals have the right not to be touched in an unwelcome, offensive manner while at work. Moreover, employees are protected from sexual and other harassment by employees and non-employees when they are working, on business premises or at work-related events elsewhere, including when they are on business travel.

The subject of a claim of unlawful sexual harassment would be the employer, not TSA, as it is the employer's responsibility to ensure that an employee is not sexually harassed while at work.

To establish a sexual harassment claim against an employer for sending a business traveler into such harm's way, the employee-traveler would have to show that: (1) the employee is in a protected group—either male or female; (2) the employee was subjected to unwelcome behavior, such as groping at an airport; (3) the harassment was based on sex—for example, the victim was groped because she is female rather than male; (4) the harassment was sufficiently severe or pervasive to alter the conditions of the victim's employment and created a hostile work environment; and (5) the employer knew or should have known of the offensive conduct and failed to take prompt and appropriate remedial action.

In many ways, employees are right to think they should be protected during a TSA security check:

- The law is well-settled that employees are protected from harassment while working, in any location, including while traveling through an airport to get to or from one's next assignment.

- Further, employees should be made aware that they are legally protected from harassment by third parties; namely, offensive non-employees an employee may encounter while doing their job. There are countless examples of unlawful "third-party harassment" that could be compared to airport screening: for example, a customer gropes a female employee; a contractor working on the employer's premises uses sexually-offensive language toward employees; a patient at a hospital assaults a health care worker; or a vendor on the premises makes unwanted advances to an employee. This could also include TSA workers through whom an employee must navigate to accomplish a business travel requirement.

- Finally, unwanted physical contact is clearly a form of sexual harassment. Most courts have adopted a "reasonable person" standard—what an objective reasonable person under a totality of the circumstances would consider offensive—for assessing whether conduct is sufficiently severe or pervasive to create an abusive work environment. Courts are clear that a single, unusually severe instance of unwanted physical touching of the most intimate areas of the body constitutes sexual harassment.

Before you lawyer up and demand millions from your employer for sending you through TSA on business travel, it's important to understand that there are several hurdles an employee who is offended by a TSA pat-down would still have to overcome to bring a successful claim.

The principal problem would be proving that the employee

was subjected to offensive behavior "because of" their sex. The victim would have to show they were being targeted for a pat-down because of their sex, whether male or female. TSA agents purport to follow a "universal" protocol. Under TSA's procedures, men and women are both subject to intrusive pat-downs. Although some TSA officers have been accused of inconsistent treatment of women, and of targeting attractive men and women to satisfy their prurient desires, it would be hard to establish that such rogue behavior is either condoned by TSA's leadership or amounts to a TSA requirement.

Further, remember that a potential claim of harassment is against the employer. Therefore, the traveler must show that the employer knew, or should have known, of the harassment by a third-party and failed to take prompt remedial action. There is little an employer can do to alter the experience that all air travelers must pass through TSA screening. The employer is held to the standard of a "reasonable" employer under the circumstances. The primary difference between an employer's liability for harassment perpetrated by co-workers and harassment committed by non-employees lies in the ability of the employer to control the conduct of the perpetrators. The greater the employer's ability to control a perpetrator's conduct, the more likely it will be found liable for that person's unlawful harassment.

An employer is not able to control a TSA screener's conduct at an airport. An employer has no power to stop the TSA screening process, and all travelers are subject to the federal government's screening procedures.

An employee could ask not to travel by air, fearing a TSA pat-down at an airport. But employees are often required to fly as part of their jobs since it is usually the most expeditious mode of distance travel. Employers could advise, but probably not require, employees to request to opt out of the full-body pat-down and elect an alternative body scanner, if available, for security screening. However, the use of body imaging raises a host of other concerns for travelers.

Finally, like Ben Affleck, many people have accepted that TSA pat-downs are now a part of life . . . and work travel. It would be hard to establish a claim of sexual or other harassment for occasionally experiencing what the rest of us experience as part of travel.

14

IS DATING A CO-WORKER AGAINST THE LAW?

The Legal Implications of Office Romance

The Impressive Clergyman: *Mawwiage. Mawwiage is wat bwings us togeder today. Mawwiage, that bwessed awwangement, that dweam wifin a dream…And wuv, twue wuv, will fowwow you foweva… So tweasure your wuv —*

Prince Humperdinck: *Skip to the end!*

—*The Princess Bride* (1987)

IMAGINE TWO EMPLOYEES, both married to others, who've been working side-by-side every working day for years, with so much time and effort in common and, suddenly, a romantic spark ignites between them. As their relationship becomes more serious, these co-workers decide to leave their respective spouses and pursue the course of their mutual feelings for each other. Many of us have known a person who has gone this route. And most of us would agree that considerable work demands and time with our co-workers, to the exclusion of your spouse, can be hard on any marriage. But is an employer liable for putting the employees in the position—a close working relationship—to wreck their marriages?

Even more commonly, two employees may simply want to go on a date. Is it any employer's business what employees do on their own time, including the time devoted to their love life?

Although work can be a strain on a marriage, an employer has no legal responsibility to preserve a marriage. Sadly, this question comes up most frequently when it involves a married employee's affair with a co-worker.

Generally, what employees do on their own time is none of an employer's business unless the activity is unlawful, interferes with a work requirement or qualification, or creates an actual or apparent conflict of interest with the job.

Employers should be cautioned that an intrusion into the private lives of employees can be considered an invasion of privacy. Some states even have laws preventing the termination of an employee for engaging in off-duty, off-premises, lawful activities. In some states, adultery is still a crime and therefore may not be a protected lawful activity, but the crime is rarely enforced. Wisely, then, few employers tread into employees' private affairs, including affairs of the heart.

However, employers often find themselves in a dilemma. Certain workplace romances inevitably spark questions of sexual harassment. Surveys consistently show that employees are frequently aware of a romantic relationship between a supervisor and a subordinate. Most employees believe such relationships cause favoritism and poor morale at work. Yet the same percentage say romantic relationships at work are personal and should not be regulated by employers.

So what guideposts are there in the workplace?

First, *quid pro quo* harassment is unlawful. *Quid pro quo* means "this for that." Failed office romances between supervisors and non-supervisors can give rise to *quid pro quo* sexual harassment claims. Under the *quid pro quo* theory of sexual harassment, an employer is liable when a supervisor or manager demands sexual favors as a condition of employment or conditions the receipt of some tangible employment benefit (such as more pay or a promotion) on a sexual, romantic, or unduly familiar relationship.

Voluntary, consensual romantic relationships rarely form the basis for a *quid pro quo* claim. It's when relationships end that supervisors and their employers are most vulnerable to claims that the relationship was not voluntary but compelled by the person in the position of authority. And, an employer in a quid pro quo harassment claim, unlikely one in a hostile environment case, may not be shielded by an anti-harassment policy.

Rampant rumors reap ruin. Allowing rumors of an employee's affair to spread, even if the rumors are mistaken, can form the basis of a hostile environment claim. In *Parker v. Reema Consulting Services, Inc.*, a male employee spread a rumor that a female employee slept with her supervisor to get her most recent promotion. The rumor went viral at work, including endorsement by the facility's manager, causing considerable reputational harm to the female employee. The U.S. Court of Appeals for the Fourth Circuit affirmed the female employee's sexual harassment complaint on the basis that spreading rumors that a woman was promoted because she used sex reinforces a pervasive gender-based stereotype that women are less qualified than men and can only achieve success by using feminine sex appeal.

Even consensual relationships may pose problems for employers, especially when dealing with employees who work with their lovers. The U.S. Equal Employment Opportunity Commission (EEOC) published its Policy Guidance on Employer Liability Under Title VII for Sexual Favoritism on January 12, 1990. At the time, the EEOC was chaired by eventual Supreme Court Justice Clarence Thomas. Sexual favoritism occurs when an employee benefits from a sexual relationship with a manager at the expense of other, more qualified, employees. The EEOC Guidelines provide that employers may be liable to employees who have been denied employment opportunities in favor of an employee who has submitted to sexual advances.

Under the EEOC guidelines, isolated instances of favoritism toward a spouse, a lover, or a friend may be unfair but are not in violation of Title VII because they do not discriminate against women or men. The employee is not being favored due to being male or female. The employee is being favored because the employee is married to, sleeping with, or best friends with a supervisor.

However, if an employee is coerced into submitting to unwelcome sexual advances in return for a job benefit, all other employees—male and female—who were qualified but denied the same benefit may be able to establish that sex was made a condition for receiving the benefit.

Finally, widespread favoritism based on the granting of sexual favors may serve as the basis of a hostile environment claim for both male and female employees who do not welcome such behavior. Female actors having to spend time on the "casting couch" with Hollywood producer Harvey Weinstein to obtain film roles is one example. This situation created an atmosphere that was demeaning to one gender. (Weinstein does not appear to have made sexual advances toward male actors.)

An office affair can conflict with an employee's job, and the conflict may be easy to establish by the employer. For example, in *Brown v. Department of the Navy*, a civilian employee of the U.S. Marine Corps, who oversaw the Morale, Welfare and Recreation Department at a military base, began an affair with the wife of an officer assigned to the base while the officer was deployed overseas. Upon discovering the affair, the Marine Corps terminated the employee for misconduct. Clearly, raising the morale of the residents of the base did not include having an affair with an officer's spouse. The employee sued, alleging that he was fired for his off-duty, lawful behavior, but the court rejected the claim and found the employee's job dealt with the care of families of Marines and therefore, his adulterous behavior was contrary to his job responsibilities. His employer lost trust and confidence in his ability to perform his duties—even if the behavior occurred while off-duty.

Similarly, a federal appeals court ruled that a supervisor who was fired for lying about his affair with a subordinate had no claims under Title VII. In *Malone v. Eaton Corp.*, rumors swirled in a manufacturing plant that a supervisor was having an affair with an employee. The plant manager confronted the supervisor about the alleged relationship, but the supervisor denied having an affair. The plant manager warned the supervisor that the company had an anti-fraternization policy that prohibited intimate relationships between supervisors and subordinates. A year later, allegations arose that the same supervisor was having an affair with a different female employee. Again, the employee was confronted about the alleged affair and was advised that the company was concerned about its exposure to sexual harassment claims. The supervisor was warned he would be fired if he was lying. Again, the employee denied having an affair. After a brief investigation, the company discovered the supervisor had lied about having an affair and fired him. The supervisor sued the employer, alleging gender discrimination; namely, that the company treated women more favorably than men. But the court rejected the former supervisor's claim. He was the only supervisor who had engaged in any wrongdoing; therefore, he could not show that any woman was treated more favorably. The case reinforces the workplace maxim: You can always fire a liar.

In fact, barring some evidence of unwelcome, *quid pro quo* harassment, people who engage in consensual affairs are rarely victorious in court under Title VII. For example, in *Smith v. AMTRAK*, a female employee of AMTRAK began an affair with a high-level executive of the rail service. The executive told his lover he could not marry her while she was an employee of AMTRAK because the company had a rule against married couples working together. Therefore, she voluntarily resigned. Months later, she realized her lover never intended to marry her, and AMTRAK had no rule barring married couples from working together! Oops. The woman sued AMTRAK, claiming *quid pro quo* harassment by her former lover. Issuing a clear lesson in life's hard knocks, the court found that, while the supervisor's behavior was deplorable, the employee's rights were not violated. The court stated that an employee "cannot deem unwelcome retroactively what she welcomed at the time." Obviously, at the time she quit, the affair was welcome. Indeed, it was the reason she resigned.

In a similar vein, the "other woman"—in this case, the one who was fired after the boss's wife discovered her husband's affair—usually has no claim under Title VII. In *Kahn v. Objective Solutions International*, a female recruiter began a consensual, sexual relationship with the president of the company. One day, after a sexual encounter, the president informed the employee he was terminating the relationship and her job. He told her their affair had become public, his family "disapproved" of their relationship, and he suggested that, if she desired, she could "call his wife and beg for her job back." The president told the employee that "if he could not be intimate with her, he no longer wanted her around." Amazingly, the scorned employee called her paramour's wife and asked for her job back. It was only after the wife rejected the employee's pleas for her job that the employee brought a claim of harassment under federal and state law. Conceding the president was a "cad," the court dismissed the claims on the grounds the romantic relationship was consensual. The fact that the employee was terminated because the boss desired to end the affair did not constitute sexual discrimination. While "unfair and certainly unchivalrous behavior," ending a consensual romantic relationship is not discrimination based on gender. The court continued: "Rejection and discrimination are not synonymous." Harsh, but fair.

In one of the most unusual cases involving extramarital affairs, *Triplett v. Belle of Orleans LLC,* a supervisor brought a race discrimination claim against his employer for firing him after discovering his affair with a subordinate. Acknowledging that he'd had an affair with one of his subordinates, the supervisor argued that he was "set up." He claimed his employer planned his termination by arranging the affair by having a female employee "seduce" him. The court dismissed the case, finding no evidence to support the allegations. Even if some of the plot was true, there was no evidence any such plot pointed to race discrimination.

Finally, home wreckers, and their employers, beware . . . There are still a few states (Hawaii, New Mexico, North Carolina, Mississippi, South Dakota, and Utah) that allow a jilted spouse to sue the person whom they claim destroyed their marriage.

Cases alleging "criminal conversation" or "alienation of affection" are rare but allow cuckolded spouses to claim damages for the injuries they've suffered—including mental anguish and humiliation—from being cheated on. Cases against employers for alienation of affection are even rarer. In 2000, in *Mercier v. Daniels*, for example, the North Carolina Court of Appeals ruled in favor of an employer in a claim for alienation of affection brought by a spouse. A married couple, the Merciers, ran a U-Haul franchise. Mr. Mercier claimed Mrs. Mercier left him for a U-Haul field manager. Mr. Mercier sued the field manager *and* U-Haul. The trial court ruled in favor of U-Haul finding that the company had not authorized or endorsed the affair. Mr. Mercier appealed, arguing that U-Haul placed the field manager in a position to have an affair when it assigned the field manager's duties and U-Haul failed to intervene when it knew (or should have known) of the affair. The appellate court concluded that the affair was obviously not within the scope of the field manager's duties, and U-Haul could not be liable for the manager's behavior outside the scope of the employee's job. Further, Mr. Mercier presented no evidence that the company had any direct knowledge of the affair and, as such, could not have "ratified" its field manager's behavior. The court never addressed whether an employer could be liable for alienation of affection had it known of the affair and failed to stop it.

Given the risk of lawsuits, particularly those premised on sexual harassment, employers are increasingly inclined to establish "anti-fraternization" rules that apply to relationships between supervisors and non-supervisors. In other words, an employer can prohibit employees from dating if the employer reasonably believes such relationships interfere with work. This might certainly be the case if a supervisor were to date a non-supervisory employee. Employers might be concerned that a supervisor would coerce a non-supervisor into an unwanted sexual, romantic, or even unduly familiar personal relationship. Even if a relationship between a manager and non-supervisor was purely consensual, other employees in the organization might fear the non-supervisor would receive undeserved favoritism, promotion, or increased apparent authority from the supervisor they were dating.

The opposite might be true as well. Much like a young athlete coached by a parent, a supervisor might treat the person with whom they are in a romantic relationship to more demanding and unrealistic expectations in order to avoid the appearance of favoritism. Some personal relationships might conflict with an organization's values or formal ethical standards. In some cases, anti-fraternization policies can even help employees lacking supervisory status to have clearer expectations of their supervisors' behavior and hold supervisors to proper boundaries between work demands and an employee's private life. Finally, even if the dating relationship was welcome and formed under acceptable circumstances, many relationships invariably end, and few employers and co-workers have the time or inclination to manage a difficult office break-up, which could sink to the level of property divisions in a cubicle, screaming at each other at the office holiday party, or even throwing office products at each other in anger.

For years, supervisors might have been permitted to troll for their love life using work as their unrestricted domain. In the wake of #MeToo and Time's Up movements, supervisors' workplace behavior toward employees has drawn considerably more scrutiny than ever before. Supervisors should be, and often are, held to the highest standards of performance and behavior as agents of an employer for whose conduct an employer can be held liable under employment laws.

15

CAN AN EMPLOYER BEAT ITS EMPLOYEES? . . . I MEAN, REALLY?

More on the Law Against Harassment

Doug: *We now consecrate the bond of obedience.*
                      Assume the position.
                      [whack with a fraternity paddle]
Chip: *Thank you, sir. May I have another?*

Animal House (1978)

IMAGINE ONE OF THOSE POPULAR corporate motivational training sessions . . . gone wild.

Janet Orlando worked for Alarm One, Inc., a Fresno, California company, selling alarm systems. Orlando was 52 years old in an office otherwise comprised mostly of workers younger than 25. Every day, before employees ventured out for another exciting day selling alarm systems, the office would hold a "pep rally" to motivate its employees. Bonuses were handed out, employees would sing for the group, some employees would get a pie in the face. Others were encouraged to eat baby food and wear diapers. Often, the employees, including Orlando, would be spanked with an Alarm One sign or a competitor's sign.

Claiming to be absolutely humiliated by the experience of repeatedly being spanked at work, Orlando sued Alarm One and its supervisors for sexual harassment, assault, battery, sexual battery, and intentional infliction of emotional distress. A California state court jury awarded Orlando $500,000 in compensatory damages and $1 million in punitive damages against Alarm One!

Before you rush to judgment—thinking "Who would spank a 52-year old woman at work?"—on appeal, the jury verdict was overturned, and a new trial was ordered. The appeals court held that the jury had been improperly instructed on sexual harassment, and conflicting evidence made a new trial necessary. There was evidence that Orlando had voluntarily participated in the spankings. What? There was also a dispute about how often Orlando had been spanked. What? Some evidence even suggested Orlando had spanked a male employee. What? And both male and female employees were spanked, thereby rebutting the necessary element of proof that the harassing conduct must be based on the victim's sex; meaning, there was no different treatment based on an employee's sex.

Regardless of the outcome favoring the employer (at least until a new trial), this form of teambuilding demonstrated exceptionally poor judgment. Encouraging the "herd mentality" of voluntarily bending over for a spanking only invites lawsuits; it doesn't avoid them.

Unless you work on a pirate ship, there is a clear line between "motivating" employees and bullying or unlawfully harassing them. Unwelcome physical contact, no matter how it's intended, may constitute unlawful sexual harassment. People have the right *not* to be touched at work.

However, there is a difference between inadvertent contact, a polite tap on a co-worker's shoulder to get their attention, or a warm embrace among friends . . . and a personal space invader. "Hostile work environment" is a legal term, not a feeling. Being a jerk or creepy at times may not be enough to constitute harassment. Having one difficult or negative interaction with a co-worker also may not be enough. Instead, there are required elements to establish a legal claim of harassment.

First, you must be in a protected group: All employees are in more than one protected group. Both women and men are in a protected group based on gender. Whites, Blacks, Asians, and Native Americans are in a protected group based on race. Hispanics/Latinx, Italians, Swedes, Kenyans, Koreans, Arabs, and the members of every other ethnic group are protected based on national origin. Jews, Christians, Muslims, Hindus, Buddhists, atheists, agnostics, Wiccans, Scientologists, and all other religious observers are in a protected group of religious adherents. Persons age 40 and older are in a protected group based on age. Persons with physical and mental disabilities are in a protected group based on their disability.

The more difficult element to prove is that the objectionable conduct was based on one's membership in a protected group. If I scream at my co-worker, "You are the worst second baseman we've ever had on the company softball team," she may be offended. However, I am not treating her differently because she's female; I'm criticizing her because she's poor at fielding grounders. Also, softball players are not a protected group. But, if I start ridiculing her because I think women can't or shouldn't play softball, then my co-worker may show that my conduct was based on her membership in a protected group; i.e., her gender.

The behavior in question must be unwelcome from the recipient's perspective. This is a subjective standard: Every human being gets to decide what is unwelcome to them. This means an employee who didn't solicit or invite the behavior and considers the behavior to be undesirable or offensive.

There must be enough of the behavior to alter the conditions of a victim's job and create an abusive and hostile working environment. The alleged harasser's conduct is assessed from the objective standard of a "reasonable person" under similar circumstances. Isolated instances of offensive verbal remarks, the occasional use of vulgar language, and merely annoying comments probably are not enough to establish a hostile work environment. Instead, the misconduct must be sufficiently severe (harmful) or pervasive (frequent) to unreasonably interfere with one's job. The more severe the behavior, such as unwelcome intentional touching of another's intimate body areas, the fewer the number of instances necessary to show harassment.

In the world of workplace harassment, bystanders have rights, too. Although you may like to be spanked or to dip-kiss your co-workers, your co-workers don't have to like it and can be offended by having to watch you engage in such offensive behavior at work.

Speaking of spanking, football players and other athletes often spank each other on the buttocks when celebrating a superior athletic achievement or game-winning effort. That appears to be welcome and builds camaraderie on a team. Is it unlawful harassment?

Every lawyer in the United States maintains the default position that a spank on the rear end at work is usually inappropriate and is simply asking for legal trouble. However, if it occurs only one time, in celebration, it may not be unlawful harassment. In *Williams v. Ocean Beach Club, LLC*, decided in 2012, Sandra Williams, who sold time shares, brought a sexual harassment lawsuit against her employer. She complained that her male supervisor slapped her on the buttocks one time, apparently in celebration of closing a particularly difficult real estate sale. Timing is always relevant in these cases. The slap on the buttocks occurred in August 2007. Williams was fired for poor attendance a little more than two months later.

More importantly, though, the context in which the behavior occurs is often determinative in harassment cases. Williams admitted that her boss never touched her before this one instance, he'd never said or done anything else inappropriate to her or other employees, she did not believe his slap was sexual in nature, and, although the slap left a hand print on her buttocks, Williams did not think her supervisor was trying to harm her. Her relationship with her boss was otherwise a good one, and she did not want him disciplined for his misbehavior. Nonetheless, the supervisor was disciplined for his conduct by the company.

Based on these facts, the court dismissed Williams's claim of sexual harassment.

Offensive behavior must be sufficiently severe or pervasive to alter the conditions of one's job and create a hostile work environment. Here, even though the misbehavior was by a supervisor, the court found a single isolated incident of physical contact was not sufficient to constitute unlawful sexual harassment.

Obviously, the more frequent or more harmful the physical contact, the more likely the behavior becomes unlawful. This is where teambuilding can get significantly out of hand. Personally, I have two simple rules for employers and their employees: Stay away from any *Animal House*-like "thank-you-sir-may-I-have-another" shenanigans . . . and never, ever, waterboard an employee.

In another example of teambuilding gone horribly wrong, Chad Hudgens worked at Prosper Inc., a financial services company, in Provo, Utah. His boss, Joshua Christopherson, was an old-school workplace sadist. Christopherson constantly humiliated employees by drawing mustaches on their faces using a permanent marker or removed their chair when they did not meet sales goals. He patrolled the office with a wooden paddle, slamming it on desks and tables as a motivator. The *coup de gras* of workplace morale came in May 2007, when Christopherson asked for volunteers for a "new" motivational exercise. When Christopherson taunted employees about their loyalty and work ethic, Hudgens felt compelled to volunteer (even without knowing what the exercise would be). Christopherson then marched the employees outside, ordered Hudgens to lie down in the grass, further ordered his co-workers to hold down Hudgens's arms and legs, and proceeded to pour a gallon of water slowly down Hudgens's nose and mouth so that he could not breathe. For the uninitiated, that's called waterboarding.

Hudgens quit six weeks later and sued his employer and Christopherson individually for assault and battery, intentional infliction of emotional distress, and wrongful termination. The company denied the allegations. In 2008, the trial court dismissed the case for failure to state the claims properly after concluding that Christopherson only intended to motivate, and not harm, Hudgens. However, in 2010, the Utah Supreme Court reversed the decision of the trial court and allowed Hudgens to amend his complaint to renew his allegations against his employer and Christopherson.

These cases are good examples of the universal legal axiom: Mean people suck, and their employers can be sued. Cases against bullies like Christopherson and the employer that unleashed him on the workforce are increasing. Employees should know their rights.

The cases above highlight some of the legal theories that employees can use to hold workplace aggressors accountable for their behavior. A claim of unlawful discrimination, including harassment, can be brought if an employee is singled out for offensive behavior due to race, color, religion, national origin, sex, age, disability, or any other category protected by federal, state, or local law. In Orlando's case, above, it appeared that both men and women were voluntarily spanking each other. Therefore, the court overturned her big-money verdict for a new trial to determine whether she was harassed *because* she was female.

Even if both men and women are being spanked, though, that doesn't make it right. Spanking is an assault. The fact that some employees appeared to be having fun does not mean everyone thought it was a welcome experience.

There are other claims available against bullies at work. The best defense against a bully might be some form of "whistleblower" claim challenging the bully's behavior as an unlawful form of violence at work. For example, the Occupational Safety and Health Act (OSHA) of 1970 contains a provision placing a general duty on private sector employers to maintain a safe work environment, free from workplace violence. Therefore, an employee may pursue a claim because they have suffered adverse action for being subject to, or objecting to, workplace violence.

Other potential claims include assault, battery, intentional infliction of emotional distress, and breach of contract. The behavior must be exceptionally outrageous to meet the standard for intentional infliction of emotional distress. Similarly, breach of an employment contract can be difficult to establish.

An employee would have to prove that the employer made a promise (for example, in an employee handbook) to maintain a safe workplace and failed to do so.

Over the course of the last twenty years, employers typically have disclaimed contractual liability based on provisions of their employee handbooks. They have scrubbed contract-like commitments from company guidelines. Of course, if an employee is physically or emotionally harmed by a bully, eligible employees of covered employers may be entitled to job-protected time away from a bully under the Family and Medical Leave Act.

In conclusion, work is no place to humiliate or otherwise hurt an employee: Be safe out there.

16

IS IT ILLEGAL TO FIRE SOMEONE WHO IS GAY OR LOOKS GAY?

Sexual Orientation Discrimination

YES, AN EMPLOYEE REALLY ASKED me this question. I still don't know exactly what it means to "look gay." But I know that people have been harassed or otherwise mistreated for looking gay. In *Doe v. City of Belleville*, a male employee who was described as a "former Marine of imposing stature," waged a relentless verbal campaign of abuse toward two 16-year-old twin brothers working in the town's cemetery. For example, he constantly called one "fat boy" and his "bitch" and the other brother (who wore an earring) "queer" and "fag." The former Marine repeatedly asked one boy whether he was a boy or a girl, threatened to take him "out to the woods" and "get up his ass," and once, having grabbed the boy's testicles, announced, "Well, I guess he's a guy." On appeal, a federal court ruled that harassment of a male employee "because his voice is soft, his physique is slight, his hair is long, or because in some other respect he exhibits his masculinity in a way that does not meet his co-workers' idea of how men are to appear and behave, is harass[ment] 'because' of his sex." The fact that one teenage boy was harassed for wearing an earring, viewed by the alleged harasser as a "feminine accouterment not suitable for male adornment," when a woman would not have been treated in such a way, supported the boy's claim of sex discrimination.

Constantly mocking a male because he appears effeminate (or harassing a female because she exhibits allegedly "masculine" traits) is usually against the law. Making fun of an employee because he or she is heterosexual, or appears heterosexual, is likewise against the law. This question is a good reminder that issues regarding "sexual orientation" and "gender expression" are part of the new frontier of gender discrimination claims. Every employer and their employees should have a firm understanding of the law of sex . . . as it relates to work.

A recent United States Supreme Court decision, *Bostock v. Clayton County*, has extended the protections of Title VII of the Civil Rights Act of 1964 to applicants and employees based on their sexual orientation or transgender status. Many state and local governments have already granted protections based on sexual orientation and gender identity.

Despite the common mistake of conflating terms, sexual orientation and gender identity are two distinct legal, biological, and social concepts. In general, sexual orientation refers to whom one is sexually, emotionally, or romantically and enduringly attracted. Depending on the biological gender of the person one desires, sexual orientation is often categorized as heterosexuality, homosexuality, bisexuality, and asexuality (lack of sexual attraction to any person).

Gender identity and gender expression are similarly complex. For purposes of workplace law, gender identity refers to how people view their own gender, regardless of their biological sex assigned at birth. Gender expression, in turn, is how one appears or acts regarding their gender identity. Stereotypes about male and female roles in our culture, and ever-changing societal views regarding masculinity and femininity, affect gender expression.

This is where a societal rift is drawn (and people can quickly become upset . . . on all sides).

An evolving taxonomy to describe various gender identities—including cisgender, transgender, pansexual, non-binary, gender non-conformant, gender queer, and gender fluid—has developed over the last few decades. This development has drawn the attention of critics who are reluctant to embrace, or simply dismissive, of the concept of a gender identity that is inconsistent with that which does not conform to one's biological sex at birth. At one end of the spectrum, there is the group that believes there are only two sexes, as determined by whether you have a vagina or a penis. Full stop. At the other end of the spectrum is Tumblr's identification of 112 different gender identities. A dizzying array of new gender pronouns, alternatives to the traditional "he/she," "her/him," including the singular, gender-neutral "they," "ze," "xe," "ey," and "hir," adds yet another level of complexity to the discussion.

Regardless of people's developing and conflicting views in our society about these categories, workplace law has clearly arced in favor of protection based on sexual orientation and gender identity. Today, at least 23 states and the District of Columbia, along with more than 400 cities and counties, protect employees in public and private sector workplaces based on their sexual orientation or gender identity, or both. In addition, federal courts have increasingly used the term "sex," which is protected under federal law, to include both sexual orientation and gender identity.

Title VII of the Civil Rights Act of 1964 specifically protects applicants and employees from discrimination "because of sex." In 1964, well before medical professionals, social scientists, and advocates for sexual minorities had emerged on this topic, "sex" was associated with biological "gender" (male or female) and there was little effort to distinguish the terms "sex" and "gender." There was no consideration of "intersex" persons (persons born with biological characteristics of both men and women). There was certainly no inclination or attempt to associate gender with sexual orientation or gender identity. Thus, the sexual orientation or gender variance of an applicant or employee was not protected under the federal prohibition against sex discrimination.

Further, as a relevant aside, "transvestism," "transsexualism," and "gender identity disorders not resulting from physical impairments" were and continue to be specifically excluded from the definition of a protected disability under the Americans with Disabilities Act. (But based upon some recent court rulings, even this may be changing.)

A watershed legal moment in an expanded view of the term "sex" occurred decades ago, in 1989, with the U.S. Supreme Court's decision in *Price Waterhouse v. Hopkins*. Ann Hopkins, a senior manager at a major accounting firm, sued her employer for gender discrimination when her consideration for partnership in the firm was placed on hold. Hopkins argued that she was not selected for partner because of "sexual stereotyping." She was described negatively in her performance reviews and was treated differently as a woman, because she was "macho," "overcompensated for being a woman," needed "charm school," and used "unladylike" profane language. Despite being one of the firm's best performing employees, she was advised that in order to make partner, she needed to "walk more femininely, talk more femininely, dress more femininely, wear make-up, have her hair styled, and wear jewelry." In other words, Hopkins was not promoted because she did not conform to a company stereotype of how a *female* accounting manager should look or act at work. A plurality of the Supreme Court endorsed the view that gender-based stereotyping could be a form of unlawful gender discrimination under Title VII.

Therefore, at least for purposes of workplace rights, sex includes something more than one's biological gender. It also includes the social and cultural constructs associated with the words "masculinity" and "femininity." Masculinity and femininity—how society deems that men and women should look, act, or behave—convey some additional meaning about gender than one's biological sex.

Sexual stereotyping is the application of stereotypical notions regarding how a man or woman should appear and behave in the context of society's view of what is masculine and feminine. The traditional view, reinforced by countless media images, like the Marlboro Man and any woman named Kardashian, is that a man should look and act like a man and a woman should look and act like a woman. This view was consistently reinforced in the law. For example, in the early years of Title VII, courts refused to advance the notion that a man could be a victim of gender discrimination because he appeared to be "effeminate."

TIMES HAVE CHANGED. While sexual stereotyping occurs and, in fact, is quite common, sexual stereotyping that adversely affects an applicant or employee may now be used as evidence to support a claim of sexual discrimination. Therefore, harassing a man because he appears contrary to the stereotypical notion of what a man "should be" may be unlawful sexual harassment.

Further, numerous federal courts have since recognized sexual harassment claims, including same-sex harassment claims, under Title VII based on mistreatment of employees for not conforming to gender stereotypes. Indeed, at least one court found that nonconformity with gender stereotypes can include harassment toward a heterosexual male employee by other male employees on the belief he was a virgin.

Finally, in 2020, the United States Supreme Court specifically ruled that discrimination based on sexual orientation or gender identity is discrimination "because of sex" prohibited by Title VII. It is now unlawful for employers covered by Title VII to fire an employee who is gay or transgender.

In *Bostock v. Clayton County*, the Supreme Court decided three consolidated cases: *Bostock v. Clayton County, Georgia*, in which ten-year employee Gerald Bostock was fired for conduct "unbecoming" a county employee after he began playing in a gay recreational softball league; *Altitude Express, Inc. v. Zarda*, in which skydiving instructor Donald Zarda was fired days after he mentioned he was gay to customers; and *R. G. & G. R. Harris Funeral Homes, Inc. v. Equal Employment Opportunity Commission*, in which Aimee Stephens, who presented as a male when she was hired, was fired after she informed her employer that she planned to "live and work full-time as a woman." The Court opined that an employer that discriminates on the basis of homosexuality or transgender status "inescapably" treats individual employees differently because of their sex:

We agree that homosexuality and transgender status are distinct concepts from sex. But, as we've seen, discrimination based on homosexuality or transgender status necessarily entails discrimination based on sex; the first cannot happen without the second.

As a result, Title VII now protects all persons based on their sex, including a person's sexual orientation and transgender status. And that includes both a person who is gay or "looks gay."

17

WHICH BATHROOM DOES A TRANSGENDER EMPLOYEE USE?

Gender Identity Protection

THE LAW CONCERNING THE RIGHTS of transgender employees is changing rapidly. Federal courts have long considered the rights of transgender persons at work. The development of that law culminated in a 2020 U.S. Supreme Court ruling that transgender status is protected under Title VII of the Civil Rights Act of 1964 (Title VII).

But first, the story of a transgender war hero would catch anyone's attention. Kenneth Ulane was a combat aviator in Vietnam who had been awarded eight Air Medals for valor in aerial flight during the war. After leaving the Army in 1968, he immediately joined Eastern Airlines and advanced from Second Officer to First Officer, accumulating more than 8,000 flight hours. Ulane maintained that, since early childhood, he had always felt like a woman. In fact, he sought psychiatric assistance while still in the military to address these feelings. After more than ten years at Eastern Airlines, in 1979, Ulane was diagnosed by a doctor as transsexual. He began taking female hormones and, in 1980, underwent sex reassignment surgery. Now Karen Ulane, she obtained a revised Illinois birth certificate identifying her as Karen, and the FAA certified her for flight status as female. Nonetheless, Eastern Airlines fired her in 1981 on the grounds that her gender reassignment surgery would "detract" from her flight crew's cohesiveness and ability to operate safely. Ulane sued, but Eastern Airlines won.

Incredibly, at least for the early 1980s, the trial court ruled in favor of Ulane on the theory that while "sexual preference" is not protected under Title VII, a person's "sexual identity" is protected. On appeal by Eastern Airlines, though, the appellate court disagreed, holding that a person's sex means "a biological male or biological female." According to the appellate court, Karen Ulane was not fired because she was a female, she was fired because she was a transsexual. Title VII does not specifically protect transsexuals. Eastern Airlines won the case but paid Ulane a sizeable settlement to end her claims. Just a few years later, in 1989, Ms. Ulane was killed in a private plane crash. Ironically, Eastern Airlines didn't last much longer, going bankrupt, and ceasing operations in 1991.

Public opinion has changed considerably since 1981 regarding transgender persons. Many states now protect a person's gender identity from unlawful discrimination in the workplace. In 2020, the U.S. Supreme Court specifically ruled that transgender status is protected under the broad meaning of "sex" within Title VII.

As for the restroom, does it really matter what restroom an employee uses? For many, it apparently matters a great deal.

On a larger scale, issues related to gender identity and gender expression, especially which restroom one may enter, have sparked enormous interest and debate in our society. Even popular advice columnists Dear Abby and Ann Landers have addressed this question in past newspaper columns. (See their advice below.) It is quite common for employers to find themselves on the front lines of the debate over developing social issues and commensurate legal protections for their employees. Employers want to avoid lawsuits and liability and, also, get it right.

But first, we should define our terms, if they haven't changed by the time you read this book. Are we talking about a "transgender," "transvestite," or "transsexual" employee? The differences may seem slight but are legally relevant.

"Transgender" is an umbrella term used to describe a person whose gender identity is incongruent with their gender assignment at birth. A transvestite, sometimes referred to as a "cross dresser," is someone who dresses as a member of the opposite gender but usually has no desire to change their sex permanently. For example, drag queens and drag kings are people who cross-dress for entertainment purposes. According to the International Foundation for Gender Education, an advocacy and education group located in Waltham, Massachusetts, most cross-dressers are heterosexual and married.

"Transsexual" has come to describe a transgender person who desires to transition permanently to the gender with which they identify and who seeks medical assistance to make the transition, which may include hormone replacement therapy and sex reassignment surgery. For many reasons, including cost, physical or emotional pain, or personal preference, not all transgender persons are willing (or able) to undergo gender reassignment surgery.

Transgender persons may also include "genderqueer," "genderfluid," or other gender-nonconformant identities. A person could also identify as "non-binary." A non-binary person has rejected some or all the normative conventions of traditional male or female gender assignments. Some non-binary people identify as transgender; others do not.

There is an important legal aside to the discussion of gender, sexual orientation, and gender identity. Transgender status, or gender nonconformity, is not a specific medical or psychiatric diagnosis. However, transgender persons may have "gender dysphoria" which is a medical diagnosis that describes the significant distress a person may experience by not identifying with their assigned gender at birth. Legal jurisprudence is developing to determine whether gender dysphoria is a disability under the Americans with Disabilities Act, thereby entitling a person to a reasonable accommodation in the workplace.

Further, gender identity, gender expression, and sexual orientation are different. Gender identity is how you define your own gender. Gender expression is how you openly express your gender identity, such as name, appearance, dress, and behavior. Your sexual orientation is to whom you are sexually, emotionally, or romantically attracted. Therefore, a transgender person may be heterosexual, homosexual, bisexual, or may even refuse to conform to normative conventions regarding sexual orientation. Cisgender persons are persons whose gender identity matches their biological sex assigned at birth. Most persons on the planet are cisgender. A cisgender person may be heterosexual, homosexual, bisexual, or may refuse to conform to normative conventions of sexual orientation.

As Ulane's case demonstrates, and the Supreme Court finally addressed in 2020, part of the problem discussing sex discrimination is that no one knows precisely what Congress meant by "sex" when it passed the Civil Rights Act of 1964 protecting persons "on the basis of sex." Indeed, most people are unaware that "sex" was added as a protected class by a last-minute amendment made on the floor of the House of

Representatives the day before the House voted on the bill. The amendment to add "sex" was a ploy by Democrat Howard Smith of Virginia, a strong opponent of racial equality, to defeat the entire Civil Rights Act. From an outsider's perspective, Congress may have been ready to protect persons based on their race—it was the height of the Civil Rights Movement— but a mostly male Congress was damn sure unprepared to pass a law which included equal protection based on sex. After all, this was back when married couples on popular television programs could not share a bed on TV, and it was downright scandalous to catch a glimpse of any woman's bare belly.

The effort to derail the law failed. The law passed, but we have little record of hearings, legislative history, or the stated intent of Congress to help us understand today how a person's sex should be interpreted under Title VII.

Despite this, the law has changed considerably since 1984, the year Ulane's case was decided. In 2012, in *Macy v. Department of Justice*, the U.S. Equal Employment Opportunity Commission (EEOC) ruled that discrimination based on transgender status is sex discrimination in violation of Title VII. In another federal sector employment case, *Lusardi v. Department of the Army*, decided in 2015, the EEOC further expanded protection for transgender persons by ruling that denying a transgender employee equal access to a common bathroom corresponding to the employee's gender identity, rather than biological gender, constitutes unlawful gender discrimination. The employer could not restrict a transgender employee to a single-user restroom to avoid access to the common bathroom unless the employer made the single-use restroom available to all employees.

In 2018, a federal appeals court ruled for the first time that Title VII protects transgender and transitioning employees, even over an employer's religious objections. In *Stephens v. R.G. & G.R. Harris Funeral Homes, Inc.*, decided by the U.S. Court of Appeals for the Sixth Circuit, Aimee Australia Stephens, a transgender woman who was born a biological male, began work as a funeral director for a Detroit funeral home in 2007 while still presenting as a man. After six years, Stephens gave the owner of the funeral home a letter indicating she struggled with gender identity disorder her entire life and intended to have sex reassignment surgery. But before the medical procedure, Stephens was required to live and work full-time as a woman for one year. The owner of the funeral home fired Stephens immediately on the grounds that, for the owner, the Bible teaches that a person's sex is an immutable, God-given gift, and he would be violating God's commands if he were to permit his male-born funeral director to wear women's clothing. He also said customers would be unnecessarily distracted and upset by the situation.

Like Ulane did in 1981, Stephens filed a gender discrimination claim under Title VII. The trial court dismissed Stephens's claim on the basis that transgender status is not a protected trait under Title VII, and further, that the Religious Freedom Restoration Act (RFRA) barred the claim because of the employer's religious beliefs against a man dressing as a woman.

On appeal, the appellate court reversed the ruling, rejecting the argument that, for the purposes of Title VII, "sex" refers only to a "binary characteristic for which there are only two classifications, male and female." Moreover, the court said discrimination against transgender persons necessarily implicates Title VII's proscriptions against sex stereotyping and gender non-conformity. Finally, the court rejected the funeral director's religious liberty defense on the basis that RFRA protects religious "exercise," not "religious beliefs." A funeral home cannot rely on presumed biases of its customers under RFRA. "Bare compliance with Title VII—without actually assisting or facilitating Stephens's transition efforts—does not amount to [a religious] endorsement of Stephens's views."

In 2020, the U.S. Supreme Court affirmed the decision in favor of Ms. Stephens. In a surprising decision (two conservative members of the Court joined four liberal members of the Court), the Court ruled unequivocally that discrimination based on transgender status constitutes unlawful gender discrimination under Title VII. However, the Court refused to address the question of access to bathrooms and locker rooms.

What, then, are the bathroom rights of a transgender person?

First, it is unwise to limit any employee's use of the bathroom at work. The Occupational Safety and Health Administration (OSHA), the federal agency that enforces private sector employers' duty to maintain a safe and hazard-free workplace, has ruled that the Occupational Safety and Health Act requires that all workers have unrestricted access to a convenient restroom. Under OSHA's Sanitation Standard 1910.141, OSHA has further taken the position that employees should be permitted to use facilities that correspond with their gender identity. For example, a person who identifies as a man should be permitted to use men's restrooms, and a person who identifies as a woman should be permitted to use women's restrooms. According to OSHA, model business practices would also include single-occupancy, gender-neutral (unisex) facilities or the use of "multiple-occupant, gender-neutral restroom facilities with lockable single occupant stalls." Not surprisingly, mega-companies like Starbucks have since adopted single-occupancy, gender-neutral restrooms in their establishments.

Regardless of the debate in federal courts about whether "sex" includes transgender status in its protection, state and local laws already hold significant protection for transgender persons. However, this may or may not include the right to use a restroom of one's choice.

In 1993, Minnesota became the first state to protect transgendered persons from discrimination. Today, twenty-one states and the District of Columbia have similar laws. Some of these states, by law or administrative regulation, grant persons the right to use a restroom or locker room facility at work that comports with one's gender identity rather than one's biological gender at birth. These states include Colorado, Delaware, Iowa, New York, Vermont, and Washington.

Even the states that grant protection from discrimination based on gender identity have not necessarily agreed that transgender persons have the right to use the bathroom associated with their gender identity. To the contrary, over the last few years, several states have considered so-called "bathroom bills." These are laws that would restrict access to multi-user restrooms, locker rooms, and other sex-segregated facilities to persons based solely on one's sex assigned at birth or "biological sex." In 2016, North Carolina became the only state to enact such a law but, facing tremendous public backlash and business boycotts, partially repealed the law in 2017.

Minnesota was the first state to protect gender identity, but not necessarily access to the bathroom associated with one's gender identity. In *Goins v. West Group*, Julienne Goins, a transgender female who had not yet undergone gender reassignment surgery, worked for West Group in Eagan, Minnesota. Ms. Goins used the female restrooms, and several women complained to management. The human resources director advised Goins not to use the female restrooms but, instead, to use the single-occupancy "unisex" bathrooms on the premises. Goins objected to the policy and later quit. Goins filed suit claiming the employer's failure to let her use the female restrooms violated Minnesota's gender identity discrimination law.

The case progressed all the way to the Minnesota Supreme Court, which held that the company's policy requiring all employees to use the restroom designated for their biological gender was not discrimination in violation of the Minnesota Human Rights Act. The "bathroom rule"—biological men use the men's restrooms and biological women use the women's restrooms—was based on gender. Goins never claimed that West Group's assignment of bathrooms by gender was illegal. Instead, she argued only that bathroom use should be based on one's "self-image of gender" to comply with Minnesota law. Ruling in 2001, the Minnesota Supreme Court disagreed. The Minnesota law does not require employers to designate restrooms by self-image of gender. Therefore, the employer's decision to assign bathroom use by biological gender was lawful. Similarly, the employer could also have assigned restroom use by gender identity and that, too, would have been lawful. Ms. Goins could not show that she was biologically a female and, as a result, she was not discriminated against when she was not permitted to use the women's restroom.

Even if state law is no help, or you live and work in a state that has no protection for transgender persons (such as Texas), large municipalities in nearly every state may still afford protections for transgender persons. For example, in Texas, five of the six largest cities—Houston, Dallas, Austin, Fort Worth, and El Paso—have ordinances banning discrimination based on sexual orientation and gender identity. This could include access to a restroom comporting with one's gender identity. Of course, the U.S. Supreme Court's opinion in 2020 protecting transgender persons under Title VII is certain to impact access to restrooms.

Employers and employees must reconcile the rights of

transgender applicants and employees regarding the use of restroom and locker room facilities with others' personal or religious objections to endorsing a transgender person's gender non-conformance in the workplace. Like Starbucks, providing single-occupancy, gender-neutral restrooms may afford the most expedient compromise.

One thing is certain: There is a small, but more visible, population of transgender persons. Every employer should have equal employment opportunity, anti-discrimination, and anti-harassment policies addressing the protections of all workers. Managers should understand federal, state and local laws and their organization's policy guidance. Employers must anticipate and plan to hire applicants who are transgender and potentially assist those who elect to transition during their employment. Given new federal protection, the differences in state and local laws, and the diverse nature and work of organizations, training all employees about their rights and obligation to report a problem is essential.

Finally, there are experts in this area with whom an employer can consult and develop a transition plan if necessary. Of course, an employer should consult with the transitioning employee, medical advisors, and Human Resources professionals to determine the timing of the transition process. The plan should include medical needs and benefits, time off or leave rights, the use of restroom facilities, preferred name and pronouns, desired communication of the transition to co-workers, and any dress code requirements affected by the transition.

Depending on the organization, its culture, and expert advice in this area, it may be appropriate to hold meetings with the co-workers of a transitioning employee to explain the transitioning person's actual and potential impacts on employees and customers, including the transitioning employee having a new name, preferred pronouns, the restrooms to which the employee will have access, and to address any issues or concerns co-workers may have regarding the transition. Ultimately, given the level of complexity and legal liability, Human Resources in most organization is the ideal resource for addressing the needs of all concerned.

What did Dear Abby and Ann Landers advise their readers?

In her column dated April 15, 1997, Dear Abby advised that transgendered persons be allowed to use the restroom matching their current gender presentation. Dear Abby relied on the medical opinion of Dr. John Bancroft, director of the Kinsey Institute for Research in Sex, Gender and Reproduction. Therefore, if a transgender female views herself as a female, she should use the women's restroom and vice versa. In her columns dated June 21, 2001 and August 13, 2001, Ann Landers suggested the transgender person should be permitted to use the restroom with which they are most comfortable.

18

IS IT SEXUAL HARASSMENT TO ENCOUNTER A TRANSGENDER PERSON IN THE RESTROOM?

The Meaning of a Hostile Work Environment

DAVID NIELSEN, a schoolteacher in Minnesota for nearly thirty years, informed his school's administration in 1998 that he identified as a transgender female, intended to transition in appearance from male to female, and would then be known as Debra Davis. To plan for the transition, the school district collaborated thoughtfully with Davis, the school district's legal counsel, the parent-teacher association, students, parents, and psychologists. Another teacher, Carla Cruzan, asked whether Davis would be allowed to use the women's faculty restroom, and the administration informed her "other arrangements" would be made. Based on some later advice by its legal counsel, however, the school permitted Davis to use the women's faculty restroom.

A few months later, Cruzan entered the women's restroom. To her surprise, she saw Davis exiting a privacy stall. Cruzan left immediately and complained to the principal about encountering Davis in the restroom. However, before the school could do anything to address her concern, Cruzan filed a complaint with the Minnesota Department of Human Rights, alleging sexual harassment.

The state agency dismissed Cruzan's complaint, stating that Minnesota law does not require or prohibit restroom designation according to self-image of gender or according to biological sex. Undaunted, Cruzan sued in federal court, alleging religious discrimination and sexual harassment under Title VII and state law.

The federal trial court also dismissed Cruzan's lawsuit, and, on appeal, a federal appellate court agreed. Cruzan never articulated her religious beliefs to the school district, never asked for any accommodation based on her religious beliefs, and never suffered any adverse employment action. Cruzan disapproved of Davis's transition and the decision to allow Davis to use the women's restroom, but she never claimed she disapproved on any religious grounds. In other words, she never invoked any religious objection to Davis using the women's restroom.

The courts also rejected the sexual harassment claim on the grounds that Cruzan could not show that allowing Davis to use the women's restroom, which occurred infrequently, created a working condition that rose to the level of an abusive work environment.

The alleged offensive behavior in this case—a one-time encounter with a transgender female in the women's restroom—was not sufficiently severe or pervasive to alter the conditions of Cruzan's job. The women's bathroom had stalls permitting all users a significant measure of personal privacy. In addition, Cruzan noted that she more frequently used the female student's bathroom closer to her classroom than the faculty restroom used by Davis. Most importantly, Cruzan never asserted that Davis engaged in any inappropriate conduct other than merely being present in the women's faculty restroom.

Therefore, no reasonable person could conclude Cruzan had been subject to a hostile work environment. To Davis's credit, she began using a private unisex restroom at the school to alleviate others' concerns which, had Cruzan permitted her principal to address the matter, might have avoided the lawsuit in the first place. Davis retired in 2001, the year before the appellate court's decision in the case, after a successful teaching career.

Although every case depends on unique facts—for example, the case might have turned out differently had the encounter in the bathroom been wildly different—*Cruzan v. Minneapolis Public School System* stands for the general proposition that allowing an employee to use the bathroom that comports with their gender identity, or merely encountering a transgender person in a restroom, and nothing more, will not be deemed unlawful sexual or religious harassment.

19

DOES AN EMPLOYEE HAVE THE RIGHT TO WEAR YOGA PANTS TO WORK?

Dress Codes and Appearance Standards

Oh, and remember: next Friday... is Hawaiian shirt day.
So, you know, if you want to, go ahead and
wear a Hawaiian shirt and jeans.

—Bill Lumbergh, *Office Space* (1999)

WILLIAM PAULY, Chief Financial Officer (CFO) for ING Securities, Futures & Options Inc., a massive global banking enterprise, frequently criticized the office receptionist, Laura Schmitz, about her "provocative" attire at work. Schmitz wore sheer skirts, which revealed her thong underwear, and would frequently ask others how she looked in the see-through clothing. She slouched at the front desk revealing much of her cleavage in low-cut blouses. Pauly called Schmitz an "exhibitionist," asking her whether her skirts were too short and outfits too tight for the office and indicating that she left "nothing to the imagination."

Schmitz was fired by ING. However, at the time, ING had no formal dress code. After she was fired, Schmitz slapped her former employer with a sexual harassment lawsuit. Schmitz claimed the CFO's comments about her personal appearance and attire created a sexually hostile work environment. The employer defended that Schmitz was fired for her poor work performance, not her appearance or attire. Dismissing Schmitz's case, the trial court found the facts were the "exact opposite" of a hostile work environment. According to the court, the supervisor's negative comments were all aimed at "bettering [the employee's] professional image" and were not frequent enough, or severe enough, to constitute a hostile work environment. The court faulted Schmitz's "misperception that she was entitled to make the rules for workplace behavior without reference to her employer's wishes."

The Navy SEALs have a saying: "The only easy day was yesterday." Working in Human Resources can be the same . . . but with more people yelling at you and fewer weapons to defend yourself.

One of the most difficult tasks at work, one that requires the utmost tact and sensitivity, is confronting a person whose appearance or attire does not meet work expectations. Talking about appearance gets messy quickly. What is "provocative attire?" Is it revealing some percentage of the body, certain areas or parts of the body, or in what manner it shows off your body? For example, is a bare midriff or low-cut blouse on a woman more or less provocative than a grown man wearing too-short shorts (like your gym teacher in high school)? Are tight-fitting yoga pants and leggings, which are extraordinarily popular, inappropriate for work? Are men and women frequently treated differently in the workplace regarding appearance standards? What about the saggy pants, skinny jeans, or tight-fitting t-shirts that some men wear? Opinions about the appropriateness of attire vary widely based on age, gender, cultural norms, as well as the nature of the work and work location.

In other words, it is wise to recognize that one person's provocative attire may be another person's expression of contemporary fashion trends. Even if you think a co-worker is dressing inappropriately, how do you tell that person they dress too provocatively? Do employers risk a lawsuit by discussing an employee's appearance in the hope of conforming his or her appearance to meet "reasonable" expectations?

Generally, even though it may ruffle a few feathers, you run little risk of a viable lawsuit when you confront an employee—politely—about work attire. That said, there is an inherent danger in targeting only one sex for comments about appearance and attire, especially when the comments may perpetuate stereotypical views of that gender; for example, women should not wear this or men should not wear that. Singling out persons of only one gender for heightened scrutiny regarding their appearance is a recipe for a sexual discrimination lawsuit.

For example, in *Drinkwater v. Union Carbide Corp.*, an appellate court found that two comments by a supervisor about a female employee's nice-looking appearance, including her makeup, eye shadow, and clothing were insufficient to support a sexual harassment claim. But such comments could be used as evidence to support the contention that employment decisions were made based on gender stereotypes. Therefore, comments about only women's appearance can support a claim of sex discrimination. Further, the court noted that "[u]ndue preoccupation with what female employees look like is not permissible under anti-discrimination laws if the same kind of attention is not paid to male employees. Traditional ideas about what a woman should look like are not legitimate criteria for evaluating women in the workplace." Despite the questionable stereo-typing, the court ultimately concluded there was not enough evidence of pervasive or regular discrimination based on sex.

The key to enforcing a dress code or appearance standard is ensuring that all employees, male and female, are held accountable for inappropriate attire at work. In this way, it is difficult to show that one gender is being singled out for differential treatment.

If a supervisor receives complaints about an employee's appearance, or thinks an employee's attire is inappropriate, the supervisor should stop and determine whether the organization has a policy or guideline regarding work appearance or attire. Human Resources is not the "fashion police" but is a good place to start to learn about any formal appearance standard and, more importantly, how it's been interpreted in the past.

Human Resources and the supervisor should address their concerns with the provocative dresser in private to avoid any humiliation or embarrassment. Frankly, it can be difficult for anyone (other than the parent of a teenager) to confront an employee about the clothing the employee is (or is not) wearing. Most people are likely to become defensive in the midst of such criticism. It makes sense to team up with a Human Resources professional and one who is the same gender as the provocative dresser. A person of the same gender may possibly be better able to identify with the employee and his or her choices in attire and convey criticism constructively and sincerely. Also, having another person in the room as a witness can minimize potential claims of sexual harassment.

Be forewarned, an undesirable exchange might go like this:

MALE SUPERVISOR: Your attire is provocative and unacceptable.

FEMALE EMPLOYEE: What do you mean by "provocative" and how often and how long have you been staring at me?

The supervisor clearly ends up on the defensive in this exchange.

You should never insult or ridicule the employee's taste or fashion sense but should simply point out the unacceptable attire. More importantly, give the employee a "why;" explain why the attire is unacceptable to the organization, even if you have no formal rule, and direct the employee to modify his or her appearance to conform to expectations.

This topic begs two follow-on questions that invariably come up in cases of dress code violations:

1. Can an employer send an employee home if dressed inappropriately?
2. Why can't employers simply adopt a casual dress code and make life easier for everyone?

If no alternative attire is available and a supervisor feels the employee must leave the premises to change clothes, there are some legal considerations. Some employers send employees who report for work inappropriately attired home without pay. This practice is legal in the case of non-exempt employees. The issue is different for exempt employees under the Fair Labor Standards Act. If an exempt employee's pay is docked for a partial day absence—in this case, having been sent home mid-day—the employer risks losing the exemption from overtime and may owe the employee for additional hours worked. Exempt employees must be paid on a fixed "salary" basis, which prohibits part-day deductions for this reason. The exempt employee could be required to use paid time off to leave and change his or her clothing. The decision to send an employee home should be based on the level of "offensiveness" of the attire (that is, does it disrupt work?), whether the employee's attire or appearance can be modified for the remainder of the day, and whether contact with co-workers and customers could be limited. Finally, think about it: Could sending an employee home with pay for a fashion violation be perceived as rewarding the behavior?

As for the second question, a growing trend in the workplace is relaxation of the traditional dress code. However, while standards are less stringent, virtually every employer still maintains rules or expectations about appropriate work attire. Today, many organizations permit employees to dress casually. Casual attire can have the effect of raising employee comfort and morale and creating an impression that management is much more approachable. And, in traditionally staid industries (like insurance, law, and banking), casual attire actually may improve the company's image and even increase productivity.

The most common problem in allowing casual attire is employees dressing too casually. Instead of dwelling on the question, "Why do people dress that way at work?" a good employer might ask, instead, "Have we told employees our expectations regarding appearance at work?" Most experts agree that an employer must specifically define what it means by "casual" or "professional" or "appropriate" attire and must clearly communicate its guidelines.

In conclusion, today, my boss is going to have to tell me I can't wear yoga pants and flip-flops to work!

PART III

MY BRAIN HURTS & OTHER DISABILITIES

2 0

IS BEING ALLERGIC TO PERFUME A DISABILITY?

Chemical Sensitivities and the Americans with Disabilities Act

Listen! Do you smell something?

—*Ghostbusters* (1984)

HUMAN BEINGS ARE extremely sensitive to smells; scientists say we can literally smell fear. Strong odors—in particular, from perfumes, colognes, cleaning products, and that damn "potpourri" in many households—can inflame the senses. One can easily imagine the smell of tuna fish reheating in the microwave oven in the lunchroom. To me, Axe men's cologne is a crippling neurotoxin. During the next public riot, police should consider releasing a group of Axe-fueled teenage boys to disperse the crowd and immediately bring rioters to their knees. The City of Detroit, Michigan, has been Ground Zero for the legal fight against noxious odors at work.

Erin Weber was a top-ranked deejay for "Detroit's Best Country" radio station, WYCD-FM (99.5). Nominated five times for the Country Music Association's Personality of the Year award, Weber had the highest ratings (and profits) for all of WYCD's shows in 2000. That same year, Weber complained that the perfume worn by a fellow radio personality, Linda Lee, literally made her sick.

Linda Lee wore *Tresor*, which is French for "treasure." The perfume is described by Lancome as "the elegance of rose, muguet (lily of the valley) and lilac along with the sparkle of peach and apricot blossom." Seems pleasant enough . . . but Erin Weber's doctor claimed that her continued exposure to *Tresor* "could result in her death." It got even more Shakespearean. Weber claimed she lost her voice after exposure to *Tresor* and was forced to take a three-month leave of absence due to her condition.

The employer had a solution: The radio station ordered Lee to stop wearing the perfume at work. And that might have worked had Lee not "intentionally" walked by Weber at the Downtown Detroit Hoedown (a popular outdoor country music festival sponsored by WYCD) wearing *Tresor*. The walk-by perfume attack caused an allergic reaction in Weber.

Later in the summer, the radio station fired Weber—the alleged victim—for taking a leave of absence due to her allergy . . . and not her perfume assailant! Weber sued her employer, Infinity Broadcasting Corporation, under the Americans with Disabilities Act (ADA), claiming she was fired for complaining about her co-worker's premeditated "perfume attack" and the station never accommodated her medical condition. Nearly four years later, in 2005, a federal district court jury awarded Weber $10.6 million, including seven million in punitive damages! Now, that is truly a *tresor*.

Detroit was also the site of the next round in the perfume legal fight.

Susan McBride, a Senior City Planner for the City of Detroit, began working with Rosalind Chaney. McBride complained that Chaney's use of perfumes, air fresheners, and potpourri—a trifecta of noxious odors—caused her to suffer migraine headaches, nausea, and other physical reactions. McBride urged the City to adopt a policy limiting scents in the workplace. However, the Human Resources Department rejected a "scents policy" on the grounds that it made no sense (no pun intended). In 2007, McBride brought a lawsuit claiming the City had failed to accommodate her medical condition in violation of the ADA. The trial court found that fragrance sensitivity could substantially limit the major life activity of breathing and, therefore, could be a disability protected by the ADA. Before trial, the case settled for $100,000. The City also adopted a scent-free workplace policy, which is simply what McBride had asked for in the first place.

Given the growing number of employees complaining of fragrance allergies, it is reasonable to ask whether chemical sensitivities are a "disability" protected by the ADA.

Multiple chemical sensitivity (MCS) syndrome is a hyper-sensitivity to trace amounts of chemicals or physical irritants. MCS is apparently more than just "the refrigerator in the lunchroom smells bad." MCS is a real problem for many. Modern-day workers have become increasingly concerned that they are being harmed by synthetic chemical creations run amok. Since the 1950s, when America's industrial machine hit full throttle, an increasing number of workers have complained of conditions described similarly but named differently, such as allergic toxemia, chemical sensitivity, environmental illness, universal allergy, toxic carpet syndrome, and "sick building syndrome." Indeed, many veterans of the Persian Gulf War in the early 1990s returned home from war complaining of MCS-type symptoms which were later dubbed "Gulf War Syndrome."

However, before you miss a lot of work because you can't stand your boss, or his or her fragrance, you should know there is considerable debate in the medical community whether MCS is a proven diagnosis or the figment of patients' overactive imaginations. This rift among doctors does not mean employees are left unprotected. The U.S. Equal Employment Opportunity Commission (EEOC) has informally stated that MCS is an impairment. The critical question in all ADA cases, though, is *whether a particular impairment* **substantially limits** *a major life activity.*

The ADA protects qualified individuals with a disability. To be a qualified individual with a disability, you must have a physical or mental impairment that substantially limits one or more major life activities. Major life activities include breathing, concentrating, lifting, seeing, sleeping, walking, and working. To date, most courts have found that MCS does not substantially limit a major life activity. Arguably, though, if the condition worsens, as in Susan McBride's case, it could limit a number of major life activities and become disabling.

Employees who have argued that working in a "sick building" is physically disabling have usually not prevailed under the ADA, since inability to work in a particular building, even a "sick" one filled with respiratory irritants, is not substantially limiting.

This may be changing. The ADA was amended in 2008, making a "disability" easier to prove. For example, if severe reactions to a fragrance aggravate a chronic, long-term medical condition, such as severe asthma, then the impairment may be a disability protected by the ADA.

What should workplaces do when chemicals and work conflict?

A severe chemical sensitivity or allergy, particularly if it substantially limits a person's ability to breath, could indeed be a disability. In that case, an employer covered by the ADA and any state law equivalent would be required to engage in an interactive process to find a reasonable accommodation; meaning, some modification that allows an employee to perform the essential functions of the job. An employee is entitled to an effective accommodation, not necessarily the accommodation the employee wants. Reasonable accommodations can include the use of paid or unpaid time off, modification of job duties, changes to facilities in which a job is performed, use of assistive devices enabling a person to do the job and, in some states, reassignment to an available position for which the employee is qualified. An employee with a chemical sensitivity should consider asking for a reasonable accommodation and be prepared to provide medical information to support such a request.

For eligible employees, they may also take leave under the federal Family and Medical Leave Act (FMLA) or a similar state law to treat a serious health condition, such as a severe allergy. Employers may require employees to provide medical certification to support a request for a medical leave of absence.

Contrary to any street lawyer's opinion, no person has the "right" to wear perfume or cologne at work. Some employers, like the City of Detroit, have instituted a "perfume-free environment" to accommodate employees with breathing impairments aggravated by environmental conditions. Obviously, a total ban on fragrances might be difficult to enforce in a workplace that is open to the public. A total ban could also upset co-workers. Recently, I was on an airline flight when they suspended service of peanut snacks due to the allergy of a single passenger and, at least in my row, the grumblings sounded like sailors plotting a mutiny.

The smell of smoke is a common irritant. Some municipalities, and employers, have issued smoking bans not only to reduce smoking in general, but to avoid the second-hand effects of smoke on others. Other employers have offered to move an employee who has an allergy or sensitivity to another work location or to provide or improve air filtration systems or allow fresh air breaks. Remember, one can never retaliate against an employee or applicant for invoking their rights under the ADA. Therefore, a supervisor should resist the temptation to move an employee who has complained of allergic reactions to the basement with a single dim lightbulb like Milton in *Office Space*.

Some employers have settled on the "airplane announcement." This is an e-mail or other communication to the entire workforce that we have a "passenger" (that is, an unidentified employee) who has a severe allergy and would appreciate employees being considerate of the allergic employee's condition by *volunteering* not to wear strong fragrances at work.

Managers have allowed employees to wear a mask at work to mute environmental hazards. Indeed, masks or other face coverings are now *de rigueur* work accessories in a COVID-19 world. Wearing a mask to work could be a little off-putting but is a low-cost and effective measure to aid a hyper-sensitive employee.

For all employees, in my experience, it is often as simple as approaching the one person in the office who wears too much cologne or perfume and privately—and politely—asking him or her to bring less of the fragrance to work.

Two things are certain: An employee should ask for help if he or she is sensitive to workplace odors, and an employer should take even minor complaints of environmental allergens seriously. Employees should also be aware that an employer may ask for medical documentation describing work limitations caused by the condition and any suggested accommodations.

Finally, an employer must do something—ideally with the least negative impact on the entire workforce—to alleviate the problem. This does not mean summarily firing the employee with a health condition! Plenty of professional resources exist to trace irritants and fumes that are allegedly impacting the workplace. Attempt to find the source of the odor; then, if found, try to abate the problem. While an employer doesn't necessarily have to appoint a Perfume Monitor, it should expect employees not to overdose on perfume or cologne.

21

CAN EMPLOYEES BE REQUIRED TO WEAR DEODORANT?

Dealing with People who Stink

You know, it is possible to be too attractive.

—Pepe Le Pew, *Looney Tunes*

EXPERTS SAY that no two people smell alike. In fact, though, some people smell like crap. In my world, this is how the work conversation begins: We have an employee with very offensive body odor. He works closely with other employees and customers. When his supervisor spoke to him about it, he said he had a medical condition and there was nothing he could do about it. Can he be fired if he can't clean up his act or is an employee's body odor protected at work?

Imagine trying to work with a person whose body odor is so offensive that it distracts you from doing your job. The problem is compounded when the person is not even aware, or is defensive about, how badly they smell.

What can you do if your co-worker smells like a rotting corpse or, worse, used hockey gear? Is horrible body odor a disability under the Americans with Disabilities Act (ADA)? Do people from some parts of the world, where regular bathing is less common, have the right to smell badly at work?

The goal here is to help your co-worker with a problem and to make work more pleasant. There are a number of ways to get there, some of which are provided here.

Foul odors can ruin your—and everyone else's—workday. Although socially limiting at times, an overpowering body odor is generally not a protected "disability" under the ADA. Nonetheless, it can be hard to manage the problem of offensive odors at work, particularly when a person who smells like week-old fish does not detect, or even likes, the smell of their own week-old fish.

Employees with strong body odor have sued their employers. In *Georgy v. O'Neill*, a New York case decided in 2002, an employee alleged he was fired because of his body odor and bad breath in violation of the ADA.

He argued his body odor was caused by "contact reaction of axilla," dermatitis of the armpit, preventing his use of deodorants, and his horrible breath was caused by chronic periodontal disease. Even with these medical diagnoses, the employee failed to prove he was disabled under the ADA. To be disabled under the ADA, you must show you are *substantially limited in a major life activity*. While he may not have been fun in a game of Twister, the employee was apparently not smelly enough to keep him from participating in the major life activities the rest of us pursue, such as breathing, eating, walking, lifting, and working. Specifically, regarding the ability to work, the smelly employee failed to show that his body odor affected his ability to do his job. In fact, his body odor subsided after he transferred to a job where he performed less manual labor and, therefore, did not sweat as much. He also failed to show his body odor substantially limited his ability to interact with others or prevented him from working in a broad range of jobs.

In *Hannoon v. Fawn Engineering*, Said Hannoon, a Middle Eastern Arab born in Kuwait, was working as an information systems (IS) manager in Iowa. One day, three weeks after his new supervisor's arrival, Hannoon's supervisor confronted him about his offensive body odor. The manager said he'd noticed a problem with Hannoon's body odor; other employees had complained to him; and good interpersonal relationships are important for the IS manager position. Less than six weeks later, Hannoon was fired for failure to meet performance deadlines. Hannoon brought a lawsuit, alleging that he was fired because of his race and national origin. Dredging up a host of negative stereotypes about Arabs, Hannoon argued that his employer's efforts to address his body odor demonstrated discrimination against Middle Eastern persons. The court refused to entertain claims of racial and ethnic discrimination, concluding that discussions about personal hygiene are "distressing to all involved," but do not necessarily demonstrate race-based discriminatory bias toward an Arabic employee. Most relevant, in their disciplinary meeting, the supervisor never suggested that Hannoon's body odor was based on his race or Middle Eastern origin.

No one likes being told they smell bad. In truth, many people do not realize how they smell. Every human being has a distinct body odor. Therefore, while discussing another person's body odor can be awkward and uncomfortable, every expert agrees you must speak to the person who smells bad and give the person an opportunity to correct the problem.

Human Resources should not necessarily be your first

resort. HR hates being the fashion police looking for wardrobe malfunctions, listening for mind-numbingly stupid comments about personal appearance, or detecting who had too much garlic for lunch. Many employees fear their co-worker will be offended, or will get defensive, if you mention that their body odor is offensive or overwhelming. Trying "hints," like opening the window in January (if even possible in a modern office building), or writhing on the office floor gasping for air like Arnold Schwarzenegger at the end of *Total Recall*, or (my least favorite) bringing it up in a staff meeting for everybody's awkward entertainment will only embarrass the employee and aggravate the problem.

Most organizations address noxious body odor as a violation of the employer's dress code or hygiene standards. Therefore, you should attempt to pull your co-worker aside, privately (the end of a workday is a good time) and kindly, but directly, tell them you appreciate them and their work performance, but their personal hygiene is a problem. Criticism is always much easier to palate if you recognize your critic cares about you and is trying to help you. You can ask the employee for suggestions how they might address their body odor. Most adults know how to care for themselves, but some may need to be reminded more than others to wash clothes more frequently and wear deodorant; permitted to use a workplace shower or nearby gym shower facilities during the day; allowed longer breaks to attend to hygiene needs; or encouraged to wear moderate amounts of cologne or perfume to mask other odors. And, as we've seen, too much perfume can be a problem too.

A word of caution: Be careful about letting an employee work from home solely because they smell bad or you can expect the entire office suddenly to smell like an NHL post-game locker room with co-workers lining up to request work from home.

Most importantly, keep in mind that one's body odor can be a symptom of a medical problem. For example, diabetics may experience ketoacidosis which can increase bad breath and body odor. Persons with hyperthyroidism (an overactive thyroid gland) can sweat excessively. Kidney or liver ailments may create body odors from buildup of toxins in the blood or digestive tract.

An employer generally can't inquire into an employee's medical condition. However, if an employee says their body odor is caused by a medical condition, then the underlying medical condition causing the body odor could be a disability protected by the ADA. An employee has no legal right to smell bad at work. But a disabled employee is entitled to some help in the form of a reasonable accommodation. An employer can send an employee who claims their body odor is caused by a medical condition to their doctor for medical certification of the condition and, more importantly, commence an interactive dialogue seeking a reasonable accommodation to alleviate the problem.

Finally, any effort to accommodate the employee must respect and maintain the confidentiality of the employee's medical condition. In such cases, a manager should look to Human Resources to provide guidance and coaching, if necessary, to address an employee's body odor caused by a medical condition. Here, you should not necessarily expect or require a smelly employee's co-workers to intervene in the problem. It might be easier for a friend to tell a friend and peer at work that their deodorant is not doing its job, but issues of personal hygiene can be difficult and embarrassing. It's ultimately the employer's responsibility to correct the problem and to avoid escalating conflict or further rift among employees.

22

ARE HEMORRHOIDS A DISABILITY?

What Is and Isn't a Disability under the ADA

WHEN I WAS MUCH YOUNGER and first heard about hemorrhoids, I remember my Dad reassuring me, "Son, many people get hemorrhoids, it's natural; but, always remember in life, there are far more **perfect** assholes in this world!" Then he'd burst into laughter, walk away, and leave me wondering whether having hemorrhoids was actually a good thing or a bad thing?!?

In the world of work, neither perfect assholes nor hemorrhoids are protected.

Charlotte Davis, a manager for BellSouth Mobility, developed a case of hemorrhoids so severe and bloody that surgery was necessary to correct the problem. Following surgery, she needed time off work to recover and additional restroom breaks when she returned to work. She was later fired for taking too many bathroom breaks. Davis complained she was fired because she had hemorrhoids; hemorrhoids are a "disability"; therefore, her employer violated the Americans with Disabilities Act (ADA). An Alabama federal court dismissed her case, making it clear that even acute medical conditions, like hemorrhoids, are not necessarily disabling conditions.

Davis's case is a good reminder that not every physical or mental health condition, poor circumstance, or disadvantage in life is a disability. The ADA is a federal civil rights law that protects qualified individuals with a disability from discrimination and harassment in all workplaces that have at least 15 employees. Every state has a similar law prohibiting disability discrimination in employment. State laws often cover even smaller-sized employers; in some cases, those with just a single employee. As a result, most workers in the United States are protected from discrimination based on having a disability.

Under the ADA, a disability is defined as "a physical or mental impairment that substantially limits one or more major life activities of such individual; a record of such an impairment; or being regarded as having such an impairment." When the ADA was significantly amended in 2008, Congress made clear its intent to define a disability quite broadly and thereby protect more individuals with significant medical impairments.

Davis was decided before the 2008 amendments to the ADA went into effect. However, the court in *Davis* made clear that even acute medical conditions are not necessarily disabling conditions. Dismissing the case, the federal court for the Northern District of Alabama ruled that acute hemorrhoids did not substantially limit Ms. Davis in *any* major life activity. She had no permanent work restrictions. Her own testimony was that she expected to make a full recovery from her hemorrhoids. The court was unwilling to "characterize such a common malady as hemorrhoids, even severe hemorrhoids, as a disability." One can imagine the decision, like the hemorrhoids, didn't sit well with Davis.

The ADA, even though it is meant to expand the protections of persons with health conditions, certainly does not cover every health condition. In fact, the ADA specifically excludes some conditions from being disabilities. For example, homosexuality and bisexuality are not considered physical or mental "impairments" and, therefore, cannot be "disabling" conditions. "Sexual behavior disorders" are specifically excluded, namely "transvestism, transsexualism, pedophilia, exhibitionism, voyeurism [and] gender identity disorders not resulting from physical impairments." And thankfully, "compulsive gambling, kleptomania, or pyromania" are not "disabilities" requiring accommodation in the workplace.

In addition, "psychoactive substance use disorders resulting from current illegal use of drugs" are excluded. Persons who currently use drugs *illegally* are not protected by the ADA. This could include persons who are prescribed drugs but use or sell them illegally. However, persons who are lawfully prescribed drugs for a disabling condition, or used to use illegal drugs and have since recovered from an addiction, or are undergoing drug rehabilitation may be protected by the ADA.

I started turning gray at a very young age and always felt it was socially limiting. However, basic physical characteristics like eye color, hair color, height or weight within "normal ranges," and being lefthanded are not considered impairments and, therefore, are not disabilities.

If you are naïve, or a poor decisionmaker, you are likely not disabled and not protected at work. Personality traits, without some underlying physical or psychological disorder—such as having poor judgment, a quick temper, or being immature or irresponsible—are not impairments. However, being significantly stressed or seriously depressed could be the result of a mental disorder and, therefore, could be protected under the ADA.

Coming from a bad home can be a disadvantage in life and work but is not a disability. Environmental, cultural, or economic disadvantages, such as receiving a poor education or having a prison record, are not impairments under the ADA. Therefore, according to the U.S. Equal Employment Opportunity Commission (EEOC), a person who has dyslexia and cannot read due to a learning impairment is disabled; a person who cannot read because they dropped out of school at an early age is not disabled.

Finally, medical conditions that are temporary and have little or no long-term impact usually are not disabilities. For example, broken limbs, sprains, concussions, appendicitis, common colds, or influenza are usually not considered disabilities. However, if an individual broke a femur—the largest, longest, and strongest bone in the human body—and the bone did not heal properly, resulting in the permanent inability to walk normally, the individual may be deemed to have a disability.

In every instance in which an applicant or employee has a physical or mental impairment that substantially limits one or more major life activities, or has a record of such an impairment, or has been regarded as disabled by others, an employer must consider the ADA and its protections. That said, not every person will prove they have a disability, and, in some cases, the individual may be excluded from the protections of the law.

2 3

CAN I BRING MY
PET MONKEY TO WORK?

Service and Emotional Support Animals

> *You can get the monkey off your back,*
> *but the circus never leaves town.*
>
> —Anne Lamott

I COULD IMAGINE the human resources manager smiling on the other end of the phone, as if posing the impossible final answer on *Jeopardy*, when she said to me, "We have an employee who brings his pet monkey to work every day. Does an employee have the right to bring his monkey to work?"

I will admit that I paused when I first heard the question—Is there some hidden meaning behind "bringing your monkey?"—but then I remembered I work in Human Resources. There is no such thing as a double entendre in HR! We always assume the person in question literally wants to bring a monkey to work.

Countless articles have extolled the positive health benefits of bringing pets to work. In fact, a study conducted in 2012 by a management professor at Virginia Commonwealth University examined a pet-friendly workplace in North Carolina and found that employees who brought their dogs to work experienced lower levels of stress, and produced less of the stress-causing hormone cortisol, than employees who did not bring a dog to work. Apparently, the very act of petting a dog immediately lowers one's stress. A monkey may be no different.

Today, well-liked companies, such as Google, Amazon, Ben & Jerry's, and Clif Bar, allow employees to bring their dogs to work. Even Replacements, Ltd., the world's largest supplier of china and crystal allows pets to roam the company's 500,000-square-foot facilities in Greensboro, North Carolina. That is bold! My wife and I wouldn't allow our dog anywhere near the china cabinet.

But "Take Your Dog to Work Day" is a privilege, held entirely by the employer, and not a right. The only "right" to have an animal present at work is found under the federal Americans with Disabilities Act (ADA) and state anti-discrimination laws. Under the ADA and similar state laws, an employer may be required to allow a disabled employee to bring a "service animal" to work. This right, though, is limited.

The ADA is divided into five separate parts, or titles, that afford broad protection for the differently abled members of our society. For example, Title I of the ADA prohibits employment discrimination against a qualified individual with a disability. Another part, Title III, prohibits discrimination on the basis of disability in all places of public accommodation, such as restaurants, retail stores, recreation centers, movie theaters, schools, daycare facilities, and medical offices.

Title I requires employers to make a "reasonable accommodation" for applicants and employees with disabilities. The duty to accommodate is a strong legal mandate. But Title I—which governs work—is silent on whether an employer must allow a service animal or any other animal as a reasonable accommodation. Title III is different. Title III requires that service animals be allowed in *all areas of public access*. The U.S. Department of Justice, in its interpretive guidance dated July 2015, said that service animals could accompany a disabled person to a self-service buffet at a restaurant, a hotel room, or a hospital room.

The rules that apply to customers and patrons in places of public accommodation—for example, the salad bar at the Country Buffet—do not apply to the workplace. Under Title I of the ADA, an employee does not have an automatic right to have a service animal at work; however, allowing a service animal can certainly be a reasonable accommodation for an employee with a disability. Unlike a customer, who needs no permission for a service dog to be present in a place of public accommodation, an employee must request a service animal be allowed as a reasonable accommodation of a disability. Employers must take such requests seriously. An employee may be asked to provide medical information to support the request for a service animal; in particular, how the presence of the service animal will enable the worker's ability to perform the essential functions of the job.

Also, one should always check state law where the employee works, since a state law may actually require the presence of a service animal in the workplace.

There is another level of legal complexity that must be considered when it comes to animals in the workplace. In 2011, the U.S. Department of Justice revised Title III of the ADA to narrow the definition of "service animal." Now, only dogs may be service animals under Title III. A monkey cannot be a service animal for purposes of the ADA.

Therefore, dogs and other species of animals, whether wild or domestic, trained or untrained, that *only* provide emotional support are not considered "service animals" under the ADA. A service animal is trained *to do work* or *perform tasks* for the benefit of an individual with a disability. An emotional support animal, also called a comfort animal or therapy animal, is not a service animal. Comfort animals can provide significant benefits, such as companionship and relief from depression and post-traumatic stress, but they are not specially trained to do work for persons with disabilities.

In fact, a growing number of states and local governments are enacting laws making it a crime to misrepresent one's entitlement to a service animal to combat people who might try to bring an emotional support animal as a "service animal" to places of public accommodation (such as stores, airplanes, and concert venues). Interestingly, though, the ADA rule also permits the use of trained miniature horses as service animals. While the definition of a service animal is limited to dogs, the regulations specifically permit the use of a miniature horse as a reasonable accommodation for a person with a disability. Miniature horses were not included in the definition of service animals to "maintain flexibility where the use of horses would not be appropriate." You have to use your own imagination here.

While the definition of a service animal is helpful and could influence courts in future cases, it does not necessarily mean other types of animals can't be considered as a reasonable accommodation under the ADA. Therefore, employers should consider all requests to have an animal (yes, even a monkey) present as an accommodation before denying such a request. Why? The U.S. Equal Employment Opportunity Commission (EEOC)—the federal agency responsible for safeguarding civil rights protections in the United States—has taken the position that a service animal *or* an emotional support animal may be required as a reasonable accommodation in the workplace.

In 2017, the EEOC sued CRST International, a trucking company, claiming the employer unlawfully refused to hire and failed to accommodate a truck driver's request to have his dog with him as he drove his trucking routes. Leon Laferriere, a Navy war veteran diagnosed with post-traumatic stress disorder, had been prescribed an emotional support dog to help him cope with persistent anxiety and frequent nightmares caused by his condition. In 2015, Laferriere applied for a truck driver position with CRST International in Fort Myers, Florida, and was admitted to the company's truck driver training program. Even though Laferriere passed the initial phase of training, the company refused to advance Laferriere to "on-the-road" training because Laferriere requested to have his dog in the truck with him. The company has a "no pet policy" and would not accommodate Laferriere's request. The case settled in March 2019 with CRST agreeing to pay Laferriere $47,500 in back pay and compensatory damages. CRST will also have to provide anti-discrimination training to all of its employees as part of the settlement.

By virtue of the case being settled, no court has answered the specific question whether an emotional support animal is a reasonable accommodation required by the ADA. Laferriere's dog, which had been "prescribed" by a psychiatrist, controlled anxiety and provided emotional support for a war veteran's post-traumatic stress disorder (PTSD). Therefore, the dog was an emotional support animal and, technically, not a service animal. However, PTSD may be a disability under the ADA for which an employer must make reasonable accommodation. The driver claimed the employer refused to consider his request to have his emotional support animal in the truck because the company had established a "no pet" policy for its vehicles. As a reasonable accommodation, the veteran with PTSD asked for an exception allowing his comfort animal.

Regardless of the outcome, Laferriere's case is the first shot in the eventual war to permit emotional support animals at work for disabled applicants and employees. So don't laugh when an employee requests to bring his emotional support boa constrictor to work!

This brings me to a common question posed by employers: "What if other employees are afraid of or allergic to the service dog?" Banning all service dogs from a place of employment would not likely be "reasonable," as it would be a disadvantage to all service dog owners and may lead an employer to unreasonably favor one disability over another. To be sure, these situations should always be discussed with legal counsel to gain sound advice, but other accommodations, such as air filters to minimize allergens or restricting animals from certain areas in the workplace, would likely be found more reasonable than automatically ruling out a disabled employee's accommodation request.

If an employee is not disabled, the only other possible way to compel a boss to accept a pet's attendance at work would be another legal protection, such as invoking a religious practice which requires the presence of an animal, which is unlikely ("Boss, I need to bring a fatted calf to work today; it's a religious thing."), or bargaining for the right to have an animal present as part of an employment or union contract, which may be even more unlikely. The best argument for pets at work might be employee satisfaction. If employees are truly valuable to an employer, the employer may be more likely to allow workers to bring dogs (or monkeys, or emus) to work to make them happier and more productive.

Individuals with a disability may request to have a service animal or emotional support animal at work. Employers, then, must consider the presence of the animal under its duty to make a reasonable accommodation. A good resource for both employers and employees interested in dog/work interactions is Pet Sitters International website (www.petsit.com), particularly their "Take Your Dog to Work Day" Action Pack. This can lay the groundwork for at least one dog-accompanied workday a year. By the way, if you are interested, Take Your Dog to Work Day is always the first Friday after June 19.

24

ARE FAT PEOPLE
PROTECTED AT WORK?

Obesity and the Americans with Disabilities Act

*A reliable study has found that women who carry a little
extra weight live longer than the men who mention it.*

—Unknown

IN 2005, the Borgata Hotel Casino & Spa, in Atlantic City,
New Jersey, gained considerable media attention when it
banned its cocktail waitresses, known as "Borgata Babes,"
from gaining too much weight during their employment. To
be a Borgata Babe (some of whom are men, by the way), an
employee must agree to gain no more than seven percent of
his or her weight upon hire. Why seven percent? Apparently,
this measure of gain equates to the next larger size in clothing.
Employees who went over the weight restriction were given
90 days to reach an acceptable weight or they would be fired.
To help employees maintain their weight, Borgata offered gym

memberships and free personal trainers for its staff.

Later, 22 women who were fired for being overweight sued Borgata claiming gender discrimination because male servers who gained weight allegedly were treated more favorably by the casino. The female employees lost; in 2013, a New Jersey court ruled in favor of the casino.

According to the court, all the employees agreed to the weight restriction as part of an employment contract made at hire. Even though they later challenged the label "babe" as offensive sexual stereotyping, the cocktail servers knowingly applied for, and freely accepted jobs, as Borgata Babes. In other words, no one was forced to be a sex object or coerced into the weight restrictions. As for the claim of unlawful discrimination, the weight limit applied to both male and female servers. The court also found the employer could require "reasonable" appearance standards based on its business model of having attractive servers to "entertain" its customers.

Although the court didn't say it, this appearance standard works at a ritzy casino but probably wouldn't have passed muster at a Church's Fried Chicken restaurant.

Finally, the female servers were unable to prove the male servers were treated more favorably than female servers regarding the weight restriction. In other words, there was no evidence of discrimination against women.

The Borgata case is even more fascinating because it's one of the few instances where employees are subject to periodic mandatory weigh-ins in order to keep their jobs. Other than professional fighters, few jobs have this particular requirement. Imagine having to "make weight" each month to keep your job (akin to a high school wrestler).

The Borgata case unfortunately reinforces the adage: size matters . . . at least in the workplace. A study conducted at

Harvard University and published in *Psychological Science* in 2019, found that implicit, or unconscious, bias based on body weight has increased over the last ten years. Obese workers are often stereotyped negatively as lazy, unmotivated, unintelligent, sloppy, and lacking willpower.

Any health professional will tell you being overweight or obese is an epidemic of gigantic portions (correction, proportions). According to the Centers for Disease Control and Prevention (CDC), more than one-third of American adults are obese and more than two-thirds of adults are overweight. ("Obesity" is defined as having a Body Mass Index of 30 or greater; "overweight" is having a Body Mass Index of 25 to 29. A 5'10" person who weighs more than 174 pounds is overweight; obese if weighing more than 210 pounds.) Recent studies show women and children, in particular, are becoming increasingly obese at an alarming rate. According to the CDC, obesity shortens lives considerably and increases medical costs dramatically.

In a country that prizes physical beauty and a slim appearance, discrimination based on weight is rampant. And generally lawful! Applicants and employees are often surprised to learn there is no federal law that specifically protects overweight and obese persons. In fact, Michigan is the only state that specifically protects applicants and employees from discrimination based on their weight.

While all that doesn't sound good for people struggling with their weight, there is evolving protection for obese and overweight workers.

In 2008, the Americans with Disabilities Act (ADA) was substantially amended to broaden its scope. As a result, in some circumstances, obesity can be considered a disability under the ADA. The U.S. Equal Employment Opportunity Commission (EEOC) and courts have taken the position that an individual with an underlying physiological impairment that results in obesity could be disabled and, therefore, protected within the meaning of the ADA. At least one federal appeals court has ruled that an employee who is "morbidly" obese (a person who weighs more than twice their optimum body weight) has a physical impairment. Therefore, if the employee is substantially limited in performing a major life activity, such as walking, or major bodily function, such as cardiovascular function, because of their weight, they may be disabled.

Finally, the ADA protects from discrimination persons who have no "impairment" but are perceived or regarded as impaired. Therefore, discrimination against a person who is obese, regardless of the cause of obesity, simply because an employer regards the applicant or employee as unhealthy or unfit for working well in an organization, would be actionable against the employer.

As an example of actual or perceived bias against over-weight persons, McDonald's rescinded a job offer to Joseph Connor, of Connecticut, solely because he was "super-sized." In August 2003, the corporate giant settled with the 420-pound giant under terms both sides declined to disclose. Mr. Connor alleged the fast-food chain promised he could start work as soon as a promised "specially-ordered uniform" arrived. But the uniform and job never materialized. The trial court refused to dismiss Mr. Connor's claim that he was "regarded as" disabled under the ADA and Connecticut state law. After the court's decision, moving the case forward to trial, the parties settled. A good lesson for employers: Don't make a promise—in this case, a "special uniform"—you can't or don't intend to keep.

On another front, in 2013, the American Medical Association voted at its annual meeting to officially classify obesity as a disease. While the vote is not legally binding, the decision certainly allows doctors to inject themselves into the obesity debate and whether or not an employee has the ability to do his or her job.

Admittedly, in the early days of the ADA, it was very difficult for an obese person to catch a break under the law. Back then, for most courts, obesity was rarely a disability because the employee usually could not establish that obesity substantially limited any of life's major activities. As an interesting aside, supporting the position that obesity itself is not a disabling condition, one may recall the "fit but fat" phenomenon of the recent past. Several medical studies published in 2012 and 2013 found physical activity and fitness, rather than weight, more likely affected one's mortality. Being fit, regardless of weight, leads to greater health outcomes. Incidentally, the "fit but fat" studies have recently come under considerable scrutiny.

This issue is evolving. Courts may continue to maintain that for obesity to be an impairment under the ADA, an applicant or employee must show his or her obesity is the result of some underlying physiological disorder or condition, such as diabetes. Under the amended ADA, which makes clear that a "substantial" limitation should be viewed broadly, courts could also find that obesity can be a covered impairment, even if it is not due to some underlying physiological condition. Federal appellate courts are sure to address the question of whether morbid obesity that does not stem from an underlying physiological disorder is a disability under the ADA.

In some ways, though, it may not matter. Protection from mistreatment for "regarding" a person as disabled has also been expanded in recent years. So an applicant or employee need now only show that an employer perceived him or her as limited or impaired because of excess weight in order to bring a claim of disability discrimination.

25

ARE FEARS AND PHOBIAS A DISABILITY?

Mental Impairments under the ADA

Fear is the path to the Dark Side. Fear leads to anger, anger leads to hate, hate leads to suffering.

—Yoda, *Star Wars: Episode I—The Phantom Menace* (1999)

CONSIDER THESE SCENARIOS. A pharmacist in New York suffers from trypanophobia (fear of needles) and refuses to give immunization shots to customers. A Connecticut taxicab driver with cynophobia (fear of dogs) won't pick up a blind customer at the airport because he is accompanied by a service dog. An art teacher in South Dakota with ergophobia (fear of being fired) is so anxious that her teaching contract won't be renewed that she can't teach. A high school teacher in Ohio claims her school district forced her to retire because of her pedophobia (fear of young children) when it reassigned her from high school to teach much younger junior high students. An Illinois bridge worker with acrophobia (fear of heights) is fired after he panicked trying to change a light bulb on a high bridge. All of these scenarios are true. All of the employees suffer from phobias.

Being afraid of danger or harm (real or imagined) is quite common. Having a phobia—a persistent, irrational fear—is much less common.

Specific or social phobias are fears that produce such overwhelming anxiety that an affected person may experience panic attacks, hysteria, and severe physical symptoms of distress when triggered. Common social phobias include fear of speaking in public, flying in an airplane, or being trapped in confined spaces. Common specific phobias include fear of dogs, spiders, snakes, darkness, germs, and clowns. Yes, clowns can be very scary!

According to the National Institute of Mental Health, approximately four to five percent of the U.S. population has one or more clinically significant phobias in a given year. These numbers don't account for the number of undiagnosed and untreated phobias prevalent in the general population.

Phobias can (and do) occur . . . and can generate lawsuits.

In the above scenarios, courts considered whether the employees had a disability under the ADA, whether an accommodation was necessary or reasonable, and whether the employee with the phobia was still qualified to do their job.

Phobias are mental or emotional "impairments" and, therefore, are arguably covered by the ADA. While the ADA prevents discrimination against a person with a mental impairment or a psychological disorder (at least if the impairment substantially limits the person's major life activities), some behavioral conditions are not protected under the ADA. The ADA specifically excludes pedophilia, exhibitionism, voyeurism, and other sexual behavior disorders; compulsive gambling, kleptomania, or pyromania; and psychoactive substance use disorders resulting from current illegal use of drugs.

Many persons with phobias, although clearly a mental impairment, have difficulty demonstrating that the condition substantially limits them in a major life activity. In other words, it may be difficult to show you are "disabled" when you have a phobia. For example, what if an employee fears abduction by aliens and their fear causes a disruption with co-workers (some of whom may wish the employee to be abducted)? Fear of abduction by aliens is a specific phobia. However, this particular phobia is rarely treated (other than perhaps being told to stop watching reruns of *The X-Files*). Even if the phobia is treated, through behavioral therapy and desensitization (for example, an incremental, systematic exposure to alien imagery might help to reduce one's fear of aliens), or medications (such as the use of sedatives or mini-bottles of vodka to reduce one's fears in general), a fear of abduction by aliens is unlikely to result in the substantial impairment of any major life activity under the ADA. Accordingly, in most instances, a person with a specific, or simple, phobia is not necessarily disabled within the meaning of the ADA. A person who fears abduction by aliens is probably not disabled.

This does not mean that an employer should do nothing when applicants and employees have phobias. Of course, an employer's reaction to a phobia is going to be gauged by the nature of the impairment. For example, an employee's fear of snakes may not significantly limit a person who lives and works in the middle of a large city. However, a fear of elevators or heights by a person who lives and works in a major metropolitan area with many tall buildings might be substantially more limiting and may necessitate some response.

Employers should address any limitation expressed by an applicant or employee with a view toward assisting the person in meeting the expectations of the job. The ADA does not require employers to eliminate the essential functions of the job as an accommodation. Furthermore, it may not be possible to accommodate some phobias. For example, how would an employer accommodate an employee who is afraid of persons of a different race or ethnicity—i.e., a race phobia—without trampling on the civil rights of others or clearly sending the wrong message in the workplace?

A better example may be the fear of flying. After the September 11, 2001 terrorist attacks on North America, many employees were reasonably reluctant (or even unwilling) to fly in aircraft. A person with a phobic fear of flying, particularly if it is a manifestation of a medically diagnosed anxiety disorder, could have a disability under the ADA. Again, the burden remains on the employee to show that a phobia substantially limits him or her in doing a job. Perhaps a pilot or flight attendant who became fearful of flying could make this showing. By the same token, a pilot or flight attendant who fears flying and will no longer fly, even if offered some accommodation, may no longer be qualified for his or her job and, therefore, may no longer be protected under the ADA. Obviously, more medical information would be necessary to address the phobia and any limitations on working.

Employees who have abject fears, particularly phobias that may impact work, should address the problem with their employer. As discussed above, the fear of flying, alone, is not likely to be a substantial impairment of a major life activity. However, flying periodically for work may be an essential function of one's job and an expectation of continued employment.

An employer may be receptive to temporary modifications

to the job, at least until a reasonable solution can be found. It would help for the employee to be prepared to present information detailing a medical reason for any limitation and proposing possible reasonable accommodations at work. While an employer may not be required to accommodate the fear of flying under the ADA, an employer may have a good business interest in addressing an employee's fears and maintaining an employee's ability to do the job.

Following 9/11 and the temporary grounding of air traffic, many employers discovered that allowing employees to participate in remote meetings via teleconference, rather than traveling to meetings in person, was an equally efficient and cost-effective way to conduct business. In some parts of the country, allowing an employee to travel by train or automobile is a reasonable alternative to flying. The decision to provide such alternatives is at the employer's discretion and is usually not required. If flying to a work location is essential, an employer may have no alternative other than to expect the employee to fly to that location or face some disciplinary action. The key is to be sensitive to an employee's limitation and have a clear mutual understanding of the essential requirements of the job.

The cases first mentioned above are instructive for employers and employees alike. The needle-phobic New York pharmacist, who was fired days after refusing to go to mandatory training on giving inoculations, was awarded $2.6 million in damages by a federal jury on his ADA and state law claims! However, on appeal, the jury award was reversed in favor of the employer and the judgment vacated. A federal appeals court held that the employer, Rite Aid, did not violate the ADA since giving immunizations was an essential function of the pharmacist's job, and requiring other pharmacists to give the shots or hiring a nurse to do so was not reasonable in a small clinic with few employees.

The Connecticut cab driver who is afraid of dogs also lost his ADA and state law claims. Federal and state law require customers with service dogs be allowed to use all modes of public transportation. In 2015, a Connecticut state court found that a dog phobia could qualify as a mental disability under state law, but providing transportation to disabled passengers and their service dogs is an essential function of being a cab driver. Therefore, the taxi driver's fear of dogs was not sufficient to overcome the legal requirement to perform the essential functions of a cab driver's job.

And the school teachers? The South Dakota teacher who feared being fired won at least the first round of her legal battle. In 2013, a federal district court ruled she had shown sufficient evidence that her anxiety was a disability, and a jury should determine whether her contract was not renewed because of unlawful discrimination on the basis of her disability. The Ohio high school teacher who was afraid of young children did not fare as well. First, the teacher's own psychologist stated that she was only incapable of teaching "children under 12." The school district had never assigned the teacher to an elementary school. Junior high children, to whom she was assigned to teach, are generally 12 and older. Further, even assuming pedophobia is a disability, no reasonable accommodation was available. The high school only had one language teacher (her teaching specialty); therefore, another position for the fearful teacher was not available. Under the ADA, an employer does not have to bump another employee out of a job or create a brand new position for a disabled employee.

Finally, the Illinois bridge worker with a fear of heights demonstrates the seriousness with which employers should take an employee's phobia. After being fired in 2007, and losing in the trial court, the bridge worker's lawsuit gained new legal life in 2011. A federal appeals court resurrected his claims, allowing the case to go to a jury to determine whether working at heights was an essential function of the job. The bridge worker had gone for years without climbing heights, and his employer had always excused him from performing any high-altitude work. Others could have changed a light bulb on the bridge in this particular case.

Lastly, the ADA protects persons who are "regarded as" disabled even if they have no physical or mental impairment. The appeals court sent the bridge worker's case back to determine whether the employer, by its response to the employee's stated fear, regarded the employee as disabled under the ADA and thereby unwittingly protected him from discrimination.

Therefore, real fears should compel sincere reactions by employers.

26

IS ADDICTION TO
TECHNOLOGY A DISABILITY?

The ADA and Addictions

Don't be obsessed with your desires Danny.
The Zen philosopher, Basho, once wrote, 'A flute with
no holes, is not a flute. A donut with no hole, is a Danish.'
He was a funny guy.

—Ty Webb, *Caddyshack* (1981)

TODAY, it is difficult to tell whether we have control over technology or it has control over us. Is your cell phone or tablet the last thing you look at before going to bed and the first thing you reach for upon waking up? Be honest, have you ever slept with your phone? For fear of missing out, do you frequently check your phone and social media accounts? Have you ever felt the phantom ring or vibration of your phone and been absolutely sure that someone is trying to reach you by call or text? Are you distracted by the Internet while watching television or talking with friends? How many times have you seen a driver reading their phone or texting while driving? (And yes, being stopped at a traffic light is considered by most law enforcement to be "operating a vehicle" aka driving.) How many hours a day are you on your laptop, tablet, or smart phone?

When it comes to our dependence on technology, there's a thin line between normal and addiction. And some of us clearly are addicted to technology. If that's the case, would an employer have to accommodate a technology addiction?

We've come a long way since Dr. Ivan Goldberg, a New York psychiatrist, made up the term "Internet Addiction Disorder" as a joke among his peers in 1995. In actuality, scientists struggle with the proper definition of an addiction. The American Psychiatric Association's *Diagnostic and Statistical Manual of Mental Disorders* (DSM-5)—the "Bible" of psychiatry—describes only one non-substance-related "addictive" disorder: Gambling Disorder. The World Health Organization (WHO) takes a more expansive view. In the WHO's ICD-10, *Classification of Mental and Behavioural Disorders*, Internet addiction might be considered an impulse or behavioral disorder.

At least one Internet addict has brought a claim of disability discrimination and sought a reasonable accommodation for his condition. James Pacenza worked for IBM inspecting computer chips rolling off the assembly line at the company's semiconductor plant in East Fishkill, New York. He worked twelve tedious hours each day using a computer-based tool that measured the thickness of silicon wafers. The work was so repetitive that Pacenza would access the Internet to help pass the time.

Pacenza was also hiding a dark secret: He had a long-standing Internet porn addiction. Years earlier, he'd been treated for sex addiction; had been hospitalized for having suicidal thoughts; and had taken leaves of absence from work for in-patient psychiatric treatment. He claimed his addictive tendencies were the result of post-traumatic stress disorder (PTSD) stemming from combat service in Vietnam and sexual abuse as a child. Nonetheless, Pacenza managed to work at the IBM plant for nineteen years without his addiction affecting his work performance.

That is, until he got caught. In late 2002 or early 2003, Pacenza's supervisor confronted him about complaints by co-workers that he'd been visiting pornographic sites during the workday using his work computer. Pacenza was warned that he could be fired for violating IBM's policy against accessing websites with sexually explicit or other offensive content using a work computer. Pacenza swore to his supervisor it would never happen again. Just a few months later, using his work computer, Pacenza visited an adult Internet chat room and joined a discussion about oral sex. In his defense, Pacenza argued that he never actually viewed pornographic images using a work computer but only that he was "chatting" about sex on his work computer. It didn't matter. He was fired immediately for violating IBM's computer use policy.

Pacenza brought a lawsuit claiming that IBM knew he was an Internet sex addict who suffered from PTSD and fired him because of his disability. Additionally, Pacenza claimed that IBM made no effort to accommodate his disability. In 2009, a New York federal court denied Pacenza's claims. Pacenza never argued that his Internet sex addiction was a disability. Instead, he claimed his PTSD—which allegedly caused his Internet addiction—was a disability. The case turned on this distinction. When confronted, Pacenza told his supervisor he had a problem with sex addiction; he never informed his supervisor he suffered from PTSD. Therefore, Pacenza was incapable of showing his supervisor fired him *because of* his disability since the supervisor never knew about his PTSD.

For the court, knowledge of an employee's sex addiction is not necessarily notice of an employee's PTSD. Moreover, IBM was able to show that *all* employees are treated in the same adverse manner for violations of its Internet and sexual harassment policies. Finally, the court found that Pacenza was not entitled to a reasonable accommodation for his Internet sex addiction. He had argued consistently that his addiction never interfered with his job and, in fact, insisted that accessing sex chat rooms actually helped him perform his job more satisfactorily. In the end, he simply could not show that he needed any accommodation to help him do his job.

The court never answered the question whether an Internet addiction is disability. No court has specifically addressed this question. It is only a matter of time, however, before someone presents the right case; that is, provides medical information that they are addicted to the Internet and the condition substantially limits one or more major life activities, such as the ability to concentrate or interact with others due to an overwhelming craving for long periods of Internet use. Given the broad interpretation of a disability under the ADA, a court might find an employee is protected. This may include the obligation to provide a reasonable accommodation. However, even if a court someday finds that an Internet addiction is a disability, it is highly unlikely an employer would have to allow an employee to cruise adult chat rooms as a reasonable accommodation.

Pacenza's problem is not unique. Misuse of the Internet at work is a significant growing problem. In April 2010, an inspector general report found that a number of senior-level federal employees of the U.S. Securities and Exchange Commission (SEC) had spent considerable time accessing porn sites during the workday . . . all on the taxpayers' dime. In one case, a senior attorney at the SEC's headquarters in Washington D.C. spent up to eight hours a day looking at, and downloading, pornography. He was allowed to resign. Another employee, an accountant, was blocked 16,000 times in a month from porn sites, yet still managed to download a large cache of porn to his hard drive. He only received a 14-day suspension. The frequency of porn visits increased as the Great Recession emerged in 2008; SEC employees diddled while Rome burned.

Despite the obvious incompatibility of a porn addiction with work, some addictions can be protected at work. Technology addicts might look to the protections drug and alcohol addicts have under the Americans with Disabilities Act (ADA).

The *current* use of illegal drugs—even if a person is addicted—is not protected by the ADA. An employee can be fired for using illegal drugs on or off the premises. However, a rehabilitating or recovered drug addict, who is no longer using illegal drugs, is protected. The ADA helps persons trying to overcome a serious addiction. Therefore, past use of drugs by a recovered drug addict usually can't be held against an applicant or employee. An employee with a drug or alcohol addiction who seeks treatment may also be protected by the federal Family and Medical Leave Act, allowing up to twelve weeks of leave while guaranteeing one's job.

Similarly, addiction to alcohol may be protected. Some, though not all, courts have held that severe alcoholism is a disability under the ADA if it substantially limits a person's ability to perform one or more major life activities. Even if alcoholism is a disability, an employer can still enforce rules limiting alcohol use at work or coming to work under the actual or apparent influence of alcohol. A reasonable accommodation for a person disabled by the disease of alcoholism is time off for treatment, like other employees with medical conditions, and not a minibar in the break room.

What can employers and employees do about our dependence on technology and its negative side effects? We may need an intervention. Allow periods of time for you and others to go device-free, particularly during meetings, meals, and interactions with family and friends. Employers should establish and enforce rules about acceptable uses of work-related technology. For example, it's generally acceptable for an employer to limit sexually offensive or illegal activity while at work or using a work computer. Some employers have taken the bold step of limiting Internet access, which is a recipe for an employee exodus, or, more commonly, using filtering or blocking software to limit access to particular types of sites. Finally, employers should educate employees about the dangers of technology addiction and encourage employees who need help to come forward.

Likewise, employees who realize they may have a problem should address their online behavior before it interferes with work and risks the loss of their livelihood.

PART IV

RULES ARE MADE TO BE BROKEN

27

ARE OFFICE GAMBLING POOLS LEGAL?

Office Pools and Betting

Gambling! I'm shocked . . . shocked to find
that gambling is going on in there.

—Captain Louis Renault, *Casablanca* (1942)

I AM SO BAD AT FANTASY FOOTBALL that I was cut from my own fantasy league. For many others, though, fantasy sports require little skill, are tremendously exciting, and can be wildly popular; maybe too popular. Gambling can be a real problem. Fidelity Investments, one of the largest mutual fund companies in the world, made national news in 2009 when it fired four male employees for playing fantasy football on work computers. At the time, during an economic downturn when many people were losing their jobs in the financial crisis, firing four employees solely for participating in a $20 fantasy football league seemed extremely harsh. From Fidelity's perspective, it was a matter of trust. Fidelity doesn't wager with other people's money and wouldn't want its employees to appear to be "gamblers" with their clients' money.

While the four Fidelity employees were fired, millions more employees participate in office fantasy sports leagues and enter office pools to pick the winners of the Academy Awards, or the final score of the Super Bowl, or the weight of their co-worker's newborn baby.

This begs the question, is participating in fantasy football leagues or office pools illegal?

It depends on the state where you work. Some states have laws making office pools or fantasy leagues an illegal form of gambling. Other states say that competing in fantasy leagues does not constitute gambling because a participant does not sustain "gambling losses." The theory is that the entrance fee to a fantasy league or office pool is not a wager or bet; and prizes of guaranteed amounts are awarded. For example, my home state, Colorado, has a "social gambling" exception that allows office sports pools as long as a social relationship exists among participants and no one other than participants profit from the game. However, under Colorado's law, corporations are not protected. Therefore, a company-sponsored Super Bowl or Academy Awards pool may not be legal.

But just because an office pool is legal in a state does not mean that an employer must permit the activity. Employers can regulate the use of work time and the use of its work equipment. Therefore, Fidelity was within its legal right to fire the fantasy leaguers if, in Fidelity's estimation, the behavior improperly conflicted with work time and the use of work equipment.

There is no question that office pools can be fun and can build morale at work. As with every fun thing, participation can also detract significantly from work time and productivity. On more than one occasion, IT managers at work have complained that so many employees live-stream Olympic events and World Cup soccer games during the workday that it bogs down their company's servers. Another concern is that fantasy league and tournament pool websites are a breeding ground for hackers and computer viruses.

There is the old adage: It's fun until someone gets hurt. Gambling is an addiction for some people and can result in personal and financial disaster. An employer may not want to sow the seeds of an employee's personal self-destruction by encouraging any form of gambling.

I know the question you want to ask right now: Is gambling addiction a disability that would require your employer to accommodate your condition by providing office pools and gambling opportunities? Nice try, but no. Compulsive gambling is not considered a disability under federal or state anti-discrimination laws. Yet.

Finally, some employers don't permit office pools because they may eventually invite union organizing efforts. The National Labor Relations Board has ruled that private sector employers cannot limit union organizing efforts while at the same time allowing employees to solicit participation in sports pools or charity fundraisers. Therefore, if you're going to have an office pool, check your state's laws, check with your employer and, most importantly, be careful about it getting out of control.

28

CAN AN EMPLOYEE BRING A SWORD TO WORK?

Weapons in the Workplace

Mom:	*Ralphie, what would you like for Christmas?*
Adult Ralphie:	*Horrified, I heard myself blurt it out.*
Ralphie:	*I want an official Red Ryder carbine action two hundred shot range model air rifle.*
Mom:	*No. You'll shoot your eye out.*

—A Christmas Story (1983)

WHILE I AM GENERALLY A BIG FAN of employees being recognized for their good work, I have never been a proponent of employee length-of-service or anniversary awards. Recognition for time served, rather than effort, reminds me of the good attendance award in grade school, or the 16th place ribbon at the summer swim meet.

That is, until I read that video game maker Blizzard Entertainment, the developer of *World of Warcraft, StarCraft,*

Overwatch, and other games, rewards employees who've worked there for five years with a sword! A real dragon-slaying sword! Ten-year employees at Blizzard are rewarded with a shield . . . Hmmm, I wonder how many years you have to work before you get a suit of armor or a castle? Now **that** is real incentive for longer service.

Swords are impressive, but the issue of weapons—particularly guns—at work is one of the major fault lines in workplace politics. Most employers have long hewed to the rule that employees and visitors are not permitted to have a weapon on the premises. For non-governmental employers, the workplace is the employer's private property and an employer can decide whether it wants weapons on its premises. A private business, like a homeowner, has the right to permit, or prohibit, weapons on its private property.

From an employer's perspective, even if one supports the right to bear arms, weapons at work raise concerns about employee safety and an employer's liability for accidental or intentional harm caused by weapons on the premises. The federal Occupational Safety and Health Act (OSH Act) demands a safe workplace, including one free from workplace violence. Similarly, insurance companies covering the risk of injury at work often insist on an on-premises "weapons ban" in order to reduce insurance risks.

Recently, though, a sea change has occurred regarding weapons in the workplace. The Second Amendment, and often a comparable state constitutional guarantee, applies to public employers. Public employers include federal, state, county, and municipal governments as well as public universities and schools. The Second Amendment addresses a *government's* ability to restrict an *individual's* right to bear arms, not a private company's right to restrict weapons on its own property. An increasing number of governmental employees are dusting off the Constitution to challenge weapons bans in public workplaces, including municipal offices and public universities. Therefore, governmental employers must navigate federal—and some state and local—laws to afford public employees the right to bear arms within the constraints of more restrictive state and local gun laws.

But another voice has arisen in this age of workplace violence: the voice of fear. Maybe it began as we watched nearly 3,000 people die while working in skyscrapers in New York and the Pentagon in Washington, D.C. on 9/11. Maybe it is the sad reality of witnessing countless senseless and terrifying school shootings. Either way, many employees fear harm at work and desire a means of personal protection. Many employees no longer feel their cell phone is the most important tool for survival; instead, they want a Glock 19. This growing concern has not gone unheard in state legislatures. To the surprise of many employers, an employer is legally required in about half of the states to permit an employee to bring a gun to work or keep a weapon in a parked vehicle on the premises—even over an employer's objection. State law varies, and a number of exceptions apply, so any employee desiring to bring a gun to work is advised to check the laws of the state where they work first before suffering the consequences of a bad decision.

Remember Blizzard Entertainment: You receive a sword after five years of work. In an interesting twist on the right to bear arms, some employees have actually sued for the right to bring a sword to work. Almost all are Sikhs. Sikhism, a 500-year old monotheistic religion with 28 million practitioners worldwide, is the ninth largest religion in the world. Most Sikhs live in India, but about 500,000 live in the United States. While few Americans know much about Sikhs or their beliefs, federal court judges have learned a great deal. Sikhs who are initiated fully in the religion must wear five outward symbols of their faith: unshorn hair, usually worn by men wrapped in a turban (expressing respect for the perfection of God's creation); a small wooden comb (representing discipline and cleanliness in thought and daily life); cotton undergarments (a symbol of chastity and a reminder to control one's sexual desire); an iron or steel bracelet (once used for hand-to-hand combat but now a symbol of dedication to God); and finally, the kirpan, or ceremonial sword or dagger (representing the courage to fight injustice and to defend the oppressed).

Sikhs have frequently challenged appearance standards and dress codes that interfere with a male Sikh wearing a turban or having a beard. Some Sikhs have brought lawsuits to enforce the right to wear the kirpan at work. Employers have a legal duty to provide reasonable accommodation of a religious belief and practice unless it would impose an "undue hardship" on their operations, such as violating a reasonable health and safety standard.

In February 2008, the U.S. Equal Employment Opportunity Commission (EEOC) filed a lawsuit against ManorCare Health Services in Sacramento, California after the nursing home fired a Sikh employee, Baljit Bhandal, for wearing a small kirpan at work. Even though Bhandal provided literature that her kirpan was an article of her faith (and not a weapon) the employer insisted the dagger violated its ban on weapons in the work-place and fired Bhandal when she refused to remove it. The case settled in 2010 with the employer's agreement to pay Bhandal $30,000 and to train all employees on preventing religious discrimination. Interestingly, in the "lightning-really-does-strike-twice-in-the-same-place" category of employment law claims, ManorCare had been sued six months earlier by the

EEOC for an identical claim by a Sikh employee who was fired for wearing a kirpan in a Detroit, Michigan worksite. The earlier case also settled before reaching the courtroom.

In 2013, a federal appeals court refused to dismiss the religious discrimination claim of Kawaljeet Tagore, an Internal Revenue Service (IRS) employee in Houston, Texas, who converted to the Sikh faith in 2005. Tagore requested a security waiver, allowing her to enter her federal office building with her kirpan, despite a federal law prohibiting "firearms or other dangerous weapons in a Federal facility." The federal weapons ban exempts law enforcement officers, military personnel authorized to carry weapons, and possession of certain weapons on federal premises incidental to hunting. Knives are allowed under the federal law but only if the blade is less than 2.5 inches long. There is no prescribed length for the kirpan in the Sikh faith and they don't consider the kirpan to be a weapon but a religious symbol.

In response to Tagore's request to wear the kirpan at work, the IRS placed Tagore on "an interim Flexiplace arrangement" so she could work at home until the matter was resolved. The IRS then convened a "working group" to discuss whether it could accommodate Tagore's request to wear a kirpan. Despite the working group's best efforts, no mutually agreeable accommodation could be found, and Tagore was formally terminated in 2006. The case settled in 2014 with terms that included removing Ms. Tagore's firing from her personnel record, permitting her to enter federal office buildings with the kirpan and allowing her to work with other federal agencies.

Ironically, given religious protections at work, the sword may be mightier than the gun. While many Americans have fought for the right to refuse to bear firearms for religious reasons (particularly in times of war), to my knowledge, no employee has ever requested to bring a gun to work *for religious reasons.*

Employers may have rules regarding the open or concealed carry of a firearm and, depending on federal and state laws, may limit the possession of a firearm or other weapon in the workplace. But a request for religious accommodation must be considered despite an employer's rules to the contrary. Employers must make an effort to understand an employee's sincerely held religious beliefs and practices when they collide with work rules and, where reasonable, accommodate differing (and even unusual) religious practices. Therefore, the employer must consider allowing an employee to wear the kirpan, as an exception to an existing dress or appearance standard, unless it would create an undue hardship on the operation of the employer's business.

29

CAN EMPLOYEES REFUSE TO HAVE TAXES WITHHELD FROM THEIR PAYCHECK?

Tax Protesters and Resisters

What is the difference between a taxidermist and a tax collector? The taxidermist takes only your skin.

—Mark Twain

FAMOUSLY, Benjamin Franklin once said, "Nothing can be said to be certain, except death and taxes." However, since the ratification of the Sixteenth Amendment in 1913, which gave Congress the power to "lay and collect taxes on incomes," I would add tax objectors (and, more recently, celebrity sex tapes) to Mr. Franklin's modest list of things that are inevitable.

My first brush with a tax objector occurred in a most unexpected manner. On his first day of work, a new employee strode confidently into the Human Resources Office and demanded that no taxes be deducted from his paycheck. Asked why, he said proudly, "I'm not an American. I'm a citizen of the Free Republic of Texas. I don't have to pay taxes." Texans, am I right? I subsequently learned this objection has been raised many times before, has even been considered by the Internal Revenue Service (IRS), and, as you might expect, suffered the same fate as the Alamo. Texans, like the rest of us, have to die or pay taxes.

In this employee's defense, ever since the ratification of the Sixteenth Amendment, and the creation of an "income tax," many employees have tried to avoid paying taxes.

Congress figured out long ago that it's easier to get money from businesses than individuals. Therefore, employers have the responsibility to collect federal income taxes from their employees' wages. Employers must also withhold a portion of Social Security and Medicare taxes. Every employee is asked to complete an IRS Form W-4 to help compute taxes to be withheld from the employee's paycheck. Federal income tax withholding is based on an employee's marital status and the number of tax allowances an employee chooses. An employee can refuse to provide a Form W-4 (which might seem like a good idea to a tax objector) but the employer is then authorized to treat the employee as single with no allowances. With no withholding allowances, a person's income tax withholding is higher and paycheck amount is smaller.

On the other end of the spectrum, a Form W-4 claiming excessive allowances, thereby lowering an employee's with-holding for taxes, must be sent to the IRS for review. Instead of refusing to complete a Form W-4, or falsely claiming to have more children than the Duggar family (of *19 Kids and Counting* fame), some employees argue they should be exempt from federal income tax withholding.

There are only a few lawful exemptions from federal

income tax withholding. The most common occurs when an employee had no income tax liability in the previous year and expects none in the current year.

Tax objectors are an entirely different matter. They fall into two general categories: protesters and resisters. Tax protesters present *legal* objections to taxation, claiming income taxes are unconstitutional or they are not a citizen of the United States and, therefore, they should not be taxed. Alternatively, tax resisters offer *moral* objections to taxation, arguing federal taxation is stealing (contrary to one's religious beliefs) or federal taxes pay for "immoral" governmental actions, such as funding the "imperialistic war machine."

Tax protesters and tax resisters are distinguished from tax evaders who use illegal means to refuse to pay taxes. Gangster Al Capone was an infamous tax evader. Tax protesters and tax resisters, on the other hand, are locked in a battle of legal or ideological differences with the federal government.

It should come as no surprise that the Internal Revenue Service (IRS) has expended considerable time and money to combat frivolous tax objections. After all, the IRS wants all of the money they are due. The IRS has even published a guide, *The Truth about Frivolous Tax Arguments*, to debunk the most common protests. Needless to say, it is risky to mess with the IRS. The willful failure to pay taxes carries criminal and civil penalties. To add insult to injury, the Internal Revenue Code imposes a $5,000 penalty for filing a frivolous tax return or for making a submission *any part of which* the IRS identifies as frivolous.

My personal favorite tax protest is when an employee, like above, says they are no longer a U.S. citizen and, instead, are a citizen of a State: I'm not an American; I'm a citizen of the Free Republic of Texas and, therefore, I don't have to pay U.S. taxes.

(Incidentally, Texas is one of seven states that does not collect a personal income tax, so Texas is a good choice if you desire to avoid state taxes as well.)

However, under the Fourteenth Amendment to the United States Constitution, "All persons born or naturalized in the United States . . . are *citizens of the United States and of the State* wherein they reside" [italics added]. Thus, all citizens are citizens of a State *and* the United States.

A person can renounce their U.S. citizenship. You may not have heard that record numbers of Americans are giving up their citizenship each year. In 2006, only 268 Americans gave up their U.S. citizenship. Just ten years later, that number climbed to 5,411. Why so many? Reasons vary but tax experts say tax laws passed in 2010, including the Foreign Account Tax Compliance Act (which brought more scrutiny to assets held by Americans abroad) encourage those with significant foreign financial holdings to renounce their U.S. citizenship.

It's not easy, or cheap, to give up your U.S. citizenship. First, you can't live in the United States, and that includes Texas, even if you believe Texas is not part of the United States. To voluntarily renounce your citizenship, you must also appear before a U.S. diplomatic official *in a foreign country* and sign a written oath of renunciation. Thereafter, you must obtain a visa to re-enter the United States—even if it's just to let the dog out or pick up your dry cleaning. You also can no longer work lawfully in the United States without obtaining separate temporary work authorization. You also don't break a military sword over your knee or cross your heart and pledge yourself a man or woman without a country as a symbol of losing your citizenship. Instead, you are charged a fee of $2,350 (the highest in the world) to renounce your U.S. citizenship. Finally, giving up U.S. citizenship is, in most cases, irrevocable, even if you change your mind later. And the biggest kicker? Renouncing U.S. citizenship may have no effect on your tax obligations, being drafted in the event of national conscription, or prosecution for crimes committed while a U.S. citizen. What's the fun of giving up your citizenship if you can't get out of the DUI you got last summer?

Similarly, in the "resistance to the government is futile" category, employees' efforts to avoid taxes on moral grounds have also failed miserably. Individuals or groups who refuse to pay federal income taxes based on religious or moral beliefs, or an objection to the use of taxes to fund certain government programs, often invoke the First Amendment in support of their position. Additionally, tax resisters often rely on the Religious Freedom Restoration Act (RFRA) in support of their moral stance. While the First Amendment of the U.S. Constitution guarantees free speech and the free exercise of religion, and RFRA further protects religious freedom, courts have consistently held that these laws do not provide the right to refuse to pay taxes for religious or moral reasons.

Therefore, as my grandfather, an immigrant, used to say, "If you make the money, you've got to pay the taxes."

30

CAN AN EMPLOYEE AVOID A DRUG TEST IF AFRAID TO PEE AROUND OTHERS?

Limits on Drug Testing of Employees

Andrew Clark:	*Hey, you're not urinating in here, man.*
John Bender:	*Don't talk. Don't talk. It makes it crawl back up.*

—*The Breakfast Club* (1985)

PEE FRIGHT. It happens. Nearly everyone has experienced the inability to urinate around others in some fashion. Remember the first time your roommate, spouse, or significant other walked into the bathroom to brush their teeth at the exact same moment you were starting to flow? And don't urinals and toilets in public restrooms often feel too darn close to each other for comfort?

Pee fright is technically called paruresis or "shy bladder syndrome." In the world of work, the only time paruresis has ever come up is as an excuse for not giving a urine sample for drug testing purposes. Employers should know, before taking any action against a person who cannot pee, the U.S. Equal Employment Opportunity Commission (EEOC) has taken the informal position that paruresis can be a disability protected under the Americans with Disabilities Act (ADA).

Courts have consistently held that the elimination of bodily wastes is a major life activity. For some more than others, I am sure. However, to establish a disability, the burden remains on the applicant or employee to show their medical condition "substantially limits" a major life activity. Without some clear medical evidence of a physiological inability to urinate normally, an employee who cannot pee in front of others is going to have a difficult time demonstrating a substantial limitation of a major life activity. Of course, an applicant or employee who desires not to participate in a mandatory drug test might likely say they cannot pee in front of an observer. However, this limitation would be self-diagnosed and infrequent, rather than a substantial limitation. Courts are clear: You can never self-diagnose your own disability.

On the other hand, an infrequent, or episodic, impairment can still qualify as a disability if it imposes a substantial limitation when it is active. For example, a male employee might try to offer evidence of a substantial limitation by citing past difficulties trying to pee at public urinals. But this supposed limitation is relieved by using a private stall with the door closed, or by waiting until others are not present in the public restroom. In other words, it could be difficult to prove a person with paruresis is substantially limited urinating at work.

Even if a person has paruresis, and it is disabling, this does not necessarily mean an applicant or employee will be released from a mandatory drug test. An employee might still be tested, particularly if the job has safety considerations, like a truck driver, pilot, or heavy machine operator.

One alternative for those with paruresis is to allow the person to give a sample in an unobserved "dry room" devoid of anything that could be used to alter or dilute a sample. An employer could also forego requiring a urine sample for other forms of drug testing, including taking a blood sample, hair sample, or using a patch to collect sweat for testing. Yes, sweat patch drug testing is a real, and effective, thing.

I am often asked: Does an employer even have the right to drug test?

Generally, private sector employers have the right to conduct drug and alcohol testing of applicants and employees. However, an employer needs to check because some states and municipalities limit drug testing. Remember, current illegal drug use is not a protected activity. Therefore, off-duty illegal drug activity, discovered later through drug testing at work, can result in termination of employment.

Recently, medical and recreational marijuana use and possession have become lawful in many states, but they still remain illegal under federal law. Employers are not required to permit or accommodate the use of marijuana by their employees. Again, some states vary on the duty to accommodate medical marijuana, and this issue is currently being tested in state courts. While some state laws may vary, especially in a state like California, pre-employment testing of applicants, post-accident testing of persons hurt on the job, and "reasonable suspicion" testing of employees under the actual or apparent influence of drugs is usually permitted. Prudent employers try to obtain an employee's express or implied consent to be tested before embarking on drug testing.

Government employees and transportation workers have special considerations regarding drug testing. Government employees are protected by the U.S. Constitution. A drug test is a "search" within the Fourth Amendment. Random drug testing and testing based on a reasonable suspicion of drug use draw considerable scrutiny by courts. However, the U.S. Supreme Court has permitted drug testing of public employees in situations where an employer has a compelling interest, such as safety-sensitive positions like law enforcement, commercial transportation, and the handling of dangerous materials.

Therefore, while no employer could ever "force" an employee to give a urine sample, an applicant or employee who refuses to give a sample for a lawful drug test could be [1] disqualified from employment or [2] terminated, if already hired.

31

WHAT HAPPENS IF AN EMPLOYEE WORKS TO DEATH?

The Legal Consequences of Overwork

THERE IS NO QUESTION Americans work hard. Just ask them. Hard work is the American way, a legacy of Puritan forefathers in New England and the Protestant work ethic, which still influences how many Americans view work.

Surveys consistently show Americans work longer hours than most other workers in the Western hemisphere. On average, you wouldn't likely work late in France, Germany, or Italy. But it's different in Asian countries. Japanese workers work *really, really* long hours. The Japanese labor so long, often without pay, that it kills them. Literally. Death by overwork is so common in Japan that they coined a word for the phenomenon, "karoshi."

How does one "commit" karoshi? In the most widely-reported case, in 2006, a 45-year-old Toyota chief engineer responsible for the worldwide manufacture of the new Camry sedan hybrid automobile died of heart failure after averaging 80 hours of overtime a month . . . Yes, 80 *overtime* hours in addition to his regular work hours during the six months before his death. He also had a soul-crushing overseas travel schedule. His body was discovered by his daughter the day before he was scheduled to make yet another long, stressful business trip to Detroit in preparation for the new car's launch.

The Toyota employee's death proved to be a watershed event in Japan. It also brought considerable worldwide attention to the problem of karoshi, or death by overwork.

In 2008, the Japanese Labor Bureau for Aichi Prefecture, the site of Toyota's headquarters, ruled for the first time that the employee's widow and children were entitled to workers' compensation insurance benefits for the employee's death. According to Forbes Magazine, Toyota Motor Company was one of the largest automobile manufacturers and the 24th most admired company in the world in 2015. Imagine the public embarrassment associated with the death of a key employee (and not its first employee to die) by overwork. This is the moral and marketing equivalent of the Walt Disney Company exterminating Mickey Mouse in the name of public health.

Despite the widespread public attention to the issue, karoshi remains a serious problem in Japan. In December 2015, Matsuri Takashi, a 24-year-old employee of Dentsu, a major advertising agency, jumped to her death from a company dormitory following her repeated complaints of overwork and harassment. She had clocked 105 hours of overtime in the month leading up to her suicide. Her death was determined to be karoshi. As a result of these cases, insurance payments and damage awards in Japanese courts continue to increase. For example, in 2012, Japanese insurance companies compensated more than 800 families for karoshi-related claims. To address the problem, the Japanese government passed a law in 2014 ordering research into overwork-related health hazards and initiating a public awareness campaign highlighting the dangers of overwork. However, the Japanese government has made no effort to limit the number of work hours of its workers or penalize corporations whose employees work extreme hours.

Could karoshi wind up on U.S. shores like Godzilla eventually did? First, while Americans work hard, Americans look at work differently. Puritans certainly aren't running most Fortune 500 companies or business start-ups in the United States. Unlike Asian culture, Americans pride themselves on rugged individualism. We really don't mind if the loser in the cubicle next to us burns the midnight oil, as long as they gain no unfair advantage over the rest of us.

Second, assume Americans do work a ton of hours. Most employees in the United States are entitled to workers' compensation insurance benefits. Workers' compensation includes medical care and treatment for work-related illnesses and injuries. Employees are entitled to temporary and, possibly, permanent disability payments if they are unable to work due to a work-related illness or injury. Stress-related workers' compensation claims can be extremely difficult to prove but would likely be raised in cases of extreme overwork.

Further, the United States workplace is one of the most regulated environments on Earth. The substantial physical or mental limitations associated with aggravated work-induced stress can support claims of discrimination and demands for reasonable accommodation under the federal Americans with Disabilities Act (ADA) as well as requests for job-guaranteed time off under the federal Family Medical Leave Act (FMLA) or their state counterparts. In other words, Americans are more likely to sue or take considerable time off if work becomes extraordinarily burdensome. Therefore, employers have more incentive to avoid liability by regulating work hours and curbing excessive amounts of work.

Finally, employers have to pay for all that work. While the federal Fair Labor Standards Act (FLSA) puts no limit on the number of hours most adult employees may be required to work in the United States, employees not otherwise exempt from the FLSA are entitled to an overtime premium for working more than 40 hours in a workweek. Most states have similar rules. Unlike Japan, where it is common for a factory worker to pull a "7-11" (arriving at 7:00 a.m. and departing at 11:00 p.m.) without compensation for overtime hours worked, most employees in the United States would rack up huge amounts of overtime pay, making it extremely cost-prohibitive for employers to try to work an employee to death.

The moral of the karoshi story? Don't work too hard yourself, and don't make employees work longer than can reasonably be expected.

3 2

DO EMPLOYEES HAVE THE RIGHT TO GO TO THE BATHROOM?

Workplace Safety and Access to a Restroom

IN THEIR 1998 BOOK, *Void Where Prohibited: Rest Breaks and the Right to Urinate on Company Time,* co-authors Marc Linder and Ingrid Nygaard detailed the disturbing lengths to which some employers have gone to keep their employees from using the restroom at work. These are typically manufacturing environments in which a brief bathroom break can mean one or two less widgets down the assembly line and thousands of dollars of lost profits over the course of a year. According to the authors, employees have encountered locked restrooms at work, been forced to wear diapers while working, and even had to void in their clothing! The work and health consequences to a worker not allowed to use the bathroom are significant: urinary tract infections, dehydration, kidney and bladder stones, and constipation—often caused by employees failing to drink fluids in an attempt to avoid taking bathroom breaks or by not going to the bathroom regularly for optimum health.

If there ever is, or should be, an inalienable right at work, it is the right to go to the restroom. Not surprisingly, though, there are myriad legal issues that arise involving restroom use at work, including disabled employees' access to restrooms and rest breaks, paying for the time it takes to go to the restroom, and the consequences, if any, of using the restroom too much.

Every employee should know that most employers are required to provide toilet facilities to their employees. The Occupational Safety and Health Administration (OSHA) is charged with enforcing safety and health standards at work. Ironically, OSHA was created by the Occupational Safety and Health Act of 1970, which is also known as "OSHA" or the "OSH Act."

OSHA (the federal agency) has promulgated a veritable mountain of regulations interpreting OSHA (the law) which few people can successfully ascend without hazarding an avalanche of confusion and government enforcement. OSHA's regulations govern most private sector workplaces but do not apply to local governments. However, local governments are usually subject to state regulations which can be as stringent as OSHA regulations.

OSHA's "sanitation standard" for general industry requires employers to provide their employees with toilet facilities. The regulations state that "toilet facilities, in toilet rooms separate for each sex, shall be provided in all places of employment." The number of toilet facilities that must be provided for each sex is based on the number of employees of each sex in the facility. An employer with 15 or fewer employees must have at least one toilet; an employer with 100 employees must have at least five toilets. An employer need not have separate toilet rooms for each sex if it has a unisex bathroom, meaning it is single occupancy, can be locked from the inside, and has at least one toilet.

A pleasant surprise in the sanitation standard for all office workers is that "no employee shall be allowed to consume food or beverages in a toilet room" and, better yet, no food or beverages can be stored in restrooms. OSHA says nothing about having a supply of reading materials in the restroom.

Farm workers and agricultural employees are covered by a field sanitation standard which mandates that toilets (fixed or portable facilities) be located no more than a quarter mile walk from the location where employees are working.

Unless it is a single, unisex restroom, toilets must be built to assure privacy—that is, have partitions; and must have running water, soap, or cleansing agents and hand-drying materials or equipment. In case you were wondering, urinals are allowed but don't count toward the number of toilets.

The sanitation standard does not necessarily say that an employee is entitled to a break to use the bathroom, or that any break must be paid. However, in a 1998 memorandum, OSHA interpreted the standard as mandating employees' "prompt *access* to bathroom facilities" and any restrictions on access must be "reasonable."

A disabled employee may have the right to a bathroom break as a reasonable accommodation under the Americans with Disabilities Act (ADA). For example, Ed Sulima was employed by defense contractor Defense Support Services LLC (known as "DS2"). In 2005, he was assigned to work as an electronics technician at Tobyhanna Army Depot in Pennsylvania. Sulima was morbidly obese and suffered from sleep apnea attributed, at least in part, to his weight. He was directed by his doctor to lose weight. One of the medications Sulima was taking to lose weight, Xenical, prevents fat in food from being absorbed into the body and, instead, forces fat from the body. You can see where this is going . . . urgent bowel movements as a side effect of the medication. Therefore, Sulima needed to take frequent restroom breaks at work. On October 28, 2005, it hit the fan for Sulima. Joe Johnson, Sulima's team leader, observed Sulima leaving his workstation several times and remaining in the restroom for a total of approximately two hours during his shift! The team leader confronted Sulima about the frequent breaks that day and, when Sulima said it was due to his medication, Johnson told Sulima to get a note from his doctor. The next day, Sulima brought in a note from his doctor saying: "Due to a gastrointestinal disorder, Ed may need to use the restrooms more than usual."

When Sulima continued to take frequent long breaks, he was transferred away from his job and, later, laid off. Sulima brought a lawsuit, alleging that DS2 violated the ADA and the Rehabilitation Act of 1973, a precursor to the ADA, which prohibits disability discrimination by the federal government and federal contractors like DS2.

Despite the side effects, the drug worked: Ed Sulima lost a lot of weight . . . and then he lost his lawsuit. Employers and their employees can learn some lessons from the case. Most importantly, a federal appeals court ruled that the side effects from medical treatment can be an impairment under the ADA. However, an impairment must substantially limit a major life activity to constitute a disability protected by the ADA. Sulima could not show his prescribed medication was required in the prudent judgment of the medical community. In fact, after Sulima was confronted by his supervisor about the excessive bathroom breaks, Sulima told his doctor, who recommended he stop taking the medication. Sulima could not show he was disabled, because he did not have to take the medication. Under a different set of circumstances, though, a court could determine that a disabled employee needs to use the restroom more frequently or for longer periods than usual.

Restrooms are also a frontline in the gender wars. Women have complained successfully in lawsuits that employers have engaged in sex discrimination by depriving them of the use of a restroom at work.

Remember, too, that an employee should be paid for going to the bathroom at work. Some state laws require rest breaks. However, under the federal Fair Labor Standards Act (FLSA), breaks, including restroom breaks, are not required. But if an employer provides breaks, employees must be paid for any break shorter than 20 minutes. This would include most bathroom breaks, unless you are reading *War and Peace* in there.

Finally, an employee, particularly a non-disabled employee, could be disciplined for taking too many bathroom breaks or taking a bathroom break at the wrong time. At least one court, in *Zwiebel v. Plastipak Packaging, Inc.*, upheld the termination of a long-term production employee who left his factory line three times, including once to use the bathroom, during a single shift. The employee argued he was fired for using the bathroom in violation of clear public policy requiring an employee's access to a restroom at work. The court disagreed, concluding that OSHA standards permit reasonable restrictions on access, such as the number of times an employee can go to the restroom each day. The employee was not fired for going to the bathroom, he was fired for leaving his production line unattended. All parties agreed that, had the employee asked a co-worker to watch his production line for him when he went to the bathroom, he'd still be employed. The fact that he left to use the restroom, versus some other purpose, was irrelevant.

Bottom time, going to the bathroom is serious business.

33

WHAT HAPPENS WHEN AN EMPLOYEE DIES ON THE JOB?

Dealing with Loss at Work

*It's not that I'm afraid to die, I just don't
want to be there when it happens.*

—Woody Allen

HOW MANY TIMES have you heard "work is killing me!"?
Sometimes it really does.

This is not a metaphysical question. If you are normal,
when an employee dies on the job, you grieve the loss of a
friend, you remember the employee well, and you comfort the
survivors, including the employee's work family. If you are in
management and Human Resources, you must also navigate a
host of legal issues.

Surprisingly, it is not uncommon for an employee to die
at work. Deaths happen with remarkable frequency. The
Occupational Safety and Health Administration (OSHA)

reported that 5,250 employees died from fatal workplace injuries in 2018. The most common cause of a fatal work injury is a roadway accident.

In many cases, deaths on the job are heart-breaking. Literally, your heart breaks. According to the Centers for Disease Control and Prevention, the leading cause of death in the United States is heart disease, followed closely by cancer. OSHA reports that about 10,000 sudden cardiac arrests occur *at work* each year.

Every workplace should be prepared for an employee to have a heart attack. Get an automated external defibrillator (AED) for your worksite. If an employee is at or near death, always call 911 to notify emergency first responders such as your local fire or police department. A paramedic may be critical to provide lifesaving or life-extending medical procedures, to determine when death has occurred, or to transport the employee's body away from work. Note that it's not the front-desk receptionist's job to clean up the body on Aisle 15, and no workplace has a ready supply of body bags to store the remains of Pat from Accounting.

Depending on the location, either an ambulance will transport, or the coroner's office will be dispatched, or, possibly, a funeral home will be contacted to move the employee's body to the morgue or a funeral home.

You will likely have to notify the federal government of a work-related death . . . *promptly.* All employers subject to the Occupational Safety and Health Act's jurisdiction must notify OSHA within *eight hours* of discovery of a work-related fatality. An employer must also notify OSHA of a work-related injury that causes in-patient hospitalization, the loss of an eye, or an amputation within *24 hours.* Be prepared: OSHA will want to know the details of the injury, including name of the business, identities of employees, location and time and brief description of the incident, and the name and telephone number of a contact person. An employer can contact the nearest OSHA area office during normal business hours, or call the 24-hour OSHA hotline at 1-800-321-OSHA (1-800-321-6742), or report online at https://www.osha.gov/pls/ser/serform.html.

Even more importantly, you must notify the employee's family. Most employers maintain an emergency contact number for employees. If the employee is in transit to a hospital, it is good practice to send a representative of the company to meet the family at the hospital. The organization must decide who is going to notify the family, or other emergency contact, of the employee's grave condition or demise. Usually, this job falls to an executive leader, a Human Resources representative, or both. The chief executive of the organization may want to contact the family, but the logistics regarding pay, benefits, and the like may be left to Human Resources. Typically, Human Resources will also notify other employees and prepare for the grieving process, including making grief counselors available (if necessary) and communicating any funeral or memorial events.

Employees can get paid, even after they die. The deceased employee's final paycheck must be paid in accordance with state law, including accrued, unused paid time off (such as vacation), and wages earned through the last day of work. In some states, the final paycheck goes to the deceased's estate administrator or executor. In other states, the final payment goes to a surviving spouse or next of kin. Some employers are even more generous. For example, when an employee dies while working at Google, Google pays the employee's surviving spouse or partner 50% of the employee's salary, every year, for the next ten years. A deceased Google employee's child receives a $1,000 monthly payment from the company until they reach the age of 19 (or 23 if the child is a full-time student).

Employees and their survivors may also have pension rights, workers' compensation benefits, health insurance or life insurance benefits, including death benefits payable to beneficiaries. The surviving spouse and unmarried minor or disabled children of a Social Security beneficiary are eligible for survivor benefit payments. Usually, a surviving spouse must be 60 years old to claim Social Security survivor benefits, but the age is reduced if the survivor is disabled or caring for children from the marriage who are under 16 or disabled.

Under a federal law called the Consolidated Omnibus Reconciliation Act of 1986 (COBRA), or a state equivalent covering smaller employers, an employee's death triggers a qualifying event for spouses and other dependents to remain on the employer's health insurance plan for up to 36 months.

In addition, the company will want to make arrangements to return the employee's personal possessions at work to the family of the deceased. Conversely, the company will likely try to obtain the return of any work-related items the employee had from the employee's family, such as keys, credit cards, and laptop.

One thing that may surprise employees or their families is that some organizations, usually financial institutions, are permitted to profit on an employee's death. Some employers take out life insurance policies on employees and collect life insurance proceeds upon the employee's death. These death benefits are tax-free and can be used for any purpose, potentially making them a good investment for a business. To many, it seems morally suspect for a business to profit on its own employees' demise. There are several legal restrictions on this practice, including the Pension Protection Act of 2006, which requires that an employee give his or her consent and that companies can only insure the highest-paid "key person" group of employees.

In the meantime, live long and prosper.

34

CAN EMPLOYEES BE REQUIRED TO WORK ON A HOLIDAY?

The Limited Right to Time Off

*Worse? How could things get any worse? Take a look
around you, Ellen. We're at the threshold of Hell.*

—Clark Griswold, *National Lampoon's
Christmas Vacation* (1989)

THE EMPLOYEE WAS IN SHOCK and asked his manager, "What
do you mean I don't get Christmas off?" He assumed he'd have
the day off, everyone gets Christmas off, even Bob Cratchit got
a Christmas holiday!

Alas, this employee might be Scrooged.

Generally, absent some specialized profession where work
hours are limited for safety reasons, such as motor carriers and
airline pilots, an employer can require an employee to work:
any day; every day; any time . . . including holidays.

Some perspective is humbling here. A critical part of the

labor force works on holidays: doctors, nurses, hospital workers, paramedics and other emergency service personnel, law enforcement employees, firefighters, dispatchers, retail and restaurant workers, gas station attendants, movie theater employees, hotel workers, airport employees, public transportation personnel, and many other professionals and businesses.

Even though Christmas is a legal holiday in the U.S., most employers can still require an employee to work. The confusion lies in the expression "legal" holiday—which gives the impression that it's "legal" to miss work and, therefore, you can't be fired. However, there are no federal laws requiring employers to recognize any holidays, give time off for a holiday, or pay a premium for working on a holiday. State law may vary, so you should always check the laws in your particular state.

The term "legal holiday" refers to days that have been declared holidays by federal, state, and local governments. The federal government, and many state governments, recognize certain holidays for public employees: New Year's Day (January 1); Dr. Martin Luther King, Jr.'s Birthday (3rd Monday in January); Presidents' Day (3rd Monday in February); Memorial Day (last Monday in May); Independence Day (July 4); Labor Day (first Monday in September); Columbus Day (2nd Monday in October); Veterans' Day (November 11); Thanksgiving Day (4th Thursday in November); and Christmas Day (December 25). While a government may elect to close its offices, it doesn't mean you are entitled to a day off.

The vast majority of employers, however, see the wisdom of giving employees holidays from work to spend time with family and friends. Many employers even pay employees holiday pay for the day off. And while employers aren't required to, many also pay a premium to employees who are required to work on a holiday as an incentive and reward.

And this gets me back to Christmas. Under Title VII of the Civil Rights Act of 1964, an employer must provide a reasonable accommodation for an employee to observe religious practices unless the time off would create an "undue hardship" on the employer's business. Therefore, an employer must consider an employee's request for a religious holiday, which could include Christmas. In most cases, the burden to request time off falls on the employee, who must be prepared for the employer to counter that the time off would result in undue hardship to the business since required work may not be completed or it would be too costly or unsafe to hire a substitute to do the work.

35

CAN EMPLOYEES WORK FOR FREE?

Wages for Hours Worked under the Fair Labor Standards Act

I WAS SURPRISED the manager called me. Maybe it sounded too good to be true. She explained that she had an applicant in an interview who offered to work for free. Yes, free. *Pro bono.* No compensation for services rendered. Dumbstruck, I asked, "Why?" The manager said, "He told me that he loves what our organization stands for and what we do. He just wants to gain experience with us and be part of a great team."

There is truly only one guiding principle in human resources management . . . No good deed ever goes unpunished. Allowing an employee to work for free is fraught with legal challenges.

However, not every worker is an employee. There is a cadre of workers in the United States who are not entitled to any compensation for services rendered.

This question comes up in a variety of different ways, especially in hard times. First, there is the "go-getter" or the "will-work-for-beer-type." These are usually industrious people who are either dedicated to the cause or want to prove their worth to a company, so they volunteer to work for free in order to get a foot in the door. Then there is the "social climber." This person, often a current or recent student, offers to work for free in exchange for the opportunity to put their experience with the organization on their resume and enhance their professional reputation and future job prospects. Finally, there's the "let's-tighten-our-belt" crowd. When the company is hurting financially, for example, during a pandemic, employees are sometimes willing to forego their pay in order to "save" the company.

Do you have to pay any of these people?

Let me keep this brief: The answer is yes, all of them. While these circumstances seem like reasonable excuses not to pay people, there is no such thing as a free employee. The federal Fair Labor Standards Act (FLSA) presents a considerable hurdle for employers who are considering not paying their employees. It doesn't help that the FLSA was passed in 1938. Modern business practices still must conform to the law's stubbornness in old age. Employers covered by the FLSA (which is most employers in the United States) must compensate "employees" under the rigid requirements of the law.

The FLSA is simple in its two fundamental requirements: [1] employees not exempt from the operation of the law must be paid at least the federal minimum wage, which was 25 cents an hour when the law was passed in 1938 and still seems the equivalent of 25 cents an hour more than 80 years later (actually, it's been $7.25 per hour since 2009); and [2] non-exempt employees also must receive overtime pay—time and a half their regular rate of pay—for each hour worked more than 40 hours in a workweek. Employees should know that at least half of the states and many municipalities have increased their minimum wage for a covered worker beyond the federal minimum wage.

The devil of the FLSA is in the details. The FLSA has an incredibly broad definition of an employee. The FLSA defines an employee as any person who is "employed" by an employer. The law does not discuss the length of employment, or in what capacity. The FLSA also has an incredibly broad definition of what it means to "employ" a worker. "Employ" means to "suffer" or "permit" to work. This is not a "whistle-while-you-work" positive view of work. The federal government takes a medieval view of work: You suffer at work, or a benevolent employer grants you the permission to work. In effect, any person who toils, or is permitted to work, for the benefit of an employer is an employee entitled to be paid under the FLSA.

However, just because someone at the office is holding a cup of coffee, or sneaking a second doughnut in the break room, does not mean they are an employee. Employees are economically dependent on the business for their livelihood. Independent contractors, trainees, interns, volunteers, prison inmates, and immigration detainees are not considered employees under the FLSA. Therefore, they are not entitled to be paid *under the FLSA*. State laws may grant these workers greater rights to be paid.

Employers are particularly intrigued by the idea of having volunteers in their service. By definition, a volunteer is a person who freely agrees to work without compensation. However, volunteers are limited to individuals who perform public service for a *public agency* or similar *nonprofit* organization for civic, charitable, or humanitarian reasons, without promise, expectation, or receipt of compensation for services rendered. Volunteers cannot displace regular employees hired to do the work. In the public sector, government employees are permitted to volunteer for their own agency. For example, a police officer could volunteer to read to children at the public library.

However, an employee can never volunteer to do his or her own job for free.

Under the FLSA, employees may not "volunteer" their time or energy to for-profit private sector employers. IBM can't make its employees—or allow them to—"volunteer" to pick up cigarette butts in its parking lots for free. Of course, an employee can always volunteer for a public agency or non-profit, such as Habitat for Humanity, on their own time. Corporate volunteerism programs and "volunteer time off" (VTO) are very popular employer-sponsored benefits, particularly for Millennials. According the U.S. Department of Labor, employers can incent their employees to volunteer for public agencies and nonprofits—by giving paid VTO days or paying a bonus for their volunteer efforts—without jeopardizing the employees' status as volunteers.

Therefore, under the FLSA, employees must be paid for their work.

If employees must be paid for their work, what can an employer do in times of economic crisis to keep the business afloat when it can't afford to pay its employees? Employers have a number of unpleasant, but perhaps necessary, options to keep the ship of business from sinking. For non-exempt employees, an employer can reduce the number of hours or days of work of an employee with a commensurate reduction in pay. If a non-exempt employee doesn't work, the employer isn't required to pay the employee.

Alternatively, an employer can reduce the wage rate of a non-exempt employee as long as the employer pays the required minimum wage in the jurisdiction where the employee works. An employer can also send a non-exempt employee home without any pay as long as the employee does not work from home.

A furlough is a full or partial reduction in an employee's

work hours without terminating the employee. Benefits, such as health care, usually continue during a furlough. A layoff is a temporary or permanent loss of employment. In many states, an employee whose hours are reduced, or furloughed, or laid off is entitled to unemployment insurance benefits.

Exempt employees must be paid a set salary for any week in which they do work, regardless of the quality or quantity of work performed. An exempt employee is not entitled to be paid for an entire week during which they do no work. In other words, an exempt employee can be furloughed without pay in full-week increments. There is a more generous rule in the public sector allowing furloughs of exempt employees in less-than-full-week increments. Also, the FLSA permits employers to reduce an exempt employee's salary to address a long-term business disruption or in cases where an exempt employee has exhausted paid leaves and voluntarily elects to take full-day absences without pay for personal reasons.

In situations where a large number of employees is being laid off or furloughed, an employer may have to give advance notice to employees under federal and some states' laws. There are usually exceptions, however, for temporary layoffs or layoffs triggered by natural disasters or unforeseen circumstances.

In all cases where employers and their employees are disrupted, and any party is considering having employees work for free, all involved should stop, seek the advice of a legal or human resources professional, and consider all of their options.

36

IF WORK CLOSES DUE TO A BLIZZARD, DO EMPLOYEES STILL GET PAID?

Business Closures and the Fair Labor Standards Act

I HAD NEVER HEARD OF a "bomb cyclone" until just a few years ago, when a foot of snow unexpectedly dropped on Denver one March day, closed my office, and canceled our vacation plans to sunny California.

Severe weather happens frequently. For example, a blizzard dumps three feet of snow, essentially paralyzing a city, and closing most of its businesses for a few days. Natural and man-made disasters occur less frequently but can impact work more harshly. For example, a Category 5 hurricane bearing down on Florida can literally shutter businesses in the storm's path for days until the storm has passed and any damage is assessed. You, though, were lucky in the event of bad weather. You weathered the storm, live nearby work, and were still planning to go to work. However, your employer decided to close the office due to bad weather or disaster.

Do you still get paid when the office is closed due to

unforeseen circumstances? What if you are on vacation or out sick and the office closes on a day you are absent; do you get your vacation or sick day back?

According to the U.S. Department of Labor, whether an employee is entitled to be paid for work closures due to inclement weather or disasters depends on an employee's status as an *exempt* or *non-exempt* employee. Exempt employees usually hold executive, administrative, or professional jobs and are not entitled to overtime. Instead, they are entitled to be paid a salary for a full week of work if they worked any part of that week. On the other hand, a majority of employees are non-exempt. They are entitled at least to minimum wage for all hours worked plus overtime pay for hours worked in excess of 40 in a workweek.

If an employee is able and allowed to work from home on a snowy day, then the employee must be paid for all hours worked at home for the benefit of the employer. Similarly, an employer may allow employees to make up missed time in the event of an unplanned circumstance, such as for weather events. Note that state or local laws and union agreements can provide greater rights to employees in the event of office closures. For example, a union member may be entitled to more protections, and more pay, under the terms of a collective bargaining agreement.

Here's the rub: Non-exempt employees are paid only for the hours they actually work. Therefore, if the office is closed, for whatever reason, a non-exempt employee is not entitled to any compensation. It does not matter if a non-exempt employee was ready, willing and able to work, and the employer closed the office, or the employee simply chose not to work on a particular day. In either case, the non-exempt employee who does not work receives no pay unless the employer elects to be more generous than the law requires or the employee is allowed to use accrued paid leave, such as vacation, for a day or part of a day in which no work is performed. Employees working in the field or at other sites not affected by the weather, such as a satellite or home office, who are still doing their jobs would be entitled to their regular pay.

Exempt employees, on the other hand, must be paid a set, pre-determined salary that is not readily subject to deduction. An employer risks jeopardizing an employee's exempt status, including not having to pay overtime, if it makes improper deductions from that employee's salary. There are just a few deductions from an exempt employee's salary that are permitted; for example, missing a full day's work for personal reasons other than accident or illness, like taking the family to an amusement park for the day. When an employer decides to close the office, if an exempt employee is ready, willing, and able to work, the employer can't make deductions from the employee's pay when the employer decides to make work unavailable. Therefore, exempt employees who do not work still get paid on a weather-related closure day.

However, if the office is open, and an exempt or non-exempt employee chooses or is unable to come to work that day due to severe weather or disaster—for example, the employee's car is under a mountain or snow or floated away in flood waters, or travel to work is otherwise restricted—the full-day absence is considered to be for "personal reasons" and can be deducted from an employee's pay. Of course, in this particular circumstance, employees are often allowed to use accrued vacation or other paid time off for the day and not lose pay.

Also, keep in mind that this rule applies only to *full-day* absences by exempt employees. If an exempt employee marshals a sled dog team and arrives to work late, or works from home on a snow day, then the exempt employee is entitled to be paid for the full day even if only present for part of the day. An employer can also require employees, whether exempt or non-exempt, to use vacation or other paid time off—for example, a personal day—for the time the office was open and the employee could not make it to work, or when the office was closed and no work was done. This could include employees who are already on vacation when the office was closed. Therefore, an employee who is out sick or on vacation may still be charged a sick or vacation day even though the office is closed unless the employer elects to be more generous.

In conclusion, the most important consideration in all cases of inclement weather or disaster is whether it is safe for employees to come to work. It is always an employer's prerogative to close the office to help ensure the safety of its employees or because work is not practical or possible in inclement weather or following a disaster. Resolving pay issues can occur after the storm has passed. That said, smart employers plan for unexpected events. For example, many employers have adopted inclement weather policies to help employees understand what to expect—including whether they will be paid—in the event of a weather-related closure. Additionally, employers may elect to be more generous when unplanned events close the business and curtail work. Employees likely didn't plan to miss work, and lose pay, for a weather closure. Therefore, employers and employees should always check their own rules, and local laws, and abide by them in the event the office is closed due to a serious weather event or disaster.

PART V

EMPLOYEE RIGHTS

37

DO EMPLOYEES HAVE THE RIGHT TO DISCUSS THEIR SALARY WITH OTHERS?

The National Labor Relations Act

THIS IS THE STORY SHE TOLD ME. Maybe it was seeing the paystub laying on his desk, but she suspected she was being paid substantially less than her new co-worker for doing the exact same job. So she flat-out asked him, "What's your salary?" He hemmed and hawed and, finally, said "I'm not allowed to tell you." He claimed the company had a rule ordering employees not to discuss their pay with other employees. The employee turned to me and asked, "Is that true? Can you get fired if you talk about your salary at work?"

One could see where an employer might be tempted to curb discussions by employees about their pay in order to minimize gripes or complaints about differences in the level of compensation. An employer could also want to avoid the morale-busting discovery by some employees that other employees are paid much more than they are . . . for no clearly justifiable reason. As a result, companies have included "salary administration" statements in employee handbooks, such as, "Salaries are confidential between employees and the company and are not to be discussed with anyone other than supervisors or Human Resources."

Are these rules enforceable? Can an employer order an employee not to disclose her own pay?

The answer, under the law, is generally a clear and compelling NO. A work rule or order prohibiting employees from discussing their salary and working conditions is presumptively unlawful, unless the employer can show a substantial and legitimate business reason for the rule.

Section 7 of the National Labor Relations Act (NLRA) makes it an unfair labor practice for employers to interfere with, threaten, or coerce employees in the exercise of their rights to engage in "concerted activities" for their "mutual aid and protection." The NLRA applies to all private employers, and not only employers with a union. "Concerted activity" is not defined in the NLRA but includes discussions of wages and other terms and conditions of employment.

Therefore, so-called "non-discussion rules"—ordering employees not to talk about pay and working conditions—are presumptively invalid since employees may wish to band together to address low or inequitable wages and other terms or conditions of their employment. For example, as recently as April 2018, the National Labor Relations Board (NLRB) ruled that a provision in Lowe's Home Center's Code of Business Conduct and Ethics prohibiting employees from discussing "confidential information," including salary information, violated the NLRA. The specific provision challenged by the NLRB is as follows:

Confidential information includes all non-public information that might be of use to competitors of the company, or harmful to Lowe's, its suppliers or

customers, if disclosed. It includes all proprietary infor-
mation relating to Lowe's business such as customer,
budget, financial, credit, marketing, pricing, supply cost,
*personnel, medical records and **salary information**.*

The NLRB relied on a December 2017 case involving The Boeing Company in which the Board held that broad prohibitions on the discussion of wages are generally "always unlawful."

The lesson for employers is that, unless a nondisclosure policy is narrowly-tailored to address a legitimate business reason, prohibitions against employees discussing wage and salary information are likely to be challenged as an unfair labor practice. Further, some states have laws protecting employees' rights to discuss their wages.

An employer can still preserve the confidentiality of its proprietary business information. In such cases, though, the employer must provide tangible, legitimate business justifications, rather than bald assertions, to support its confidentiality rule.

38

DO EMPLOYEES HAVE THE RIGHT TO DISCUSS POLITICS?

Politics at Work

Commissioner Brumford:	*[On phone.] Hello? He did what? How many animals escaped? Oh, my god.*
Frank:	*Hello, Commissioner. You're looking lovely this evening.*
Commissioner Brumford:	*Do you realize that because of you this city is being overrun by baboons?*
Frank:	*Well, isn't that the fault of the voters?*

—*The Naked Gun 2½: The Smell of Fear* (1991)

POLITICS AND WORK rarely mix well. This is particularly true when politically divided co-workers must work together in the midst of contentious campaigns, elections, and their aftermath.

Consider this case. Jeffrey Heffernan, a City of Paterson, New Jersey police detective stopped by the headquarters of the candidate challenging the city's mayor in a coming election and picked up a yard sign. At the time, Heffernan was a 20-year veteran of the Paterson Police Department. While he knew and was friends with the challenger for mayor, Heffernan did not live in Paterson, could not vote in the mayoral election, and was not publicly supporting any candidate in the election. He was only picking up the sign at the request of his mom, who lived in Paterson, but was bedridden and could not pick up a sign herself. He's an admirable son.

Other police officers, who saw Heffernan show up at the challenger's campaign headquarters and take a yard sign, immediately informed ("ratted" in New Jersey) the police hierarchy, including the police chief, who—you guessed it—were appointed by (and strongly supported) the incumbent mayor.

Based solely on the *mistaken* belief that he supported the challenger in the local election, Heffernan was demoted *the next day* to uniformed patrol officer walking a beat. Heffernan brought a lawsuit under the First Amendment of the U.S. Constitution claiming he was demoted for exercising his free speech rights. This case took ten long years to reach the U.S. Supreme Court but justice was served! Ruling in Heffernan's favor, the Supreme Court upheld the legal principle that a government entity cannot discipline a public employee for engaging in partisan political activity—even when relying on a mistaken belief—when the activity is not disruptive to the agency's operations and the punishment has a chilling effect on others' exercise of free speech; i.e., other employees would be discouraged from participating in politics if they thought they could be fired for their outside political views.

Even longer ago, remember 2004: Bush v. Kerry? Lynne Gobbell was fired from her job at a Moulton, Alabama factory for allegedly displaying a John Kerry bumper sticker on her car in the factory's parking lot. She may have been the only person in Alabama with a Kerry bumper sticker on her car! The Kerry campaign hired her after learning of her firing.

The same week Gobbell was fired, a man who allegedly heckled President Bush at a campaign rally in Hedgesville, West Virginia was fired from his job as a graphic designer. He purportedly embarrassed and offended a business client of his employer who had provided the tickets to the event for the company's employees. Neither case prompted a lawsuit.

Perhaps the greatest urban legend at work is that all political expression is protected. Employees, especially employees with strong opinions (and often little sense), are shocked to learn that there is no federal law specifically protecting employees *in the private sector* who inflict their political opinions on others while at work. In other words, there is little right to free speech on the job. You might recall the "middle finger seen around the world." In October 2017, Juli Briskman, an employee for a government contractor in the Washington, D.C. area, twice "flipped off" President Trump's motorcade during a bicycle ride in Northern Virginia. A photograph of the incident received worldwide attention. Briskman was fired after she admitted to her employer that she was the expressive cyclist. Even though Briskman was off-duty and not wearing any gear to identify her employer, the employer claimed Briskman's action violated the company's social media policy and conflicted with her duties as a marketing employee of a company that is dependent on contracts with the federal government. Briskman filed a lawsuit claiming wrongful termination and breach of contract in 2018. However, her lawsuit was dismissed later in 2018 after a finding that there is no free speech protection for an employee in the private sector.

Certainly, the First Amendment of the U.S. Constitution

protects free speech. Free speech includes freedom of expression. Political expression is clearly a form of free speech. However, the U.S. Constitution stands as a shield against a *government's interference* in our individual liberties. Therefore, only *public sector employers*, such as federal, state, county, and municipal governments and school districts, are subject to the First Amendment's protection of free speech. Government workers are protected against the very governments they serve. But a government employee is protected only when speaking as a *private* citizen on a matter of *public* concern.

Generally, speech and other forms of expression (e.g., signs, t-shirts, buttons, ballcaps) while on the premises, or while working (even in a government job), are not "private" speech and, therefore, can be restricted by an employer.

However, there are exceptions: Some forms of expression may be accepted, or difficult to regulate, by an organization. For example, an entire body of conflicting case law has developed about whether a public employer can prohibit a public employee from displaying a bumper sticker on his or her private vehicle on the employer's premises.

Off-duty, off-premises political speech and activity by a public or private employer is protected—unless an employer can show that the activity interferes with an employee's job. Every state recognizes an employee's right to privacy, and some states protect the lawful, off-duty, off-premises activities of employees. These states—California, Colorado, Illinois, Iowa, Louisiana, Minnesota, Missouri, Nebraska, Nevada, New Mexico, New York, South Carolina, Utah, and West Virginia—specifically protect employees from discrimination or retaliation for engaging in political activities or expressing their political opinions.

Finally, the National Labor Relations Act (NLRA) affords

some protection for a discussion of politics at work. The NLRA applies to all *private sector* workplaces. Under the NLRA, employees, who are not supervisors, have the right to engage in speech or other protected concerted activity for their "mutual aid and protection." As many political causes could affect the terms and conditions of work (e.g., organized labor, safety, wages, health and welfare benefits), employees have some liberty at work to participate in political activities. While employers can generally limit such activities to non-working time, employees could discuss politics during lunch, after work, and, more commonly today, on social media platforms.

Google's experience with its employee, James Damore, provides a cautionary tale for both employers and their employees. In July 2017, Damore, an engineer for Google, lit his employer on fire by writing and then disseminating by internal e-mail an incendiary memo criticizing Google's diversity training. The ten-page memo, entitled "Google's Ideological Echo Chamber," stated that Google discriminated against white men and persons with conservative political views. Damore was fired in August 2017 for violating Google's code of conduct. Damore filed a charge alleging unfair labor practices with the National Labor Relations Board (NLRB) but later withdrew his complaint and filed a discrimination lawsuit against Google in January 2018. A NLRB internal memo released in 2018 had concluded that, while parts of Damore's memo criticizing Google could be considered protected concerted activity under the NLRA, Damore was fired for his unprotected comments deriding women in violation of the company's anti-discrimination policy. Damore opted to enter arbitration to settle with Google, and a California court ruled in July 2019 that Damore's case could proceed to trial if the matter did not settle.

A complete ban on all political discussions at work would likely be unlawful under the NLRA, impractical to enforce, and, in many instances, a buzzkill for morale. Employees spend so much time at work—and discussions about the coffee, pets, favorite concerts, and sports only go so far—that it is natural to express one's political views. Most of us just want to be heard and can also live in a world in which people disagree. Indeed, a truly diverse workplace should recognize diversity of thought and political opinion. The problem arises when employees simply cannot agree to disagree or they drift into disrespect. Employers should always insist that employees be respectful toward their co-workers. Even better, employees should always insist that their co-workers treat them respectfully. Respect should start at the top and be reinforced at every level of any organization.

Finally, employers can, and often do, limit political discussions that interfere with work or the relationships between employees. Some political rhetoric can even spark allegations of unlawful discrimination and harassment. For example, an employee may have strong opinions about U.S. immigration policy and desire to secure the border of the United States from persons entering or remaining unlawfully. However, another employee with opposing political views may hear the same words as offensive and exclusionary rhetoric toward persons based on their national origin. I recall an upset employee telling me, when dealing with this very issue, "He keeps saying he wants to secure the southern border, but I never hear him say he wants to secure our border with Canada. I think he doesn't like or trust Mexicans." Two people can hear the same words entirely differently. I had another case in which a manager drew fire for removing an employee's small "rainbow flag," supporting LGBTQ rights, yet left a New England Patriots pennant to adorn a neighboring co-worker's workstation. Apparently, flags were acceptable in this workspace, just not rainbow flags.

We all have our political opinions, and biases. A mature person learns to manage them in the company of others.

39

ARE EMPLOYEES ACCOUNTABLE FOR THEIR SOCIAL MEDIA POSTS?

Employee Expression

HAD THE POET ELIZABETH BARRETT BROWNING worked in Human Resources, she might have altered her famous poetic first line to, "How do I fire thee? Let me count the ways." There are countless ways employees have been fired for oversharing on the Internet.

Just ask Juli Briskman, Curt Schilling, Scott Bartosiewicz, Kimberly Swann, or Ellen Simonetti.

In a dizzying example of just how quickly the Internet can change one's life, let's revisit Juli Briskman's situation from the previous scenario. Briskman was riding her bike on Saturday, October 28, 2017, when she was overtaken by President Trump's motorcade leaving the Trump Country Club in Sterling, Virginia. As the cars passed, Briskman "extended her middle finger as an expression of disapproval of the President." The moment was captured by a member of the press corps following the motorcade. The image was published online the same day and went viral immediately. Although the photograph didn't show Briskman's face, or otherwise identify her in any way, the next day, Sunday, Briskman updated her personal Facebook page and Twitter page with the photograph of herself, making it her cover photo or profile background on the two social media networks. Her profiles and posts never identified that she worked for Akima, LLC, a defense contractor with headquarters in Herndon, Virginia. However, back at work on Monday, October 30, 2017, Briskman informed Akima's Human Resources Department about the photograph. Briskman was fired the next day, on Halloween.

According to Briskman's subsequent complaint, alleging wrongful termination, she was told she was being fired for two reasons: [1] the photograph could link her to Akima, and Akima, being a government contractor, feared retaliation by the President or his Administration and, [2] the photograph amounted to "obscene content" on her Facebook page in that it could discredit Akima. Briskman lost her wrongful termination case but was awarded the severance pay promised her at termination. In November 2019, Briskman was further rewarded by winning a seat on the Loudoun County (Virginia) Board of Supervisors.

Other examples abound:

- On April 20, 2016, ESPN announced the network had fired former pitching great, and Boston World Series hero, Curt Schilling, from his job as an ESPN baseball analyst after he shared a Facebook post critical of transgender persons' use of restrooms and added his comments: "A man is a man no matter what they call themselves. I don't care what they are, who they sleep with, men's room was designed for the penis, women's not so much. Now you need laws telling us differently? Pathetic."

- In 2011, Scott Bartosiewicz, a contractor doing (iron-ically) marketing work for Chrysler, the automobile manufacturer, mistakenly posted the tweet, "I find it ironic that Detroit is known as the #motorcity and yet no one here knows how to fucking drive," on Chrysler's company Twitter feed instead of his personal Twitter account. After discovering the tweet critical of Detroit, the epicenter of the U.S. auto industry, Chrysler elected not to renew its contract with New Media Strategies, Bartosiewicz's employer, effectively firing him.

- As a 16-year-old clerical worker for a product develop-ment company in Clacton-on-Sea, England, Kimberly Swann made international news in 2009 after she was fired solely for posting on her own Facebook page how "dull" and boring her new job was. Teenagers, right? Swann's boss discovered the post while surfing the Internet and summarily fired her.

- Ellen Simonetti was a flight attendant for Delta Airlines who started a blog, Queen of the Sky: Diary of a Dysfunctional Flight Attendant. She was fired in 2004 for posting photos of herself in company uniform posing seductively in the cabin of a passenger aircraft. Even though Simonetti never identified her employer online, Delta still fired her for bringing, in the airline's view, discredit to the airline. Ms. Simonetti later sued for gender discrimination and retaliation and the case settled for an undisclosed amount.

Social media has become a dominant force in the world. For some of us who are of a certain age, we were still trying to figure out how our e-mail worked when social media was born and raced right past us. Now, I'm worried that my kids won't even friend me on Facebook . . . and I didn't even know what Facebook was ten years ago . . . and my kids have already moved on from Facebook. Except for occasional use by Shakespeare, to "unfriend" a person wasn't even a thing until recently.

Most of us are now very familiar with what social networking is and how much sway it holds. In this age of change, most even understand some of the new technologies and distribution platforms that give social networks their force at the speed of going "viral."

Social networking forums, like Facebook, YouTube, Instagram, Twitter, and LinkedIn, have exploded in a relatively short period of time. For example, Facebook was founded in 2004, and, sixteen years later, has 2.5 billion active users. Twitter, a 280-character micro-blogging site launched in 2006, had 330 million active monthly users as of November 2019. YouTube, which shared its first video in 2005, has two billion logged-in monthly users. In the United States, more adults use YouTube than Facebook. According to Pew Research, YouTube is the most popular online platform in America.

There are over 1.7 billion websites on the Internet today and it's estimated that over 600 million of them have web logs ("blogs"). According to Blubrry, the world's largest podcast directory, as of 2019, there are more than 600,000 podcast titles and the number rises by about 2,000 every week.

Employers live, and may die, by the Internet. People in the technological age have an unquenchable appetite for new technologies and applications. As is often the case, employers have adapted their business practices, including recruiting and hiring, to capitalize on these technologies, including social media. A 2017 Careerbuilder.com survey found that 70 percent of employers use social media to verify applicants' background information or search for inappropriate activity that might disqualify an applicant from employment.

Social media is an excellent way to bolster an organization's connection with its customers and the public, brand products, keep an eye on the competition, and communicate instantly with followers and the public. However, such use of social media and other Internet technologies is not without risk.

In making a decision as to whether to check applicants' social media profiles or monitor employees' Internet use, at work or even at home, employers are primarily concerned with:

- the inadvertent or intentional disclosure of confidential or proprietary business information, such as trade secrets;

- acts of disloyalty or reputational harm wrought upon the employer as a result of an employee's Internet activities; and

- employees' misuse of company time and resources or lost productivity while online, otherwise referred to as "cyberloafing."

Ironically, despite these concerns, many employers not only allow, but actively encourage, employees to use Internet technologies. For example, today, employers allow employees to remotely access work networks from their home computers, thereby blurring the distinction between our work and home lives. Some employers further allow employees' use of social media while they are working.

Most of us equate the Internet, a vast playground of

information and opinion, with free speech. You can say or do anything on the Internet. At the same time, though, very few people want to be held accountable for what they say or display on the Internet, especially by their employer. Is information on the Internet even any of an employer's business?

Courts have consistently held that employees do not have a reasonable expectation of privacy when using their employer's Internet, computer, or e-mail system. Workplace policies reinforcing an employer's right to monitor its own communications systems have essentially eroded any reasonable expectation of privacy with respect to such systems. More recently, though, employers have stepped beyond their own computer systems to employees' off-duty activities on the Internet.

Generally, information posted on the Internet is not private unless the information is secured behind a password-protected site. Information in the public domain may be relied upon by an employer or a third party to the detriment of an employee. *Moreno v. Hanford Sentinel* is an early example of the negative consequences of putting too much information on the Internet for public view. Cynthia Moreno, a college student at the University of California, Berkeley, posted an "Ode to Coalinga [California]," containing negative references about her hometown, on her MySpace page. Her high school principal sent the Ode, identifying Moreno by name, to the local newspaper which, in turn, published the Ode as a letter to the editor. Upset residents sent death threats to Moreno's family in Coalinga, shot at her home, and, ultimately, forced the family to close its business and move out of town. Moreno sued the newspaper, its editor, and the high school principal for invasion of privacy and intentional infliction of emotional distress. The cases against the newspaper and its editor were dismissed under state law and First Amendment free press grounds. The lower court also dismissed the case against the principal. In 2009, a California appellate court agreed, holding that Moreno's decision to post the Ode on the "hugely popular" MySpace website (perhaps in 2008 but, today, Facebook has 50 times the number of users) rendered the post public as a matter of law. Therefore, the principal's decision to forward the Ode to the newspaper was not an invasion of Moreno's privacy.

Social media platforms as a recruiting tool may invite scrutiny by the U.S. Equal Employment Opportunity Commission (EEOC) and applicants claiming discrimination. The majority of employers use social networking sites, such as LinkedIn, a professional networking site, to recruit and fill open positions. However, social networking sites can represent limited social groups. For instance, surveys consistently show that a surprisingly low number of LinkedIn users are Black or Hispanic. Therefore, an unsuccessful applicant of color might argue that exclusive use of social networking sites adversely impacts the hiring of minority candidates. An employer who uses social networking sites as a recruiting tool would be best advised to rely on other recruiting methodologies as well in order to broaden the pool of potential applicants. Of course, the EEOC and the U.S. Department of Labor's Office of Federal Contract Compliance Programs, which regulates federal contractors, expects employers to document their recruiting efforts. The informality of using social networking sites may lead to relaxed documentation efforts and subsequent lack of proof in the defense of a claim.

Unless otherwise restricted, employers and recruiters, both external and internal, may have access to and rely on information posted on an individual's website, blog, or other Internet posting to make employment decisions. However, before an employer "Googles" an applicant, there are some important words of warning. An Internet search may disclose an applicant's not otherwise obvious membership in a protected group, such as race, ethnicity, religion, disability, or sexual orientation. If the applicant is rejected and can show the Internet search may have influenced the decision, an employer could be inviting a discrimination lawsuit. The same concern applies if an employer is inconsistent in whom it searches online or who is doing the online searches. If an employer is doing Internet searches, then an unbiased arm of the organization should be conducting them—not the hiring manager. In addition, the employer should maintain a record of the searches and any information on which it relied to make an employment decision. Finally, in a world of "fake news," content on the Internet is often unreliable or can be easily misconstrued, so an employer should carefully weigh the limited value of the information it may receive in making an overall employment decision with the potential risks of a discrimination or other claim that may arise.

The infamous "Cisco Fatty" story illustrates the dangers of posting one's thoughts on an unrestricted Twitter account. In 2009, newly hired 22-year-old Connor Riley tweeted, "Cisco just offered me a job! Now I have to weigh the utility of a fatty paycheck against the daily commute to San Jose and hating the work." A Cisco associate who received the tweet responded to Riley that her concern would be passed along to the hiring manager who "would love to know that you will hate the work." The job offer, and potential "fatty" paycheck, was rescinded.

An invasion of privacy claim or, for employees in the public sector, a violation of the Fourth Amendment's privacy protection, may be successful when the applicant or employee's information on the Internet is not accessible to the public at large, i.e., "private" web information.

In *Pietrylo v. Hillstone Restaurant Group*, a federal court in New Jersey addressed the limits of an employer's ability to monitor social networking sites. Two employees of a restaurant were fired for the offensive content of their private MySpace "gripe site," which contained negative posts about the restaurant. Membership in the site was by invitation only. A hostess at the restaurant who had been invited to join the private group shared the offensive content on the site with a restaurant manager, and, after being asked, gave another manager the site's login and password for access. The managers accessed the gripe site using the hostess's login and password. The employees were fired for their unprofessional and discourteous behavior in violation of company policy. The court ruled in 2009 that the employer violated the federal Stored Communications Act and invaded the employees' privacy. The Stored Communications Act makes it unlawful for an employer to access, without authorization, communications stored at a facility which provides an electronic communications service. The facts that the gripe site was password-restricted, there was no evidence of use of any work computer or work time to disparage the company, and a sincere question was raised as to whether the hostess who gave the managers access to the site did so only out of fear of losing her job influenced the outcome in favor of the employees.

Employees who are expressive online should know that the outcome would have been different if a co-worker had voluntarily given the other employees' social media posts to the employer. Strident employees may abandon their privacy to their friends on Facebook or other social media. In 2013, a federal court in New Jersey revisited the issue of an employer's access to an employee's social media content in *Ehling v. Monmouth-Ocean Hospital Service Corp.* A New Jersey paramedic posted a critical comment on her Facebook account about the actions of District of Columbia police and paramedics following a deadly shooting at the Holocaust Museum in Washington, D.C. One of the employee's Facebook friends, a fellow paramedic and co-worker, forwarded the negative posts to their manager who, in turn, forwarded the posts to the company's director of administration. The employer disciplined the paramedic for the posts on the grounds her posts demonstrated a "deliberate disregard of patient safety." In her subsequent lawsuit, like in *Pietrylo*, Deborah Ehling argued that her employer violated her right to privacy by coercing her co-worker to divulge her private Facebook content. The court disagreed. By inviting another employee to "friend" her on Facebook, and allowing the co-worker to view her posts, the co-worker was an authorized user of Ehling's social media account and could divulge the content to others. Also, unlike *Pietrylo*, there was no question in the case that the co-worker voluntarily, and without any pressure, disclosed Ehling's Facebook posts to the manager.

Generally, employers are permitted to monitor electronic communications, such as e-mail, under exceptions to the Electronic Communications Privacy Act of 1986; namely, where a party consents to monitoring, such as working for an employer with a handbook provision that makes clear the employer will monitor computer systems; an employer can monitor its own systems as administrator of the system; or where monitoring is part of the ordinary course of business, e.g., to ensure quality of service or customer satisfaction.

Federal and state laws prohibit discrimination on the basis of race, color, religion, national origin, gender, age, disability, genetic information, Armed Forces Reserve or National Guard status, and other protected categories including, in many jurisdictions, sexual orientation and gender identity or expression.

An employer's duty to protect applicants and employees extends to online communications. An employee could be held accountable for blogging, posting, or even being associated with online content that is sexist or racially, ethnically, or religiously offensive. For example, a number of employees of private sector businesses were reportedly fired in 2017 after pictures of them participating in a white supremacist rally in Charlottesville, Virginia, which turned deadly, were posted on the Twitter account, "Yes, You're Racist." Public employees, discussed below, have greater protections for their off-duty behavior under the First Amendment's freedom of expression and association standards.

An employer could be held liable for online offensive conduct directed to an employee by another employee or a third party where the employer knew or should have known of the offensive behavior and failed to take immediate, appropriate corrective action. Liability of an organization is magnified when the offending party is a supervisor or manager. A supervisor who attempts to give a whole new meaning to the term "friend," and makes unwanted advances to a subordinate employee in person, or by text, tweet, or post online, may expose the employer to damages for unlawful harassment.

Similarly, as recurring events constantly remind us, employers may have a duty to take action to prevent workplace violence, threats, or criminal misconduct using a work computer. For example, in *Doe v. XYC Corp.*, a New Jersey court remanded a case for trial after an employer, who had discovered one of its employees was using the employer's computer system to visit pornographic websites while at work, failed to investigate or take decisive action to address the problem. The employer was sued for negligence after the discovery that the employee was taking illicit pictures of his 10-year-old stepdaughter and using his work computer to publish the photos on Internet porn sites.

An employer who desires to punish an employee for his or her online activity must consider state laws that protect employees' activities outside work or that safeguard "whistleblowers." Nearly every state has common law or statutory provisions that prevent an employer from retaliating against an employee for complaining about matters of public concern, such as whistle blowing about illegal or unsafe practices; holding an employee's political activities against him or her; taking adverse action against an employee who refuses to perform unlawful acts; or firing an employee who engages in lawful, off-duty, off-premises legal activities.

Publicly traded companies are reminded that the Sarbanes-Oxley Act, a federal law passed in 2002 in the wake of corporate fraud scandals such as Enron and MCI Worldcom, protects employees who are retaliated against for reporting corporate fraud or accounting abuses. An employee of a publicly traded company who unveils corporate fraud on the Web may be protected. An employee of any company who creates online posts that rail against alleged organizational fraud, waste, or other abuses—as unpalatable and offensive as the comments may seem—may be protected by federal or state whistleblower protections or the common law claim of wrongful discharge in violation of public policy. For example, if an employee posts information that accuses the employer of violating legal or professional standards, then terminating the employee for the post may constitute wrongful discharge in violation of public policy. Better to investigate the underlying allegations in order to frame the best response to the allegations if they are significant or harmful enough to warrant a response.

Employees are usually not protected if they divulge an employer's work or trade secrets.

Also, employees are usually not protected if they falsely impugn the reputation of the employer or otherwise engage in acts of disloyalty while employed.

The National Labor Relations Act (NLRA) covers both unionized and non-unionized private sector employers and protects an employee's right to engage in "concerted activity" for "mutual aid and protection," including discussions relating to wages, hours worked, and other terms and conditions of employment. Taking adverse action against an employee who vents online about pay, working conditions, workplace safety, or organizing other workers could result in legal liability for an employer. In 2017, in a case involving The Boeing Company, the National Labor Relations Board (NLRB) issued guidance indicating it would scrutinize more closely employers' rules limiting employees' rights under the NLRA, particularly rules barring employees from making disparaging remarks about a company or offering criticism of an employer. This would likely include restrictions on employees' use of social media. Indeed, where an employer permits personal use of e-mail, cell phones, and access to the Internet by employees using work computers, the employer must be careful not to interfere with protected concerted activity using such permitted technologies. Of course, employers may generally limit use of their own computer equipment and networks, and employees' use of such equipment and networks, to work-related activities. An employer can also regulate excessive personal use of work-issued equipment or property.

Countless Internet complaint sites, or gripe sites, have sprung up for disgruntled employees or dissatisfied customers to vent about businesses or their products; for example, walmartsucks.org and complaintsboard.com. Many of these sites contain one-sided attacks, often exaggerated or just plain false. But if the site is set up by employees and invites other employees to comment on the organization, its executives, or its policies, then the commentary may be considered protected concerted activity. Now, if employees are engaging in defamation—that is, maliciously posting false information that causes actual damages (which can be a very hard claim to prove given that much of the information is couched in the public's interest)—or employees are divulging confidential information or violating trademark laws, then an employer has courses of action against its attackers.

Public employees are more protected on social media platforms. Generally, governmental employees have the privacy and free speech protections provided under the U.S. Constitution. Some states, such as California, extend privacy protection to all employees under their State Constitution. What does this mean? A public employee cannot ordinarily be punished when speaking as a private citizen on a matter of public concern under the First Amendment and is free from unreasonable searches and seizures under the Fourth Amendment.

Employees should know that freedom of speech at work is not absolute. Consider the seminal case of *Garcetti v. Ceballos*. Garcetti refers to Gil Garcetti, the former District Attorney of Los Angeles County. He allegedly retaliated against Richard Ceballos, one of his employees, after Ceballos wrote an internal memo criticizing the County Sheriff's conduct in a pending criminal matter before the District Attorney's Office, recommending dismissal of the charges, and actually testifying for the defense in the case. Ceballos alleged the memorandum constituted free speech that could not be held against him in his public employment. The United States Supreme Court disagreed, finding that an internal memo generated solely in one's capacity as an employee, rather than as a private citizen, is not protected speech.

So there is a distinction between speaking as a private citizen, which is substantially more protected, and the job-related speech of an employee, which may be regulated by an employer. Courts apply a balancing test to determine whether the employee's speech—if on a matter of public concern—is outweighed by the employer's legitimate interest in curbing such speech.

For example, in 2007, in *Curran v. Cousins*, the U.S. Court of Appeals for the First Circuit upheld the firing of a corrections officer who was terminated for his blog entries comparing the county sheriff to Hitler and speaking approvingly, and threateningly, of the plot during World War II to take Hitler's life. Still, public employers must be cautious about treading into matters related to free speech, particularly by employees commenting in their private capacity as citizens. Purely private speech that is not related to any public concern—in essence, a personal gripe or grievance—is not protected under the First Amendment. If private speech is on a matter of public concern—matters of political, social or community interest—then the burden shifts to the employer to demonstrate that the speech interferes with the employer's legitimate interests.

Social media sites are here to stay and will continue to evolve. So will employees' participation in social media activities. Employers have a few options: Ignore employees' online activities, embrace them, or address them as a matter of policy. Some employers are of the opinion that the Internet is a vast universe, and even negative information will be swept away by the massive amounts of information on the Web. Other employers actively encourage employees' use of social media, citing the business and marketing advantages, and may place only common-sense restrictions on employees. For example, when social media was in its infancy, Microsoft took a basic "don't be stupid" approach to its blogging policy. Similarly, IBM's Social

Computing Guidelines used to end simply with the cautionary reminder: "Don't forget your day job." Now, IBM's guidance ends: "Remember to always use good judgment and common sense in deciding what you post." All good advice.

Some employers address social media by imposing an absolute ban on their use at work. There are myriad reasons for a ban: to preserve staff productivity and the organization's reputation, maintain security of computer networks and data, and to reduce potential liability. But a ban may also make it difficult to attract a growing labor force that clearly has expectations regarding the use of social networking sites.

Finally, some employers take a conditional approach, attempting to allow, monitor, and control the content of employees' Internet activity as it relates to work, including disciplining employees who overstep the bounds of reasonable behavior.

The benefits of social media cannot be overstated. Web technologies are a low-cost way to brand products or people online. Think of the recent successful uses of social media sites in political campaigns, including the last few elections for President of the United States. Some social media, including video and audio podcasts, allow portable and innovative learning delivery methods for employees. Social networks encourage conversation, sharing of information, timely feedback from staff and members of the public, and allow leaders to gain a consensus of thought from people who have a shared interest in a cause, an organization, or a product. Most businesses and organizations, public or private, want to understand their consumers. Social networks are a great way to hear from the ultimate consumer.

At the same time, in the United States, complaining is time-honored . . . long before we had the Internet . . . have you heard of the Boston Tea Party . . . and can be protected. Employees have a number of federal and state privacy protections as long as their online behavior does not interfere with their job or create an actual or apparent conflict of interest. For public employees—people who work for federal, state, or municipal governments—complaining may also be protected by the First Amendment of the U.S. Constitution. Complaints by private sector employees may be shielded by the National Labor Relations Act.

In closing, as a practical matter, an employee's safest harbor online lies in their anonymity on the Internet. If an employer does not know who is posting, and cannot discover the identity of an employee making disparaging comments online, then the employer can do very little.

40

ARE CONFEDERATE AMERICANS AND THE CONFEDERATE FLAG PROTECTED?

More on Employee Expression

CURTIS STOREY WORKED as a security guard at a Sony plant in Newton Station, Pennsylvania. Storey placed a small Confederate flag, the "Stars and Bars," on his lunch box and two Confederate flag bumper stickers on (yep) his pickup truck. One bumper sticker included the slogan, "The South Was Right," and the other sticker proclaimed, "Heritage not Hate."

Storey's supervisors pulled him aside one day and told him that he'd have to remove or cover the Confederate flag stickers while on company premises. Storey apparently resisted the effort to remove the stickers, and, doubling down with his own volley, requested boldly that sensitivity training around "Confederate-American issues" be included in his employer's new diversity training program.

That was not going to happen. Storey was fired for his failure to cover or remove the Confederate flag stickers. Storey filed a lawsuit claiming discrimination on the basis of his national origin, "Confederate Southern-American," and his religion, Christian. Storey argued that Confederate Southern-Americans share a "common culture and history of persecution" dating back to the Civil War era. Further, for Storey, the Confederate flag is a "religious symbol," akin to the Star of David. In fact, the Confederate flag is said to incorporate the Cross of Saint Andrew (the familiar x-shaped cross) or the Greek letter "X"— both venerated symbols for Christ.

Even assuming Storey's arguments were sincere, a federal appeals court upheld his termination and the dismissal of his claims in 2004. Storey could never show his national origin, or religion, *required him* to display Confederate symbols at work. The court noted that a similar issue arose before, in *Swartzentruber v. Gunite Corp.*, where an employee failed to show that his employer's directive to cover his Ku Klux Klan tattoo at work conflicted with his religious beliefs. Like Storey, the KKK member was fired lawfully for failing to cover his "religious" symbol at work.

Storey is a reminder that the Confederate States of America (the Confederacy) holds a unique place in American history. In 1860 and 1861, eleven states seceded from the Union. The resulting civil war among the divided states produced this nation's deadliest conflict. Today, the Confederacy, and the Confederate flag in particular, stand for some as both a point of cultural pride and heritage. However, for others, the Confederate flag represents a continuing emblem of white supremacy, support for slavery, and hatred toward Blacks.

While displaying a Confederate flag in public has some protections under the First Amendment of the U.S. Constitution, being a Confederate American does not bring you any additional rights. There are a surprising number of cases involving modern-day Confederates. How these cases arise is often more interesting than the legal conclusions drawn by the courts.

Courts have consistently found that being a "Confederate American" or one's "Southern-ness" (*a la* Paula Dean) are not protected traits in the workplace. On the contrary, the display of the Confederate flag can be offensive toward others and create a hostile work environment.

In 2012, the U.S. Equal Employment Opportunity Commission (EEOC) found that a Black postal worker's treatment by his co-workers could constitute a racially hostile work environment. The Black employee was continually exposed to other employees wearing Confederate t-shirts. The employee asked his supervisors to address the problem but was ignored repeatedly. The EEOC determined that repeated exposure to the Confederate flag could be a form of racial harassment for a Black employee.

However, another court, in Alabama, found that "isolated" exposure to the Confederate flag—such as occasionally seeing the flag on t-shirts, ball caps, and stickers in the workplace— is not sufficiently severe or pervasive to alter the conditions of an employee's job and, therefore, cannot constitute a racially hostile work environment. In this case, the court was particularly influenced by the fact that the employer removed the Confederate flags and changed its dress code to ban Confederate flags on t-shirts and ball caps immediately after an employee complained.

Further, no one has the right to wear the Confederate flag on another's private property. Any private—that is, non-governmental—employer has the right to limit display of the Confederate flag on its own premises.

Employees in the public sector have more protection. For employees who work for governmental entities, such as a city, county, state or federal government, their employers must navigate the First Amendment's protection of "free speech" in assessing whether to limit any display of the Confederate flag. Still, even in the public square, the arc of public opinion has swayed substantially against display of the Confederate flag as an offensive symbol of racial hatred.

In November 2012, on the day President Obama was re-elected to a second term in office, a police captain for Clayton State University, a public university in Georgia, posted on his Facebook page the image of a Confederate flag with the phrase, "It's time for the second revolution." The employee, Captain Rex Duke, was demoted for the posting.

In his defense, Duke was an exemplary employee. He posted the image on his personal Facebook page and he was off duty when he posted the image. Neither the post, nor the Facebook page, referenced Duke's employment at Clayton State University. The university had no social media policy prohibiting the post; Duke made no disparaging comments about his employer; and he took down the post within one hour of having posted it. So how did he get in trouble?

This is a good lesson for employees. During the one hour the image was posted on Duke's Facebook page, a "friend" sent the image to an Atlanta television station. A reporter descended on the university immediately and, by that night, the station ran a news story about the post referring to Duke's position as a deputy chief of police.

Relying on a long-standing balancing test to weigh the free speech rights of government employees when they are speaking in their capacity as private citizens on matters of public concern (such as giving one's opinion of the President), the court found that Duke was not protected when he posted the Confederate flag even if on his own time and personal Facebook page. The university police department's interest in maintaining its reputation and preserving good relationships with all members on campus outweighed Duke's free speech rights. The court highlighted the fact that the Confederate flag is considered offensive by many. More importantly, the use of the Confederate flag, associated with a senior law enforcement officer who was also calling for a "second revolution" in the midst of a presidential election, only fuels racial disharmony and distrust of the police in a community.

In the end, times have changed for the Confederate flag and its admirers. Given the symbol's racial divisiveness today, employers and others are much more likely to ban the Confederate flag from open display. Following a mass shooting in the Emanuel African Methodist Episcopal Church in Charleston, South Carolina, on June 17, 2015, in which a gunman murdered nine African American worshipers in an attempt to start a race war, Warner Brothers Entertainment announced it would stop production of "The General Lee" toy cars—bearing a Confederate battle flag on the roof—popularized by *The Dukes of Hazzard* television program of the early 1980s. Even more recently, in June 2020, amidst intense protests following the death of an unarmed black man, George Floyd, during his arrest by police officers in Minnesota, the National Association for Stock Car Auto Racing (NASCAR), the operating company of the "most Southern sport on Earth," banned the Confederate flag from all of its events and properties.

If a uniquely Southern institution like NASCAR can ban the Confederate flag, every person should use their best judgment in displaying any symbol that might reasonably offend or unnecessarily distract others at work.

41

IS IT AGAINST THE LAW TO SECRETLY RECORD CONVERSATIONS?

Electronic Monitoring in the Workplace

IT HAPPENS MORE OFTEN than you think. A supervisor, with a pained look on his face, will say to me, "Employees have been recording me . . . at work. That can't be right, it's got to be illegal." On the contrary, surreptitious recording can easily occur at work, does occur, and, most surprisingly, it is not necessarily illegal—depending on the state in which you work.

In 2018, a secret tape recording made front page news when Omarosa Manigault-Newman, a former aide to President Trump, divulged she had recorded others in the White House by sneaking a cellphone into the Situation Room. The Situation Room is a Sensitive Compartmented Information Facility, or SCIF, in which classified information is stored and sensitive information may be discussed. Cellphones are not allowed and anyone in the room should have felt comfortable they weren't being secretly recorded. Manigault-Newman also secretly recorded her termination of employment by White House Chief of Staff John Kelly in December 2017.

Setting aside for a moment the personal impropriety and national security lapses of sneaking an electronic recording device into a secure area, as a practical matter, it is not uncommon for an employee who feels they are being treated unfairly to memorialize the perceived injustices. It often starts with diary entries and escalates to surreptitious recordings in the workplace.

Every new cell phone on the market has both audio and video recording function. Therefore, it's not difficult for any employee to go all *Inspector Gadget* on the workplace. On the other side of the workplace equation, nothing is more likely to upset a co-worker than to learn an employee is keeping a secret log or recording conversations *with them* at work.

Perhaps the more important first question for any employer is, why do your employees distrust this work environment to the extent they feel the need to "protect" themselves in this manner? Building trust and better communication often obviates the need for "self-help" recording.

Contrary to popular opinion, it is not illegal (under federal and most states' laws) to record a conversation to which you are a party. In other words, you can usually consent to record yourself, even if the other party to the conversation does not know, let alone consent to the activity. This rule varies from state to state, so check first, before recording, or you could go to jail.

Federal wiretap law clearly prohibits the recording of conversations to which the listener is *not* a party to the conversation; for example, electronic eavesdropping on others is prohibited. The word "eavesdrop" originated in 17th century England, when passers-by could stand hidden beneath the eaves of a house and overhear the conversations in the house. Who hasn't put a glass up to a wall to overhear a conversation in the next room? Okay, maybe that's just me and weird people like me.

What can an employer do? Even if secret recordings are legal in your state, it doesn't mean an employee can't be fired. There is no inherent right to record yourself and others at work. Taking secret video or audio recordings of others without their permission is viewed by most workers as invasive, highly offensive, and potentially disruptive if co-workers discover the behavior.

In *Bodoy v. North Arundel Hospital*, Angelo Bodoy was terminated for secretly recording his conversations with his supervisors, lying about it, and later refusing to turn over the recordings. Bodoy then sued his employer for racial and ethnic discrimination. The employer won. The court relied on the fact that it is illegal in Maryland (where Bodoy worked) to record a conversation without the permission of all parties.

If an employer knows an employee is recording, and orders the employee not to record, then the employer may be justified in disciplining the employee who does not comply. In *Hernandez v. McDonald's Corp.*, an employee walked into a disciplinary meeting at work with a recorder expressing her desire to record the meeting. The employee was warned, "If you use that tape recorder, you no longer work here and that is insubordination." The employee continued to record the meeting and, as a result, was fired immediately. The court dismissed the employee's discrimination claims finding that the reason for firing the employee was nondiscriminatory.

There is one way an employee may be protected when recording the workplace: engaging in concerted activity under the National Labor Relations Act (NLRA). Under the NLRA, employees have the right to engage in "concerted activities for the purposes of collective bargaining or other mutual aid or protection." Protected concerted activities include talking with co-workers about the terms and conditions of employment, such as pay and health benefits, investigating or speaking out about workplace problems, and considering a union. The NLRA covers *union* and *non-union* private sector workplaces.

In 2017, a federal appeals court upheld a National Labor Relations Board (NLRB) finding that Whole Foods' blanket ban on *all recording* in the workplace was overbroad and violated the NLRA. Whole Foods adopted a policy that prohibited employees from recording conversations, phone calls, and meetings without first obtaining a manager's approval. Whole Foods argued that the recording ban was never intended to interfere with its employees' rights to discuss terms and conditions of employment; instead, it was to promote candid communication at work by assuring employees that they weren't being recorded.

However, there are times when an employee might *desire to be recorded*; for instance, during an internal investigation where the employee fears discipline or wants to make sure their words are not misconstrued. An employee may want to record a meeting that involves challenging a workplace practice. An employee may want to make a recording as protection against retaliation. An employee may also want to record a video for media consumption if protesting at the front gate of their facility.

On subsequent review by the U.S. Court of Appeals for the Second Circuit, the appellate court found that Whole Foods' policy could "chill" an employee's exercise of rights under the NLRA. In other words, a complete ban on all recording could have a chilling effect on exercising one's rights. The Second Circuit didn't say employers couldn't ban some recording. There may be very good policy reasons to prevent some types of recording. For example, a company may want to ban video recording of trade secrets or proprietary business information in order to prevent theft, or in hazardous work areas to reduce distractions that could lead to injury, or to protect a person's privacy in the bathroom.

Under the NLRA, a savvy employee might justify surreptitious use of a recording device as a protected concerted effort to gather evidence of unlawful discrimination. But this is no guarantee of protection.

In 1989, the Second Circuit held that recording a conversation at work, in violation of a no-recording policy, might not be enough reason to fire an employee. In *Heller v. Champion Int'l Corp*, the Second Circuit found that an employee's secret tape recording of a meeting with his boss could be justified considering his reasonable belief he was about to be demoted based on his age. According to the court in *Heller*, the employee's surreptitious tape recording represented "a kind of disloyalty" to the company but not necessarily the kind of disloyalty that would warrant dismissal as a matter of law. While bold, this course is risky for an employee. Not only does the employee have to establish they are engaging in protected activity, but the employee also faces potential claims, such as invasion of privacy, for secretly recording others.

It may not be a crime to record others without their knowledge, but it's still a problem.

So how do employers address this situation at work?

First, for most employers, it's not only appropriate, but advisable these days to inform employees that recording at work without authorization can be rude, offensive, have a chilling effect on the free exchange of words, and is not tolerated.

Second, if an employee recording is discovered, a better approach may be simply to ask the employee why they feel it necessary to record conversations or video others at work. If the employee distrusts management or co-workers to the degree that the employee feels the need to resort to secret recording, then the employer and employee may have a difficult conversation in store. The employer needs to consider changes to the environment that fostered this level of distrust. Alternatively, the employee may need to stop working in such an unsatisfactory environment. No one should work in a job in which they distrust others so much.

Third, if there is a viable concern or threat to the organization created by recording, the employer should craft a prohibition on recording that is narrowly tailored to the threat. For example, it is reasonable to ban audio or video recording in a restroom or locker room in order to protect the personal privacy of occupants.

Even if an employer discovers an employee has recorded openly or surreptitiously, the employer should refrain from a knee-jerk reaction, such as immediate termination, without first asking the following questions:

- Why was the employee recording and what was the recording ostensibly used for; for example, to prove alleged discrimination or harassment?

- Were the recorded conversations or images intended to be kept private? For instance, there could be a huge difference between taping a private meeting versus the activities in a crowded breakroom.

- Was the information shared with others?

- Had the employee been directed not to record?

- Did the recording disrupt or harm the workplace; e.g., result in complaints by co-workers who were monitored or the recording of proprietary trade secrets or confidential business information?

- Does the particular state in which the recording took place prohibit such behavior?

Finally, for both sides of this debate: Just because an employee records others at work does not mean the information is automatically admissible in a lawsuit. Written notes, audio and video recordings are a form of hearsay. Hearsay is inadmissible in court unless it falls into a specific exception to the rule. Any evidence sought to be admitted must be trustworthy, and the statements offered would have to be more "probative" to the point than "prejudicial" to a party. In other words, the recording must be offered to prove unlawful conduct, such as racial harassment, rather than show that the person recorded uses foul language or makes offensive statements. Not surprisingly, surreptitious bad recordings (garbled, too much background noise, inability to distinguish voices or frame the context in which comments occur, or lengthy blank spots) have been excluded as unduly prejudicial. And the information sought to be admitted must have been lawfully obtained.

In closing, surreptitious recording, while tempting, may not always achieve the desired result sought by an employee.

42

CAN AN EMPLOYEE BE FORCED TO TAKE A LIE DETECTOR TEST?

Polygraphs and Work

YOU WORK IN A BANK. The bank has tons of money in it. One day, a few thousand dollars is discovered missing in a random audit. Naturally, like an Agatha Christie novel, suspicion falls on every employee with access to the missing funds. The boss demands that every employee take a lie detector test to prove their innocence or record their guilt. Good idea or bad idea?

The answer to this is simple: It is very difficult for an employer to meet the legal standard to be able to require an employee to take a polygraph test.

Flying under the radar scope of most employers is a little known federal law called the Employee Polygraph Protection Act of 1988 (EPPA). President Reagan signed the EPPA which prohibits most *private sector* employers from using a lie detector test to screen applicants during hiring or (with limited exceptions) during the course of employment. According to the EPPA, employers generally may not require, or request, an employee or job applicant to take a lie detector test, or discharge, discipline, or discriminate against an employee or job applicant for refusing to take a test, or for exercising other rights under the EPPA.

However, some employers are exempt from the federal law. The EPPA permits lie detector tests to be administered to certain applicants for jobs with security firms (such as armored car or alarm companies), and pharmaceutical manufacturers, distributors, and dispensers. In addition, the EPPA does not cover federal, state, and local government agencies. Therefore, to get a job as a law enforcement officer or investigator, you may be required to take a polygraph test.

There is another provision which applies to suspected thieves. The EPPA allows a lie detector test in cases of suspected theft at work. In such cases, though, employees are afforded a host of rights before a polygraph may be administered. An employer who desires to administer a polygraph may need the help of a reputable outside firm. The polygraph examiner must be licensed and bonded or have professional liability coverage. An employee must be given specific notice of the loss being investigated, a description of the loss incurred, and a detailed description as to why the employee is suspected.

The EPPA restricts how information derived from a polygraph test may be used. During polygraph testing, the examiner cannot ask unduly intrusive or degrading questions, questions about religious or political beliefs or affiliations, race-related questions, or questions about sexual attitudes and behaviors. Most importantly, an employee must be allowed to stop the test at any time. Also, an employee can avoid the test if they provide certification from a doctor that the employee has a medical condition, or is undergoing treatment, that might cause abnormal responses during a test. Employees can never waive their rights under the EPPA.

As an attorney, I would never "force" a polygraph test, and I would be cautious about recommending the polygraph examination of an employee. The EPPA is enforced by the U.S. Department of Labor, and employers who violate the EPPA may be subject to substantial penalties. The Secretary of Labor can bring court action to restrain violators and assess civil money penalties up to $10,000 per violation. An employer who violates the law may be liable to the employee, or prospective employee, for appropriate legal and equitable relief which may include employment, reinstatement, promotion, and payment of lost wages and benefits. Some states, like California, have their own polygraph statute an employer in that state must navigate as well.

Besides, the admissibility of the results of a polygraph test varies widely from state-to-state, court-to-court, and case-to-case. It is left to the discretion of a judge who may refuse to allow the results of a polygraph to be used in court.

In closing, an employer in the private sector should consider investigatory techniques other than a polygraph, and employees should always consider their rights before consenting to a polygraph.

43

CAN AN EMPLOYER SPY ON ITS EMPLOYEES?

Electronic Monitoring

I know I've made some very poor decisions recently, but I can give you my complete assurance that my work will be back to normal. I've still got the greatest enthusiasm and confidence in the mission. And I want to help you.

—HAL 9000, *2001: A Space Odyssey* (1968)

BIG BROTHER IS WATCHING YOU. A 2007 survey by the American Management Association is still trotted out regularly to warn of employees' potential misuse of technology. According to the survey, more than a quarter of supervisors had fired an employee for misusing company e-mail. Even more had been fired for Internet misuse. Two-thirds of employers regularly monitor employees' Internet use. About the same percentage of employers actively block connections to "inappropriate" websites, including adult sites, gaming sites, social networking sites like Facebook, entertainment and shopping sites, and external blogs.

Indeed, a booming industry of monitoring software and services has developed over the last decade to watch potentially wayward workers. In 2018, the magazine *Wired* profiled voice analysis software called Cogito which was being used by call centers to detect the mood of both customers and employees. About half of employers surveyed stated that they monitor employees' computer use by tracking content and length of time or number of strokes on a keyboard. Similarly, about half of surveyed employers conduct video monitoring to combat theft or violence. Today, most employers use Smartcard technology to control physical access to work premises. Many employers use Global Positioning System (GPS) technology to track company vehicles. Some employers even use GPS to track company cell phones. Big Brother is not only watching employees, but Siri and Alexa are making him feel comfortable in the lobby.

To many employees' surprise, very few states require any notice to employees that they are being monitored by their employer.

Employers can, and often do, monitor their employees at work. The rules surrounding an employer's electronic monitoring of employees are evolving. Therefore, a brief overview of federal law on the topic may be helpful. Courts have long held that an employee has no legitimate expectation of privacy in the use of an employer's e-mail system. After all, e-mail is the employer's communication system, owned or managed by the employer. Therefore, an employer can usually monitor the use, or misuse, of its own e-mail system.

However, there are still several restrictions on electronic monitoring. The Omnibus Control and Safe Streets Act of 1968 ("federal wiretap law"), as amended by the Electronic

Communications Privacy Act of 1986, prohibits the unauthorized, nonconsensual interception of "wire, oral, or electronic communications" by government agencies and private parties. Law enforcement must obtain a warrant to authorize a wiretap or the monitoring must fall within an exception to the law.

There are three exceptions to the federal wiretap law that permit employers to monitor employees' electronic communications at work. The first exception is consent by employees to monitoring. Consent to be monitored may be express or implied. In today's litigious society, employers can attempt to avoid lawsuits by essentially having employees consent to being monitored as a condition of employment. Therefore, most large employers have a policy, buried deep in an employee handbook, that says employees consent to being monitored, and the employer is allowed to administer, search, and retrieve computer and telephone communications of its employees. By accepting employment, or continuing to work, employees have already consented to being monitored at work. If you have a union in your workplace, though, electronic monitoring may be the subject of collective bargaining regarding the treatment of employees.

The second exception to monitoring employees is the "business extension" exception. Employers are permitted to monitor their own telephone and computer systems in the "ordinary course of business." For example, many employers monitor telephone communications and e-mail transmissions to ensure quality of service and customer satisfaction, investigate suspicions of theft or other illegal activity, or simply to determine whether an employee spends too much time on personal matters.

Although wise to obtain, consent is not required for the business exception rule to apply. Therefore, random monitoring to assure service to customers and productivity is acceptable. An employee could be disciplined for violation of a company policy prohibiting excessive personal phone calls or inappropriate company computer use.

There is a limit on employers, however: Monitoring must be for business reasons. An employer should not monitor personal calls on work equipment once it becomes clear the call is personal. For example, in *Deal v. Spears*, an employer, who monitored 22 hours of employees' phone calls to determine whether they had committed a theft of company property (monitoring that otherwise would have been legal) was found to have violated federal wiretap law because the employer insisted on listening to the private sex-laced conversations between one of the employees and her paramours. Two of the employees being monitored for suspicion of theft recovered $40,000 in damages.

Also, informing employees that you can monitor their e-mail does not mean an employee consents to being monitored. As an example, an insurance company was found liable for violating the federal wiretapping statute by recording not only all business calls but all personal calls at work. In *Smith v. Devers*, the employer was prevented from asserting the consent exemption, even though the employer had a detailed policy outlining its monitoring of phone calls, because the employee denied he received the handbook and, therefore, had never consented to be monitored.

Under the third exception, "service providers" can always monitor communications stored on their own computer systems. Therefore, if the employer owns its computer system for employees' use, then it can examine communications stored on the system. This does not mean employers can divulge the contents of such messages to third parties without authorization.

Employers should exercise good judgment regarding electronic monitoring. The more intrusive the monitoring, the more likely it will spur an invasion of privacy claim and, for government employees, federal and state deprivation of a constitutional right to privacy.

Although it seems counter to the culture of many organizations, employers are continually pressed in today's litigious environment to minimize employees' expectations of privacy at work. Employers expressly advise employees that e-mail and other electronic communications systems are the property of the employer. Written policies, often found in employee handbooks, are essential. Employers state that any personal use of communication equipment must be incidental and sporadic (even if it happens all the time) to avoid creating an expectation of privacy. Advance notice can be given that the premises may be monitored by the employer at all times.

At the same time, employers should not monitor or intrude into personal telephone calls or e-mails employees are allowed to make or in any way attempt to gain information behind an employee's personal password-protected social media account.

If you have a union at work, employers and employees should both be aware that monitoring may be the subject of mandatory collective bargaining.

Finally, if you are an employer who is going to monitor the workplace, please have a compelling reason to do so. And, most importantly, talk to a lawyer before electronically monitoring anyone at work.

44

ARE HIDDEN CAMERAS LEGAL?

Limits of Video Surveillance

My Dad:	*When I was a kid, you could go to the store with a dollar and get enough food to feed an entire family.*
Me:	*Dad, now they have security cameras.*

SOME EMPLOYERS can't resist a hidden camera. In 1998, the Sheraton Boston Hotel agreed to pay more than $200,000 to settle a lawsuit claiming the hotel had violated Massachusetts privacy law by secretly videotaping its employees in the employee locker room.

Between 1990 and 1994, Colgate-Palmolive installed eleven hidden surveillance cameras on its premises ostensibly to curb employee theft and other misconduct. An employee discovered one of the cameras hidden in an air vent located in the men's restroom! The company removed the camera from the bathroom immediately. The union filed a grievance and the National Labor Relations Board (NLRB) found that the presence and placement of video cameras in a unionized workplace should be the subject of collective bargaining.

These cases beg the question: Why would an employer install a hidden camera in a restroom or changing room? One manager, with the glee of an undercover cop who'd just busted the Colombian drug cartel, informed me, "That's where the drug deals go down."

In a more recent twist on video surveillance gone wrong, the City of Pocatello, Idaho, its mayor, and police chief were sued by a veteran police officer who was the subject of covert video recordings by his employer. While on an authorized medical leave under the Family and Medical Leave Act (FMLA), Officer Johnnie Walker (best name ever) discovered his own police department had set up a surveillance camera on his neighbor's fields to surveil Walker's property, apparently suspecting Walker was taking leave by false pretenses and hoping to catch him doing something outside his medical restrictions. In 2018, an Idaho federal court ruled that the video surveillance of the open property was not a violation of Walker's Fourth Amendment right of privacy but could constitute unlawful retaliation against Walker for taking FMLA leave. Describing the employer's actions as "an extraordinary response to FMLA concerns," the court permitted the case to go to trial.

Video surveillance cameras are a ubiquitous, and usually legal, part of American life. The real question in modern life is: When are you *not* monitored by a video camera?

An employer who wants to install cameras at work is best advised not to use sound recording unless it is critical for business purposes. If the camera has an audio component and can pick up the "sound" of the subjects being monitored, it falls within the restrictions of federal wiretap law. Therefore, you can't monitor the sound of others unless you obtain a warrant or fall into one of the exceptions allowed under federal and most states' wiretap laws. Federal and state wiretap law does not apply to passive, *video-only* surveillance.

However, state laws often apply to monitoring; so, depending on where the business is located, an employer should get legal advice before installing hidden cameras on its premises. This is especially true in a state such as California which has significant privacy protections for workers. Further, an employer should be able to articulate a legitimate reason for its video surveillance of work premises. Of course, a good answer is to maintain the security of the premises, including monitoring for possible theft or other crimes.

More importantly, video surveillance can still violate invasion of privacy rules and, in the case of a unionized work force, collective bargaining agreements. The NLRB has ruled repeatedly that it is an unfair labor practice to install hidden surveillance cameras without bargaining with the union, or to videotape employees engaged in union or protected concerted without proper justification.

Video cameras peering into restrooms, changing rooms, or locker rooms clearly are unreasonably intrusive and unlawful. Any camera at work, particularly a hidden camera, ideally should be focused toward common areas only, such as hallways, general work premises, and break rooms.

I have been asked frequently whether an employer can install a hidden camera in an employee's office to investigate possible misconduct, including misuse of a work computer by unlawful activity. The answer to this question often depends on the extent to which an employee has a reasonable expectation of privacy in his or her office and on what the employer intends to focus the hidden camera; for example, the whole office, or just the employee's computer screen, or a safe holding valuables? You can imagine the problem of hiding a camera in an employee's office only to discover later that this particular employee uses the office to change clothes at the beginning or end of each workday. Too much information! ... and a possible lawsuit.

While privacy at work is limited, it is not entirely absent. Most offices have a door, which may or may not lock, behind which an employee expects some measure of privacy (including being able to change clothes at the end of a workday or to go out for a lunchtime jog). Therefore, most lawyers would advise an employer to limit any monitoring to the least intrusive method. For example, if an employer believes an employee is misusing a work computer during the day, the employer could monitor the websites an employee is accessing using his or her work computer. This might raise a reasonable suspicion of improper activity. If the employer then desires to surveil an office computer for improper activity, a hidden camera installed in the office—which is extremely intrusive and sure to offend the sensibilities of some—should be focused only on the computer workstation in question. Using an abundance of caution, any actual surveillance should not run the full day but should be limited in time to the period the employer suspects the improper activity is occurring (such as after regular work hours). In the alternative, an employer should consider notifying the police if any criminal activity is suspected and let the experts do their job fighting crime.

45

DOES AN EMPLOYEE HAVE THE RIGHT TO MISS WORK FOR MALE ENHANCEMENT SURGERY?

The Family and Medical Leave Act

Excuse me while I whip this out.

—Sheriff Bart, *Blazing Saddles* (1974)

SOCIETIES THAT PRIZE physical beauty also value cosmetic surgery. In November 2018, the International Society of Aesthetic Plastic Surgery released the results of its annual Global Aesthetic Survey for procedures completed in 2017. The survey showed that the United States, Brazil, Japan, Mexico, and Italy accounted for nearly 40% of all cosmetic procedures in the world. Breast augmentation surgery remains the world's most popular cosmetic surgical procedure followed closely by liposuction. By far, the most popular non-surgical cosmetic procedure is injection with Botulinum Toxin (BoTox). Looking at prior years' surveys, it stands out that, in 2016, the total number of penis enlargements in Greece was ten times the average of all the countries that made up the top five list. This information begs two questions: What's up with Greek men? . . . and Given the popularity of such cosmetic procedures, does an employee have the right to miss work for cosmetic surgery?

Dorsey Bellanger provides a lesson learned. She brought a lawsuit alleging that she was fired from her job in 2010 after missing work to undergo a "tummy tuck." At the time, Bellanger was the Activities Director for Flannery Oaks Guest House, a nursing home. She was fired her for excessive absenteeism. Bellanger claimed the four weeks she missed following her surgery should have been protected time away from work under the Family and Medical Leave Act of 1993 (FMLA). However, a Louisiana federal court ruled in 2012 that, barring serious complications, cosmetic surgery is not a serious health condition allowing job-protected time off under the FMLA.

The FMLA is our federal leave law. The FMLA requires that an employer grant an eligible employee a total of up to twelve workweeks of job-protected, unpaid leave during a twelve month-period for the following reasons: birth and care of the employee's child or placement for adoption or foster care of a child with the employee; to care for an immediate family member (spouse, child, parent) who has a serious health condition; or for the employee's own serious health condition. There is an additional leave entitlement for military-related circumstances.

In other words, to gain the right to time off, an employee must work for an employer covered by the FMLA, be eligible for leave, and have a qualifying family or serious health need. FMLA leave is an entitlement. Once earned, there is no emergency exception, undue hardship defense, or particularly forceful supervisor that can prevent an eligible employee with a qualifying event from taking FMLA time off. It's a right to miss work.

In effect, only employees of larger organizations are protected by the FMLA. FMLA covers all governmental employers, public and private schools, and all private sector employers with 50 or more employees. However, to be eligible for FMLA leave, an employee must be employed at least 12 months (which do not have to be consecutive), must have worked at least 1,250 hours during the twelve months immediately before starting FMLA leave, and work at a site which has at least 50 employees within 75 miles of the worksite. Employees who work for smaller employers, or have worked for less than a year, or work very few hours in a year are not eligible for FMLA leave.

Many states have their own state leave law which can be more generous. Therefore, check state law, particularly if you work for an employer not covered by the FMLA.

The FMLA has considerable notice requirements for employers and employees who seek leave. Also, employers can require [1] medical certification from a health care provider to prove whether leave is necessary due to a serious health condition; [2] periodic recertification of a medical condition; [3] reports regarding an employee's status and intent to return to work; and [4] a "fitness-for-duty" certification upon return to work in appropriate situations. Many different types of health care providers can certify that an employee needs FMLA leave: medical doctor, dentist, podiatrist, physician's assistant, clinical psychologist, optometrist, nurse practitioner, nurse midwife, chiropractor, clinical social worker, Christian Science practitioner, licensed foreign health care provider, and anyone from whom an employer's health plan benefits manager will accept certification.

FMLA grants a number of rights to employees. An employee can stay on the employer's group health insurance plan during FMLA leave. FMLA leave is unpaid, but an employee may elect or the employer may require the employee to substitute accrued paid time, such as vacation and sick leave, toward the FMLA-qualifying absence. Therefore, an employee can be paid during FMLA leave. Similarly, payments under state workers' compensation or private disability benefit programs may run concurrently with FMLA-related absences. Where medically necessary, the 12 weeks of FMLA leave may be taken intermittently (e.g., hour, day, week or month-long periods) or on a reduced schedule basis (e.g., moving from a full-time to part-time schedule). Most importantly, an employee has the right to their job back and any accrued benefits, such as retirement plan participation. FMLA time off can't count against attendance or otherwise be held against the employee in performance evaluations or the opportunity for advancement.

Now...as to an employee's request for time off for male enhancement surgery. Male enhancement is a nice way of saying male enlargement. Penile enlargement surgery, also referred to as phalloplasty, is a serious medical procedure to increase the length and girth of the penis permanently. Assuming the employee is eligible for FMLA leave, he must prove he has a qualifying FMLA event, in this case, a serious health condition.

The definition of a serious health condition is broad. An employee may be entitled to FMLA leave for the employee's or an immediate family member's overnight stay in a hospital, hospice or care facility; brief absences due to a chronic serious health condition (e.g., asthma, diabetes, epilepsy, migraines, depression); time off during which an employee or family member is under the continuing care of a doctor; and leave for prenatal care, periods of incapacity for permanent or long-term conditions (such as a stroke, terminal illness), or to undergo multiple treatments (e.g., chemotherapy, physical therapy, dialysis).

Ordinarily, cosmetic surgery is not a serious health condition unless serious complications develop. The FMLA's regulations specifically exclude minor health conditions and cosmetic surgery. Minor conditions include routine physical, eye, or dental examinations. Unless complications arise, the common cold, flu, earaches, upset stomach, minor ulcers, headaches (other than migraines), and routine dental or orthodontia problems are not serious health conditions under the FMLA.

Cosmetic treatments (such as for acne, botox, hair replacement, and plastic surgery) are not serious health conditions unless inpatient hospital care is required or complications develop. Some cosmetic surgery, however, can be a serious health condition under the FMLA. For example, restorative dental or plastic surgery following a disfiguring injury or after the removal of cancerous tumors are serious health conditions.

In conclusion, the FMLA affords significant protection for employees who need time off for medical reasons, including surgery to alter their physical appearance. However, many questions remain unanswered. Could an employee take job-protected FMLA leave for gender reassignment surgery? Being transgender is not necessarily a serious health condition. But being depressed is. If a doctor diagnoses an employee struggling with their gender identity as depressed and certifies that gender reassignment surgery is necessary to treat the employee's depression, then the time off may well be protected under the FMLA. Breast augmentation surgery or a rhinoplasty (nose job), under the FMLA's rules, are outpatient cosmetic treatments not protected by the FMLA. However, breast reduction surgery to alleviate serious chronic neck and back pain would probably be covered by the FMLA. A rhinoplasty to repair blunt force trauma to the nose in a car accident or to repair a serious breathing impairment would likely be protected under the FMLA. Employers must consider allowing time off work for eligible employees with qualifying medical conditions. Therefore, employees should consider asking for time off work for medical reasons, including medical procedures that might seem out of the ordinary.

AFTERWORD

IT IS TRULY AWKWARD to end a book with a chapter on male enhancement surgery. But that's how I roll. This book has been fun, and I feel it is just the beginning, not the end. A number of questions did not make it into the book: Can an employee who accidentally ingests edible marijuana products get fired? Can an employer demand a meat-free workplace? Do smokers have any rights at work these days? In the midst of a pandemic, can an employer have a preference for hiring super-immune employees who are more resistant to illness and disease? Can an employee be harassed by another employee's computer avatar?

There's always more to learn about work. Therefore, I invite your additional questions. Please feel free to send your questions to me at www.defendwork.com. Who knows, your question may end up in the next volume of *Can I Take my Pet Monkey to Work?*

Chuck Passaglia

ACKNOWLEDGMENTS

I APPRECIATE ANYONE who took the time to read *Can I Take my Pet Monkey to Work?* It is my sincere hope that you learned a little bit about work law and smiled a few times in the process.

This book would never have become a reality without the encouragement and help of many friends and colleagues. I spoke to a number of people who have written work-related books in order to assess the relative pain-to-reward ratio before embarking on this project. In particular, Debra Fine, Lynne Eisaguirre, and Lynne's literary agent, Michael Snell, provided much advice, encouragement and, most importantly, the way ahead.

I am thankful for three fellow attorneys, colleagues and friends, Marci Kearney, Allan Estroff and Mark Parcheta, for starting me on my journey in employment law and, better yet, teaching me how to resolve complex human resources issues successfully, while maintaining my sense of humor, and stressing the importance of giving good advice to people in need.

I must thank the many friends who have encouraged and guided me along the way. You know who you are. In particular, Scott Olson is a professional writer, an author in his own right, my neighbor, and a good friend. He was the first person to read the rough draft of this book and he provided invaluable assistance regarding structure, style, and content. Dave and Cheryl Tabor have shared many meals and many more bottles of wine with me and my wife over the years hearing tall tales about a mythical book I was writing, bouncing ideas off of each other, and always encouraging me to bring this book to life.

This book would be unreadable but for the work of Debi Chernak, HR Cert Prep Pros, who edited the book with the keen eye of both an editor and human resources professional. I am lucky to have found her, even more fortunate to have gotten to know her, and I very much appreciate her good work.

My biggest thanks go to Chris Leh, Leh Law Group, LLC, a brilliant, kind employment law attorney who edited this book and made me sound like I knew what I was talking about.

Finally, my best and most fulfilling work has been as the husband of Sarah VanScoy and the father of our girls, Rachel, Rita and Lucy. I am grateful for my girls who inspire me to work hard, have fun, love much, and be a better person.

ABOUT THE AUTHOR

CHUCK PASSAGLIA is one of the top lawyers in America . . . if measured by happiness. He is from Colorado. He was a lawyer in the United States Navy and is a veteran of combat support operations in the Middle East and East Africa. He was a litigation associate with Moye Giles (now Moye White) in Denver, Colorado, and in-house employment law counsel for a large employers' association. In 2003, he founded Employment Law Solutions, Inc., which specializes in giving damn good advice and counsel in employment law matters, conducting thorough, impartial workplace investigations, and training the entire workforce in critical human resources and legal compliance topics, including ethical decisionmaking, employees' right to time off, compensation and benefits, and protections under federal and state anti-discrimination laws.

Chuck received a degree in Philosophy from St. Louis University in St. Louis, Missouri, and his law degree from the University of Denver.

Chuck is a popular speaker and trainer, conducting over 150 "entertraining" sessions annually, and is a regular contributor to legal and human resources publications.

For more information about Chuck Passaglia, please visit www.defendwork.com.

NOTES

1: BLONDES

Shramban v. Aetna, 262 F. Supp. 2d 531 (E.D. Pa. 2003).

D. W. Greene, "Title VII: What's Hair (And Other Race-Based Characteristics) Got To Do With It?" *University of Colorado Law Review*, Vol. 79, No. 4, 2008; D. W. Greene, "Black Women Can't Have Blonde Hair . . . in the Workplace," *Journal of Gender, Race and Justice*, Vol. 14, No. 2, 2011.

Santee v. Windsor Court Hotel Ltd. P'ship, No. Civ. A. 99-3891, 2000 WL 1610775 (E.D. La. Oct. 26, 2000).

For an excellent overview and to follow the progress of the CROWN Act, please visit the Official Campaign of The CROWN Act at https://www.thecrownact.com/.

Strong v. Terrell, 195 P.3d 977 (Wash App. 2008).

2: UGLY

"It's Time To Expose The Attractiveness Bias At Work," *Forbes Magazine*, July 17, 2019, https://www.forbes.com/sites/tomaspremuzic/2019/07/17/its-time-to-expose-the-attractiveness-bias-at-work/#209c79d21324.

Goodwin v. Harvard Coll., No. 03-11797JLT (D. Mass. May 17, 2005); "Librarian Files Suit Against Harvard," New York Times, September 22, 2003, https://archive.nytimes.com/www.nytimes.com/uwire/uwire_ZOEV092220034710108.html.

"US librarian loses 'sexy' lawsuit," *BBC News*, April 5, 2005, http://news.bbc.co.uk/2/hi/europe/4412665.stm.

Yanowitz v. L'Oreal USA, Inc., 32 Cal.Rptr.3d 436, 36 Cal.4th 1028, 116 P.3d 1123 (Cal. S. Ct. 2005).

Lewis v. Heartland Inns of America, L.L.C., 591 F.3d 1033 (8th Cir. 2010).

Nelson v. Knight, 834 N.W.2d 64 (Iowa 2013).

"Abercrombie & Fitch Bias Case Is Settled," *The New York Times*, November 17, 2004, https://www.nytimes.com/2004/11/17/us/abercrombie-fitch-bias-case-is-settled.html; "Supreme Court Rules Against Abercrombie & Fitch In Discrimination Case," *Huff Post*, June 1, 2015, https://www.huffpost.com/entry/supreme-court-abercrombie_n_7464534; "Why 62,000 Abercrombie & Fitch Employees Are Suing The Company," *Huff Post*, July 22, 2015, https://www.huffpost.com/entry/abercrombie-fitch-lawsuit-look-policy n_55ae70e6e4b08f57d5d29286.

"The strange loophole that lets Hooters hire only female servers," *Business Insider*, September 2015, https://www.businessinsider.com/how-can-hooters-hire-only-women-2015-9.

Wilson v. Southwest Airlines, 517 F. Supp. 292 (N.D. Tex. 1981).

3: N-WORD

Comparison of Black persons to monkeys is not a recent phenomenon. Sports fans of some vintage may recall that sports announcer Howard Cosell—who was a tremendous advocate for Black athletes—drew significant criticism in 1983 for his comment during a Monday night football broadcast when he referred to Washington Redskins' receiver Alvin Garrett, who is Black, after his sixth reception of the game, as "that little monkey gets loose doesn't he."

In *Spriggs v. Diamond Auto Glass*, 242 F.3d 179, 185 (4th Cir. 2001), permitting a Black customer service representative's racial discrimination case to go forward to trial, the Fourth Circuit Court of Appeals stated that the "continuous daily" use of the words "nigger" and "monkey" by the white supervisor toward the Black employee was sufficient to support a claim of racial harassment. The court held, "Far more than a 'mere offensive utterance,' the word 'nigger' is pure anathema to African-Americans. Perhaps no single act can more quickly alter the conditions of employment and create an abusive working environment than the use of an unambiguously racial epithet such as 'nigger' by a supervisor in the presence of his subordinates.' [quoting Rodgers v. Western-Southern Life Ins. Co., 12 F.3d 668, 675 (7th Cir.1993).]" Further, the supervisor's "constant use of the word 'monkey' to describe African Americans was similarly odious. To suggest that a human being's physical appearance is essentially a caricature of a jungle beast goes far beyond the merely unflattering; it is degrading and humiliating in the extreme."

Burlington v. News Corp., 759 F. Supp. 2d 580 (E.D. Pa. 2010). The case finally reached trial, and on June 15, 2015 a jury reached a verdict in favor of the employer, agreeing that the television station had legitimate, non-discriminatory reasons for terminating Burlington for using the n-word.

Please read Randall Kennedy, *Nigger: The Strange Career of a Troublesome Word* (First Vintage Books, 2003).

Ash v. Tyson Foods, Inc., 546 U.S. 454 (2006).

If there are any doubts that Black employees have also been fired and sued for use of the n-word, see *Weatherly v. Alabama State Univ.*, 728 F.3d 1263 (11th Cir. 2013). The Eleventh Circuit Court of Appeals upheld a jury award in the amount $1,078,611 to three Black female administrative employees who were repeatedly subjected to the n-word by a Black female supervisor at a state university. Despite repeated complaints to Human Resources, the university not only failed to address the complaints but warned the employees against going to the EEOC. One of the plaintiffs testified that "she heard [the female supervisor] use the word 'nigger,' 'nigga,' 'nigga shit,' 'bitch,' 'stupid bitches,' 'fat bitch,' and 'white bitch' in the office; . . . I'm sick of this nigga shit. These stupid bitches can't do anything right. And, they ain't nothing but some niggas. . . . [and] called Burkhalter's seven-year-old son 'a nigger,' upsetting him so much that he crawled under his mother's desk and curled up in the fetal position." The Court stated, "[W]e are unnerved by the apparent acquiescence to, if not outright condoning of, the abusive work environment created by [the university's] high-level employees. Such conduct simply has no place in a work environment, especially at a publicly funded university." See also *Johnson v. Strive East Harlem Employment Group*, 990 F. Supp. 2d 435 (S.D.N.Y. 2014) (upholding compensatory damages award in the amount of $128,109.59 and punitive damages in the amount of $30,000 against an employer and Black Puerto Rican supervisor for his repeated use of the words "nigger," "whore," and "bitch" toward a Black female subordinate).

4: COOL NAME
M. Bertrand and S. Mullainathan, "Are Emily and Greg More Employable than Lakisha and Jamal? A Field Experiment on Labor Market Discrimination," *The American Economic Review*, Vol. 94, No. 4, (September 2004), pp. 991-1013.

For more on "testers," see EEOC, Enforcement Guidance No. N-915.002 ("Enforcement Guidance: Whether 'Testers' Can File Charges and Litigate Claims of Employment Discrimination") (May 22, 1996), http://www.eeoc.gov/docs/testers.txt. See also *Kyles v. J.K. Guardian Security Services*, F.Supp.2d 77 FEP 1473 (N.D. Ill. 1998), aff'd, 222 F.3d 289 (7th Cir. 2000).

5: WICCAN

For a review of Wiccanism, see Dettmer v. Landon, 799 F.2d 929, 932 (4th Cir.1986). Wicca is a form of neo-paganism, a belief system and way of life based upon a modern reconstruction of pre-Christian Celtic traditions. Wicca recognizes both male and female manifestations of divinity, and its festal times are tied to the cycles of nature. It emphatically dissociates itself from the popular conception of "witchcraft" as worship of Satan or evil powers. *Id*. The court in *Dettmer* estimated in 1986 that there were 10,000 to 100,000 Wiccans in America. *Id*. The "Wiccan religion (also known as Wicca, the Craft, or the Old Religion)" has also been described "as a monistic and pantheistic, positive, shamanistic, nature-based religion that is predicated on a simple set of ethics and morality which promulgates avoidance of harm to other people, promoting brotherly love and harmony with, and respect for, all life forms." *Van Koten v. Family Health Management, Inc.*, 134 F.3d 375, 1998 WL 54615 (7ᵗʰ Cir. 1998) (unpublished opinion) (upholding dismissal of Title VII claim where employer had no knowledge of employee's religion; knowledge of employee's interest in astrology and one-time statement to co-workers that Halloween was the holiest day of year in his religion not sufficient to impute knowledge of Wiccan beliefs to employer); *Hedum v. Starbucks Corp.*, 546 F.Supp.2d 1017 (D.Or. 2008); *Saemodarae v. Mercy Health Services*, 456 F.Supp.2d 1021 (N.D. Iowa 2006).

The cases discussed in this chapter include *Brown v. Pena*, 441 F. Supp. 1382 (S.D. Fla. 1977)(eating Kozy Kitten Cat Food is a personal preference, not a religion); *International Society for Krishna Consciousness, Inc. v. Barber*, 650 F.2d 430 (2d Cir. 1981); *EEOC v. United Health Programs et al.*, E.D.N.Y., No. 1:14-cv-03673 (September 30, 2016); *Chenzira v. Cincinnati Children's Hosp. Med. Ctr.*, S.D. Ohio, No. 1:11-cv-00917 (Dec. 27, 2012) (vegan nurse who refused to get a flu shot for religious reasons); *Peterson v. Wilmur Communications, Inc.*, 205 F.Supp.2d 1014 (E.D. Wisc. 2002).

EEOC v. Chi-Chi's Restaurants, Inc., complaint filed, No. L96-1692 (D. Md., June 26, 1996) (Chi-Chi's Restaurants settled the case on December 10, 1997 by paying the terminated employee $53,000 and by adopting a new corporate religious discrimination policy); *Cook v. Cub Foods Inc.*, 99 F. Supp. 2d 945 (N.D. Ill. 2000); *Slater v. King Soopers, Inc.*, 809 F. Supp. 809 (D. Colo. 1992) (membership in KKK not a religion but could be an off-duty, legal activity). See also *McGlothin v. Jackson Mun. Separate Sch. Dist.*, 829 F. Supp. 853 (S.D. Miss. 1992) (African American teacher fired for wearing traditional African head garb in violation of school district rules was not protected on the basis of religion, since her attire was a reflection of her heritage and culture); *United States v. Meyers*, 95 F.3d 1475 (10ᵗʰ Cir. 1996); *Chalmers v. Tulon Co.*, 101 F.3d 1012 (4th Cir. 1996). *See also Venters v. City of Delphi*, 123 F.3d 956 (7ᵗʰ Cir. 1997) (permitting police dispatcher's Title VII religious harassment claim where police chief constantly proselytized religious beliefs at work, including calling police station "God's house," giving employee a Bible and other religious materials, expressing disgust with employee's refusal to be saved, and stating he believed she was sacrificing animals in Satan's name and having sex with family members); *Grant v. Joe Myers Toyota*, 11 S.W.3d 419 (Tex. Ct. App. 2000) (requiring Christian employee to read "New Age" motivational book for sales training may constitute religious discrimination); *EEOC v. Red Robin Gourmet Burgers, Inc.*, 2005 WL 2090677 (W.D. Wash., Aug. 29, 2005) (denying employer's motion for summary judgment); EEOC Press Release, "Burger Chain to Pay $150,000 to Resolve EEOC Religious Discrimination Suit," September 16, 2005, https://www.eeoc.gov/eeoc/newsroom/release/9-16-05.cfm.

6: MARK OF THE BEAST

Cassano v. Carb, 436 F.3d 74 (2nd. Cir. 2006).

EEOC v. Consol Energy, Inc., No. 16-1230 (4th Cir. June 12, 2017).

EEOC v. Allendale Nursing Centre, 996 F. Supp. 712 (W.D. Mich. 1998) (requirement that employee provide Social Security number is a requirement imposed by law, not the employer).

Weber v. Leaseway Dedicated Logistics, Inc., 5 F.Supp.2d 1219 (D.Kan.1998), aff'd in an unpublished opinion, 166 F.3d 1223 (10th Cir. 1999).

"666 W-2: Walter Slonopas, Christian Employee, Quits Over Mark Of The Beast On Tax Form," *Huff Post*, February 7, 2013, https://www.huffingtonpost.com/2013/02/07/666-w-2-walter-slonopas; "Tax Evasion: 'Mark of the Beast' Belief Doesn't Save Man From Conviction," *Newsmax*, March 9, 2017, https://www.newsmax.com/TheWire/tax-evasion-mark-of-the-beast/2017/03/08/id/777696/.

7: FLU SHOT

A "pandemic" is a global "epidemic." The world has seen four deadly influenza pandemics since 1900: the deadly "Spanish Flu" of 1918; the milder "Asian" flu (H2N2) of 1957 which killed approximately 116,000 persons in the United States; the "Hong Kong" flu of 1968 (H3N2) which killed approximately 100,000 persons in the United States; and the H1N1 outbreak of 2009 which killed approximately 12,000 persons in the United States. The severe acute respiratory syndrome (SARS) outbreak in 2003 was considered a pandemic "scare." The novel SARS coronavirus that caused COVID-19 was declared a pandemic on March 11, 2020 by the World Health Organization. See https://www.cdc.gov/coronavirus/2019-ncov/faq.html#covid19-basics. See also "Pandemic Preparedness in the Workplace and the Americans with Disabilities Act," October 21, 2009, http://www.eeoc.gov/facts/pandemic_flu.html.

Chenzira v. Cincinnati Children's Hospital Med. Ctr., No. 11-917 (S.D. Ohio Dec. 27, 2012); *Virginia Mason Medical Center*, 358 NLRB No. 64 (2012).

Fallon v. Mercy Catholic Medical Center of Southeastern Pennsylvania, 200 F.Supp.3d 553 (E.D. Pa. 2016), affirmed, No. 16-3573 (3d. Cir., December 14, 2017); *Hustvet v. Allina Health System*, No. 17-2963 (8th Cir., Dec. 7, 2018) (appellate court ruled that healthcare employer can require rubella immunization as a condition of employment under the ADA).

Horvath v. City of Leander, Texas, et al., No. 18-51011 (5th Cir., Jan. 13, 2020) (transfer of firefighter to code enforcement job or wearing a respirator during the day were reasonable accommodations offered to firefighter who refused a vaccination on religious grounds).

In the event of a pandemic, employers must consider responses to the impact on an organization. The websites www.pandemicflu.gov and www.cdc.gov/business contain business pandemic influenza checklists that employers may find helpful. Employers will also need to consider difficult questions, such as the following: Is influenza a serious health condition under the Family Medical Leave Act entitling employees to leave? Would an employer have to pay, or consider paying, employees for time they are out of work with the flu or caring for a family member with the flu? What legal responsibility do employers have to allow employees time off from work to care for sick children or children that have been sent home from school or day care centers that have closed? Can an employer require an employee to stay home from work to minimize getting or communicating influenza? Can an employer require an employee not to take vacation or travel to countries/locations where the influenza virus is prevalent? Can an employer require employees to wear personal protective equipment (PPE) such as masks and gloves or take other measures to control the spread of infection? Can an employer monitor the temperatures of its employees? Can an employer require employees to have medical exams or present medical certification related to whether they are sick or carriers of the virus or healthy enough to work before allowing them in the workplace? Could an employer be held liable if its employees or other third parties contract influenza at the workplace? If the employer has unionized employees, does that affect how an employer handles issues related to a pandemic?

8: YOUNG PEOPLE

The legislative history of the ADEA is discussed in *General Dynamics Land Systems, Inc. v. Cline*, 540 U.S. 581 (2004). In the case, employees age 40-49 were treated less favorably than employees age 50 and older in retiree health benefit plan changes. The Supreme Court rejected the claims, finding that the ADEA does not prohibit discrimination against "younger" workers, even if the claimants were also over age 40.

9: SINGLE PEOPLE

According to the Sloan Work and Family Research Network, Alaska, California, Connecticut, Delaware, Florida, Hawaii, Illinois, Indiana, Maryland, Michigan, Minnesota, Montana, Nebraska, New Hampshire, New Jersey, New York, North Dakota, Oregon, Virginia, Washington, and Wisconsin prohibit marital discrimination at work. Found at https://wfrn.org/resources/policies-laws-legislation/. Michigan is one of the states that protects persons based on marital status. In *Russ v. City of Troy*, the Michigan Court of Appeals permitted a Michigan police officer to present his case under Michigan's marital status anti-discrimination law that he was denied promotion to sergeant solely because he was single. Despite scoring high on the promotion list, he had allegedly been informed by the Chief of Police that his department looked "at married men favorably" for promotion. This reinforces age-old stereotypes that married men are viewed more favorably by employers because they are more loyal; have more "mouths to feed" and, therefore, will work harder; and are less likely to leave a well-paying position with opportunities for advancement. *Russ v. City of Troy*, LC No. 98-005525-NZ (Mich. App. April 6, 2001) (unpublished opinion).

11: PREGNANCY

Some of the relevant cases cited by the EEOC include *Pacourek v. Inland Steel Co.*, 858 F. Supp. 1393, 1401 (N.D. Ill.1994) (plaintiff asserted a Title VII claim where she alleged she was undergoing in vitro fertilization and her employer disparately applied its sick leave policy to her in favor of men); *Hall v. Nalco Co.*, 534 F.3d 644, 648-49 (7th Cir. 2008) (employee terminated for taking time off to undergo in vitro fertilization was not fired for gender-neutral condition of infertility but rather for gender-specific quality of childbearing capacity; therefore, she was able to bring a claim of sex discrimination under Title VII).

12: SHORT HAIR

Willingham v. Macon Telegraph Publishing Co., 507 F.2d 1084 (5th Cir. 1975). See, e.g., *Harper v. Blockbuster Entertainment Corp.*, 139 F.3d 1385 (11th Cir. 1998), cert denied, 525 U.S. 1000 (1998) (court rejected sex discrimination and retaliation claims of former male Blockbuster employees who were terminated for violating a hair length policy); *Tavora v. New York Mercantile Exchange*, 101 F.3d 907 (2d Cir. 1996); *Barker v. Taft Broadcasting Co.*, 549 F.2d 400, 401 (6th Cir. 1977); *Earwood v. Continental Southeastern Lines, Inc.*, 539 F.2d 1349, 1351 (4th Cir. 1976); *Longo v. Carlisle De Coppett & Co.*, 537 F.2d 685 (2d Cir. 1976); *Knott v. Missouri Pacific Railway Co.*, 527 F.2d 1249, 1252 (8th Cir. 1975) ("Minor differences in personal appearance regulations that reflect customary modes of grooming do not constitute sex discrimination within the meaning [of Title VII]."); *Baker v. California Land Title Co.*, 507 F.2d 895, 898 (9th Cir. 1974); *Dodge v. Giant Food, Inc.*, 488 F.2d 1333, 13337 (D.C. Cir. 1973); *Fagan v. National Cash Register Co.*, 5 FEP Cases (BNA)

1335 (D.C. Cir. 1973) ("Good grooming regulations reflect a company's policy in our highly competitive business environment. Reasonable requirements in furtherance of that policy are an aspect of managerial responsibility."). *EEOC Compliance Manual* § 619.1 (BNA 1989).

Jespersen v. Harrah's Operating Co., Inc., 444 F.3d 1104 (9th Cir. 2006).

13: TSA PAT-DOWN
29 C.F.R. Part 1604, Guidelines on Discrimination because of Sex, section 1604.11, Sexual harassment.

The case addressing the immunity of TSA screeners from assault and false imprisonment claims is *Pellegrino v. Transportation Security Administration*, 896 F.3d 207 (3d Cir. 2018) (TSA screeners are not "investigative or law enforcement officers" for the purpose of assessing liability for intentional torts under the Federal Tort Claims Act).

14: DATING
Regarding rumors of having an affair, see *Spain v. Gallegos*, 26 F.3d 439 (3d Cir. 1994) (plaintiff's allegations that managers at three levels recognized that plaintiff was being ostracized by co-workers based on their erroneous belief that she was having affair with her supervisor were sufficient to withstand summary judgment on her hostile environment sexual harassment claim).

Sexual favoritism. See, e.g., *Womack v. Runyon*, 147 F.3d 1298 (11th Cir. 1998) (male employee not selected for promotion given to female paramour of decision-maker does not have Title VII claim based on favoritism); *Taken v. Oklahoma Corp. Comm'n*, 125 F.3d 1366 (10th Cir. 1997) (preference for paramour does not violate Title VII); *Ayers v. American Tel. & Tel. Co.*, 826 F. Supp 443 (S.D. Fla. 1993) (Federal district court dismissed the claim of a female store manager who was transferred to a store at a poorer location because her supervisor sought to reward a young and attractive, but less qualified, employee who was "bestowing her sexual favors upon him." According to the complaint, at the time of the transfer, the paramour had recently broken up with the supervisor and he was seeking to rekindle the romance. It must have worked: The couple later married. The court related the obviously unfair conduct of the supervisor to nepotism, rather than sexism, and held that hiring one's sweetheart or lover, or favoritism to a paramour, is not a violation of Title VII. However, the court noted that the result might have been different if the paramour had entered the sexual relationship in order to procure her transfer or if an element of coercion on the part of the supervisor had existed. In this case, based on the facts, the romance appeared entirely consensual.); *Dirksen v. City of Springfield*, 842 F. Supp. 1117 (C.D. Ill. 1994) (Police chief's favoritism towards his lover, who replaced plaintiff as his secretary after plaintiff rejected his sexual advances, was actionable where supervisor told employee that sexual favors were necessary for appointment as secretary); *Broderick v. Ruder*, 685 F. Supp. 1269 (D.D.C. 1988) (Female S.E.C. staff attorney who was not harassed but was offended by "open affairs" of top male management attorneys in regional office with female attorneys and secretaries. Failure of plaintiff to "get along" in the office was found by the court to be based on offensive work environment.).

Parker v. Reena Consulting, Inc., 2019 WL 490652 (4th Cir., February 8, 2019).

Brown v. Department of the Navy, 229 F.3d 1356 (D.C. Cir. 2001).

Malone v. Eaton Corp., 187 F.3d 960 (8th Cir. 1999).

Smith v. AMTRAK, 25 F. Supp.2d 578 (E.D. Pa. 1998).

Kahn v. Objective Solutions International, 86 F. Supp.2d 377, 381 (S.D.N.Y. 2000).

Triplett v. Belle of Orleans LLC, 2000 WL 264002 (E.D. La. Mar. 8, 2000).

Mercier v. Daniels, 139 N.C. App. 588, 533 S.E. 2d 877 (N.C. App. 2000).

15: BEATINGS
See *Sandra Williams v. Ocean Beach Club, LLC*, No. 2:11cv639 (E.D.Va., Sept. 25, 2012); *Hudgens v. Prosper, Inc.*, 243 P.3d 1275 (Utah 2010).

16: SEXUAL ORIENTATION
Much of the information cited in this answer, including the discussion of terms, is available by credible open source research. The older Title VII cases referred to in the answer include *Smith v. Liberty Mutual Insurance Co.*, 395 F. Supp. 1098 (N.D. Ga. 1975) (rejecting employee's claim under Title VII that he was not hired because he appeared effeminate); see also *DeSantis v. Pacific Tel. Co., Inc.*, 608 F.2d 327 (9th Cir. 1979) (Title VII does not protect against discrimination because of effeminacy).

Price Waterhouse v. Hopkins, 490 U.S. 228, 109 S. Ct. 1775, 104 L.Ed.2d 208 (1989) is a landmark Supreme Court case. Ann Hopkins left Price Waterhouse in early 1984 after filing her charge of sex discrimination against the firm with the EEOC in 1983. She filed a federal lawsuit in 1984. After the Supreme Court remanded the case back to the trial court in 1989, Hopkins eventually prevailed in the lower courts. In 1991, Hopkins was reinstated by Price Waterhouse—as a partner with seniority dating back to 1983—and recovered back pay for the seven-year period she had left the firm. Her attorneys recovered $500,000 in fees from Price Waterhouse. In 1998, Price Waterhouse merged with Coopers & Lybrand and became

PricewaterhouseCoopers. Hopkins retired from PricewaterhouseCoopers in 2002 at the age of 59.

Doe v. City of Belleville, 119 F.3d 563 (7th Cir. 1997). See also *Nichols v. Azteca Rest. Enter. Inc.*, 256 F.3d 864 (9th Cir. 2001) (citing *Price Waterhouse*, employee taunted with "faggot" and repeatedly insulted for the way he walked and carried a tray in the restaurant was subjected to unlawful harassment); *Bibby v. Philadelphia Coca-Cola Bottling Co.*, 260 F.3d 257 (3d Cir. 2001) (distinguishing harassment based on sexual orientation from harassment based on noncompliance with gender stereotypes; concluding harassment based on gender nonconformance may be unlawful discrimination because of sex; sexual orientation of the victim becomes irrelevant); *Higgins v. New Balance Athletic Shoe, Inc.*, 194 F.3d 252 (1st Cir. 1999); *Jones v. Pacific Rail Services*, 2001 WL 127645 (N.D. Ill., Feb. 14, 2001) (employee repeatedly harassed by men in the locker room at work may "advance a theory of same-sex harassment based on his perceived non-conformance to gender-based stereotypes"); *Centola v. Potter*, 183 F. Supp.2d 403 (D. Mass. 2002) (gay postal employee could bring gender discrimination claim alleging that co-workers harassed him because they considered him to be "impermissibly feminine for a man").

In 2017, in *Hively v. Ivy Tech Community College*, 853 F.3d 339 (7th Cir. 2017), involving a gay teacher denied full-time work, a federal appeals court ruled for the first time that sexual orientation discrimination violates Title VII. In 2018, the Second Circuit joined the Seventh Circuit in ruling that Title VII of the Civil Rights Act of 1964 prohibits sexual orientation employment discrimination under the category of "sex." In *Zarda v. Altitude Express, Inc.*, No. 15-3775 (2d Cir. 2018), a skydiving instructor brought a gender discrimination claim, alleging that he was fired because he is gay. The appellate court ruled:

"[B]ecause sexual orientation is a function of sex and sex is a protected characteristic under Title VII, it follows that sexual orientation is also protected."

There was a split on this issue in the federal courts. See *Wittmer v. Phillips 66 Company*, No. 18-20251 (5th Cir., Feb. 6, 2019) (joining 11th Cir., Title VII does not prohibit discrimination on the basis of sexual orientation).

The U.S. Supreme Court resolved the split among the circuits with its decision in *Bostock v. Clayton County* (GA), No. 17–1618 (U.S., June 15, 2020).

Currently, 21 states have statutory bans on discrimination based on both sexual orientation and gender identity in the public and private sector: California, Colorado, Connecticut, Delaware, Hawaii, Illinois, Iowa, Maine, Maryland, Massachusetts, Minnesota, Nevada, New Hampshire, New Jersey, New Mexico, New York, Oregon, Rhode Island,

Utah, Vermont, and Washington. Two additional states, Michigan and Pennsylvania, have such protections through executive orders, court rulings, or binding decisions by their respective civil rights commissions.

Further, two more states, Indiana and Wisconsin, prohibit discrimination based on sexual orientation only.

17: GENDER IDENTITY

For more information, please visit the Transgender Law and Policy Institute at http://www.transgenderlaw.org/.

Ulane v. Eastern Airlines, Inc., 742 F.2d 1081 (7th Cir. 1984); *Macy v. Dep't of Justice*, EEOC Appeal No. 0120120821, 2012 WL 1435995 (April 20, 2012); *Lusardi v. Dep't of the Army*, EEOC Appeal No. 0120133395, 2015 WL 1607756 (April 1, 2015) (restrictions on transgender female's ability to use a common female restroom facility constituted disparate treatment on the basis of sex, and the restroom restrictions combined with hostile remarks, including intentional pronoun misuse, created a hostile work environment).

Stephens v. R.G. & G.R. Harris Funeral Homes, Inc., No. 16-2424 (6th Cir., March 7, 2018), affirmed in *Bostock v. Clayton County* (GA), No. 17–1618 (U.S., June 15, 2020).

Goins v. West Group, 635 N.W.2d 717 (Minn. App. 2001).

18: BATHROOM ENCOUNTER

Cruzan v. Minneapolis Public School System, 294 F.3d 981 (8th Cir. 2002).

19: YOGA PANTS

Schmitz v. ING Securities, Futures & Options Inc., 10 F.Supp.2d 982 (N.D. Ill. 1998); *Drinkwater v. Union Carbide Corp.*, 904 F.2d 853 (3d Cir. 1990). See also *Bellissimo v. Westinghouse Electric Corp.*, 764 F.2d 175 (3d Cir. 1985) (female attorney fired from her job could not use the fact that her male supervisor told her to "tone down" her attire as evidence to support a Title VII sex discrimination claim where employer aimed for conservative image and counseled men on their attire).

20: PERFUME

Weber v. Infinity Broadcasting Corp., 17 AD Cases 804, 98 FEP Cases 523 (E.D. Mich. Dec. 14, 2005) (The original $10.6 million verdict was later reduced to $814,000, plus $423,807 in attorneys' fees and costs, but the parties reached a confidential settlement while the case was on appeal.)

The no-scent policy adopted by the City of Detroit in 2010 is as follows:

Our goal is to be sensitive to employees with perfume and chemical sensitivities. In order to accommodate employees who are medically sensitive to the chemicals in scented products, the City of Detroit requests that you refrain from wearing scented products, including but not limited to colognes, aftershave lotions, perfumes, deodorants, body/face lotions, hair sprays or similar products. The City of Detroit also asks you to refrain from the use of scented candles, perfume samples from magazines, spray or solid air fresheners, room deodorizers, plug-in wall air fresheners, cleaning compounds or similar products. Our employees with medical chemical sensitivities thank you for your cooperation.

21: SMELL BAD

Georgy v. O'Neill, 2002 WL 449723 (E.D.N.Y., March 25, 2002); *Hannoon v. Fawn Engineering Corp.*, 324 F.3d 1041 (8th Cir. 2003); *Clem v. Case Pork Roll Co.*, Civil Action No. 15-6809 (D. N.J., July 18, 2016) (employee subjected to numerous comments about her co-worker/husband's extreme gas and foul body odor following gastric bypass surgery were not severe or pervasive enough to give rise to an associational disability discrimination claim under the ADA where employee did not allege the comments interfered with her job); *Ofori-Awuku v. Epic Security*, No. 00 CIV. 1548 AGS, 2001 WL 180054, at 3 n.3 (S.D.N.Y. Feb. 23, 2001) ("In order to constitute a disability under the ADA, [a] hygiene problem must involve a physical or mental impairment that substantially limits one or more of the major life activities of the individual. Plaintiff has failed to establish this to be the case, and, therefore, has not proven that he is a person with a disability within the meaning of the ADA, which is necessary to establish a prima facie case." (citation omitted)). See also *Seeman v. Gracie Gardens Owners Corp.*, 794 F.Supp.2d 476 (S.D.N.Y. 2011). In *Seeman*, Jonah Seeman, a 63-year-old doorman in New York, was suspended twice for his body odor, bad breath, and poor hygiene. He suffered from diabetes, causing ketosis, an increase in ketones in the blood, which resulted in bad breath. Nonetheless, the court found that Mr. Seeman never showed that any other malodorous employee would have been treated differently; therefore, he had no claim of discrimination.

22: HEMORRHOIDS

See Americans with Disabilities Act, 42 U.S. Code §§ 12102, 12211; U.S. Equal Employment Opportunity Commission (EEOC), *Technical Assistance Manual for Title I of the Americans with Disabilities Act (ADA)* (January 1992).

Davis v. BellSouth Mobility, LLC, NO CV01-AR-0986-S, 2002 WL 31720597 (N.D. Ala., Nov. 1, 2001). Since *Davis*, a number of cases have come to a similar conclusion that hemorrhoids are not a disability. See *Allred v. Boise Cascade Wood Products, LLC*, No. 1:17-cv-01534-CL, (D. Ore., Jul. 18, 2017) (citing *Racier v. Upper Cumberland Human Res.*

Agency, 171 F. Supp 3d 751, 758-59 (M.D. Tenn. 2016) (internal hemorrhoids are not a disability under the ADA).

23: MONKEY

"More companies, citing benefits, allow pets at work," *USA Today*, February 27, 2013, https://www.usatoday.com/story/money/business/2013/02/27/pets-reduce-stress-welcome-workplace/1951957/.

Sharan E. Brown, "Service Animals and Individuals with Disabilities under the Americans with Disabilities Act (ADA), ADA Knowledge Translation Center Legal Brief No. 2.1, *ADA National Network* (2019), https://adata.org/sites/adata.org/files/files/Legal%20Brief%20-%20Service%20Animals%20and%20the%20ADA%20-%20final%20LP.pdf.

2019 *EEOC v. CRST International Inc./CRST Expedited Inc.*, complaint, No. 3:2017cv00241 (M.D.Fla., March 2, 2017); "CRST to pay driver $47,500 as part of lawsuit settlement," *Overdrive*, March 12, 2019, https://www.overdriveonline.com/crst-to-pay-driver-47500-as-part-of-lawsuit-settlement/.

The use of miniature horses as service animals was addressed by the Sixth Circuit in *Anderson v. City of Blue Ash*, 2015 WL 4774591 (6th Cir. 2015). Anderson brought an ADA claim against the town in which she lived to allow her disabled daughter to use a miniature horse as a service animal in the family's backyard. The city had adopted an ordinance prohibiting farm animals on residential premises in the city limits. The appeals court denied the City's effort to dismiss the claim and allowed Anderson's case to move forward under Title III of the ADA.

24: OBESITY

Early cases favorable to obese employees include *Cook v. Rhode Island Dep't of Mental Health, Retardation & Hosps.*, 10 F.3d 17 (1st Cir. 1993) (Decided under the Rehabilitation Act of 1973, a precursor to the ADA, the federal appeals court found that morbid obesity was a disability since the employee was foreclosed from a broad range of jobs as a healthcare worker.); *Vicsik v. Fowler Equipment Co.*, No. 51855 (N.J., March 28, 2002) (New Jersey Supreme Court ruled that morbidly obese female billing clerk was a handicapped person protected by broader New Jersey Law Against Discrimination); *EEOC v. Texas Bus Lines*, 923 F. Supp. 965 (S.D. Tex. 1996) (The employer regarded an obese applicant as disabled when it refused to hire her as a bus driver, relying on a cursory medical exam saying the applicant could not obtain a required Department of Transportation (DOT) certification, when the court found no blanket exclusion based on weight under DOT rules.) But see *Walton v. Mental Health Ass'n of Southeastern Penn.*, 168 F.3d 661 (3rd Cir. 1999) (finding no evidence that employer regarded obese person as disabled); *Francis v. City of Meriden*,

129 F.3d 281 (2d Cir. 1997) (firefighter's inability to meet fire department's weight standard, alone, was insufficient evidence that firefighter was regarded as disabled).

More recent cases favorable to obese persons include *Lowe v. American Eurocopter*, LLC, 2010 WL 5232523 (N.D. Miss. Dec. 16, 2010) (allowing hostile work environment disability harassment claim brought by obese employee) and *EEOC v. Resources for Human Development, Inc.*, 827 F. Supp. 2d 688, 693 (E.D. La. 2011) (Obesity alone, even without an identifiable physiological cause, may constitute an impairment without further medical proof.) But see *Morriss v. BNSF Railway Co.*, 817 F.3d 1104 (8th Cir. 2016) (5'10, 280-pound railway machinist not selected for safety-sensitive position due to his BMI of 40 or greater was not protected by the ADA since he could not show his weight was the result of a physiological disorder or condition that affects a major body system.)

The Harvard study is T. E. S. Charlesworth, M. R. Banaji, "Patterns of Implicit and Explicit Attitudes: I. Long-Term Change and Stability From 2007 to 2016," *Psychological Science*, (January 3, 2019), https://journals.sagepub.com.

25: PHOBIAS

The cases relied on are *Stevens v. Rite Aid Corp.*, Nos. 15-277(L) (2d Cir., March 21, 2017) (pharmacist with trypanophobia, fear of needles); *Ahmad v. Yellow Cab Co.*, 49 F. Supp. 3d 178 (D. Conn. 2014) (cab driver with cynophobia, fear of dogs); *Huiner v. Arlington School District*, No. 11-4172-KES (D.S.D., September 23, 2013) (art teacher with ergophobia, fear of being fired); *Waltherr-Willard v. Mariemont City Schools*, No. 14-3168 (6th Cir. February 11, 2015) (Spanish teacher with pedophobia, fear of young children); *Miller v. Illinois Department of Transportation*, No. 3:07-cv-00677 (7th Cir., May 10, 2011) (bridge worker with a fear of heights, acrophobia).

I mentioned fear of snakes. I am afraid of snakes. See *Anderson v. North Dakota State Hospital*, 232 F.3d 634, 636 (8th Cir. 2000) (Fear of snakes, with brief hysteria and impairment, does not constitute a substantial limitation on switchboard operator's ability to work. "A comfort level with snakes is simply not a requirement for most jobs.").

26: ADDICTION

"Dr. Goldberg gains notoriety for naming a disease he says doesn't exist: "Internet addiction disorder" (I.A.D.)" *The New Yorker*, January 13th, 1997.

Pacenza v. IBM Corp., No. 04 Civ. 5831 (PGG), 2009 U.S. Dist. LEXIS 29778 (S.D.N.Y. Apr. 2, 2009).

"SEC and Pornography: Workers Spent Hours on Porn Sites Instead of
Stopping Fraud," *ABC News*, April 22, 2010, https://abcnews.go.com/
WN/sec-pornography-employees-spent-hours-surfing-porn-sites/
story?id=10451508.

Americans with Disabilities Act of 1990, Pub. L. No. 101-336, § 2(a), 104
Stat. 327, 328-29 (codified as amended at 42 U.S.C. § 12101 et seq.).

27: GAMBLING
"Fidelity Fires Four Employees For Playing Fantasy Football," *Business
Insider*, December 16, 2009, https://www.businessinsider.com/
fidelity-fires-four-employees-for-playing-fantasy-football-2009-12;
"Allowing Gambling at Work: A Good Bet or Bad Odds?," *HR Hero
Line*, January 26, 2012, https://hrdailyadvisor.blr.com/2012/01/26/
allowing-gambling-at-work-a-good-bet-or-bad-odds/.

28: WEAPONS
Most state gun laws permitting an employee to bring a weapon to work are
so-called "parking lot" laws because, even if a weapon is prohibited from
a building, an employee is allowed to secure a weapon in their personal
vehicle on company premises. Each state's law is different and can depend
on whether the employer secures its parking area from public access. As of
2018, at least 23 states had parking lot laws, including Alabama, Alaska,
Arizona, Arkansas, Florida, Georgia, Illinois, Indiana, Kansas, Kentucky,
Louisiana, Maine, Minnesota, Mississippi, Nebraska, North Dakota,
Ohio, Oklahoma, Tennessee, Texas, Utah, West Virginia, and Wisconsin.
These laws vary and may depend on whether an employer maintains
a "restricted" parking lot which is fenced or otherwise made secure.
Source: Society for Human Resources Management (SHRM), "Guns in
Parking Lots Laws by State," https://www.shrm.org/resourcesandtools/
legal-and-compliance/state-and-local-updates/xperthr/pages/guns-in-park-
ing-lots-laws-by-state.aspx.

29: TAXES
See IRS Publication, *The Truth about Frivolous Tax Arguments* (March
2018), https://www.irs.gov/pub/taxpros/frivolous_truth_march_2018.
pdf. There is a great deal of information online about renouncing one's
U.S. citizenship. A logical starting point is "Renounce or Lose Your U.S.
Citizenship," found on the U.S. Government's official website at https://
www.usa.gov/renounce-lose-citizenship.

30: PEE
See *Linkous v. Craftmaster Manufacturing, Inc.*, No. 7:10-CV-00107
(W.D.Va., July 16, 2012); *Kinneary v. City of New York*, 601 F.3d 151
(2d Cir. 2010); *Molman v. Metropolitan Government of Nashville,*

2010 WL 3063805 (M.D. Tenn. 2010) (despite paruresis being covered under the ADA, employer was justified in following U.S. Department of Transportation regulations governing mandatory drug testing of commercial bus drivers, affording a complete defense to a claim under the ADA).

31: KAROSHI
See "Japan is facing a 'death by overwork' problem — here's what it's all about," *Business Insider*, October 18, 2017, https://www.businessinsider.com/what-is-karoshi-japanese-word-for-death-by-overwork-2017-10.

32: BATHROOM USE
The OSHA sanitation standard for general industry is at 29 C.F.R. 1910.141(c)(l)(i). The field sanitation standard is at 29 CFR 1928.110. The Memorandum for Regional Administrators dated April 6, 1998, entitled "Interpretation of 29 CFR 1910.141(c)(1)(i): Toilet Facilities," contains helpful guidance. The cases cited are *Sulima v. Tobyhanna Army Depot*, No. 08-4684 (3rd Cir. April 12, 2010) and *Zwiebel v. Plastipak Packaging, Inc.*, Ohio App., 2013-Ohio-3785 (September 3, 2013).

33: DEATH
Bureau of Labor Statistics, National Census of Fatal Occupation Injuries in 2018, released December 17, 2019, https://www.bls.gov/news.release/cfoi.nr0.htm.

"Saving Sudden Cardiac Arrest Victims in the Workplace," Automated External Defibrillators, OSHA Publication 3185-09N 2003, https://www.osha.gov/Publications/3185.html.

"Here's What Happens To Google Employees When They Die," *Forbes*, August 8, 2012, https://www.forbes.com/sites/meghancasserly/2012/08/08/heres-what-happens-to-google-employees-when-they-die/.

Social Security Administration, Survivors Benefits, 05-10084, ICN 468540, June 2019, found at https://www.ssa.gov/pubs/EN-05-10084.pdf.

34: TIME OFF
Looking for new holiday celebrations for your workplace? Many states have unique and unusual holidays that provide fodder for creative excuses to miss work. Depending on the state in which you work, consider these recognized holidays: Robert E. Lee's Birthday/Confederate Heroes Day (January 19); Franklin Delano Roosevelt Day (January 30); Casimir Pulaski's Birthday (1st Monday in March); Cesar Chavez Day (March 31); Patriots Day (3rd Monday in April); Jefferson Davis's Birthday (June 3); Flag Day (June 14); Defender's Day (September 12); All Saints Day (November 1). Interestingly, a number of states recognize Good Friday (Friday before Easter Sunday).

Like many states, my home state, Colorado, has had several interesting public holidays. For example, from 1893 until repealed in 1995, in all Colorado cities with a population of 25,000 or more, every Saturday from noon to midnight during June, July, and August was considered a public holiday. Good Roads Day, the second Friday in May, was observed between 1911 and 1995. Still on the books in Colorado: Arbor Day (3rd Friday in April), Susan B. Anthony Day (February 15), and Leif Erikson Day (October 9). Leif Erikson? Leif Erikson, an Icelandic explorer, is often credited as the "discoverer of the North American continent" in or about the year 1000 A.D.

35: WORK FOR FREE

The Fair Labor Standards Act of 1938 is found at 29 U.S.C. §§ 201 et seq.

An employer may hire an independent contractor, providing compensation in exchange for services, without being liable for wages under FLSA. The U.S. Supreme Court has, on several occasions, indicated that there is no single rule or test for determining whether an individual is an independent contractor or an employee for purposes of the FLSA. Generally, courts will look to whether a worker is "economically dependent" on the employer or works for him or herself. Among the factors the Court has considered significant are: (1) the extent to which the services rendered are an integral part of the principal's business; (2) the permanency of the relationship; (3) the amount of the alleged contractor's investment in facilities and equipment; (4) the nature and degree of control by the principal; (5) the alleged contractor's opportunities for profit and loss; (6) the amount of initiative, judgment, or foresight in open market competition with others required for the success of the claimed independent contractor; and (7) the degree of independent business organization and operation. See Department of Labor, Wage and Hour Division, "Fact Sheet 13: Employment Relationship Under the Fair Labor Standards Act (FLSA)" (July 2008), https://www.dol. gov/whd/regs/compliance/whdfs13.htm.

Trainees are persons who are in "training" for a job and, therefore, not yet employees subject to FLSA coverage. However, trainees must be distinguished from current employees who receive training for which they must be paid. The Department of Labor relies on six factors for determining whether a worker is a trainee: (1) training is similar to that which would be given in a vocational school; (2) the training is for the benefit of the trainee; (3) the trainee does not displace regular employees but works under close observation; (4) the employer derives no immediate advantage from the activity; (5) the trainee is not necessarily entitled to a job at the completion of the training period; and (6) the employer and the trainee understand that the trainee is not entitled to wages for the time spent in training. It is not necessary that all six factors be met to preclude determination that trainees are employees. See Reich v. Parker Fire Protection Dist., 992 F.2d 1023 (10th Cir. 1993); Nesbitt v. FCHN Inc., 811 F.3d 371 (10th Cir. 2016); (10th Cir. 2016) (massage therapy students were not employees entitled to be paid for giving massages to the public which was required as part of their training). If you have heard about an applicant being required to undergo a "working interview," without being paid, this is often the legal mechanism for doing so. Applicants are not usually "trainees," but in some instances an applicant may be asked to demonstrate his or her skills. For example, it is common for a restaurant to require an applicant for a chef position to show how he would prepare a dish or a trucking company to make an applicant show how she would handle a large vehicle. See *Nance v. May Trucking Co.*, No. 12-cv-01655-HZ (9th Cir., Mar. 29, 2017) (truck driving applicant's mandatory, three-day-long "orientation" program was not compensable since it was part of a valid application process).

Interns are persons involved in education or training programs that are "designed to provide students with professional experience in the further-ance of their education and training and are academically oriented for their benefit." Department of Labor, Wage and Hour Division, "Fact Sheet 71: Internship Programs Under The Fair Labor Standards Act" (January 2018), https://www.dol.gov/whd/regs/compliance/whdfs71.pdf. In 2018, the Department of Labor adopted a seven-part test to determine whether a person can be an unpaid intern: (1) the extent to which the intern and the employer clearly understand that there is no expectation of compensation; (2) the extent to which the internship provides training that would be similar to that which would be given in an educational environment, including the clinical and other hands-on training provided by educational institutions; (3) the extent to which the internship is tied to the intern's formal educa-tion program by integrated coursework or the receipt of academic credit; (4) the extent to which the internship accommodates the intern's academic commitments by corresponding to the academic calendar; (5) the extent to which the internship's duration is limited to the period in which the intern-ship provides the intern with beneficial learning; (6) the extent to which the intern's work complements, rather than displaces, the work of paid employ-ees while providing significant educational benefits to the intern; and (7) the extent to which the intern and the employer understand that the internship is conducted without entitlement to a paid job at the end of the internship. The DOL makes clear "no single factor is determinative"; instead, the "economic reality" of the intern-employer relationship governs. Unpaid internships in the public sector and for non-profit charitable, religious, civic, or humanitar-ian organizations "are generally permissible."

Volunteers are individuals who perform hours of service for a public agency for civic, charitable, or humanitarian reasons, without the promise, expecta-tion, or receipt of compensation for services rendered. 29 C.F.R. § 553.101. See DOL Wage and Hour Opinion Letter FLSA 2019-2 (March 14, 2019). The FLSA contains no similar provisions with respect to private sector employees. See Department of Labor, Wage and Hour Division, "Fact Sheet #14A: Non-Profit Organizations and the Fair Labor Standards Act (FLSA)" (August 2015), https://www.dol.gov/whd/regs/compliance/whdfs14a.pdf.

36: WEATHER CLOSURE

See 29 C.F.R. §541.602(a). See also U.S. Department of Labor Opinion Letter, FLSA2005-46, October 28, 2005, https://www.dol.gov/sites/dolgov/files/WHD/legacy/files/2005_10_28_46_FLSA.pdf; U.S. Department of Labor Opinion Letter, FLSA2005-41, October 24, 2005, https://www.dol.gov/whd/opinion/.

37: NLRA

NLRA, 29 U.S.C. § 157 reads as follows:

Employees shall have the right to self-organization, to form, join, or assist labor organizations, to bargain collectively through representatives of their own choosing, and to engage in other concerted activities for the purpose of collective bargaining or other mutual aid or protection, and shall also have the right to refrain from any or all of such activities except to the extent that such right may be affected by an agreement requiring membership in a labor organization as a condition of employment as authorized in section 158(a)(3) of this title.

See *The Boeing Co.*, 365 NLRB No. 154 (2017); *Lowe's Home Centers, LLC*, Case No. 19-CA-191665 (NLRB 2018).

38: POLITICS

Heffernan v. City of Paterson, 136 S. Ct. 1412, 194 L. Ed. 2d 508 (2016).

"Bumper Sticker Insubordination: A Kerry fan gets fired, and then hired, for her politics," *Slate Magazine*, September 14, 2004, https://slate.com/news-and-politics/2004/09/the-insubordinate-bumper-sticker.html.

"Worker fired for heckling president," *Washington Post*, August 23, 2004, http://archive.boston.com/news/nation/articles/2004/08/23/worker_fired_for_heckling_president.

"Google discrimination case first brought by James Damore can proceed," *The Mercury News*, June 7, 2019, https://www.mercurynews.com/2019/06/07/google-discrimination-case-first-brought-by-james-damore-can-proceed/.

39: SOCIAL MEDIA

Briskman v. Akima, LLC., Case No. 2018-5335, complaint (Circuit Ct., Fairfax Cty., Va., filed April 4, 2018); "The Woman Who Flipped Off Trump Has Won an Election in Virginia," *The New York Times*, November 6, 2019, https://www.nytimes.com/2019/11/06/us/juli-briskman-virginia-election.html.

"Curt Schilling, ESPN Analyst, Is Fired Over Offensive Social Media Post," *The New York Times*, April 20, 2016, https://www.nytimes.com/2016/04/21/sports/baseball/curt-schilling-is-fired-by-espn.html.

"Man fired over obscene Chrysler tweet is sorry," *Associated Press*, March 17, 2011, http://www.nbcnews.com/id/42132041/ns/business-autos/t/man-fired-over-obscene-chrysler-tweet-sorry/#.XnoWJG5FyUl.

"Fired for saying job was boring on Facebook," *Express UK*, February 27, 2009, https://www.express.co.uk/news/uk/86663/Fired-for-saying-job-was-boring-on-Facebook.

"Fired Flight Attendant Finds Blogs Can Backfire," *The New York Times*, November 16, 2004, https://www.nytimes.com/2004/11/16/business/fired-flight-attendant-finds-blogs-can-backfire.html.

Moreno v. Hanford Sentinel, Inc., 172 Cal. App. 4th 1125 (Cal. Ct. App. 2009).

"Tweeted out of a job: The "Cisco Fatty" story," *Network World*, March 18, 2009, https://www.networkworld.com/article/2234939/tweeted-out-of-a-job-the-cisco-fatty-story.html.

Pietrylo v. Hillstone Restaurant Group, No. 06-5754, 2009 WL 3128420 (D.N.J. Sept. 25, 2009).

Ehling v. Monmouth-Ocean Hospital Service Corp., 961 F.Supp.2d 659 (D.N.J. 2013).

"Charlottesville white nationalist demonstrator loses job at libertarian hot dog shop," *The Washington Post*, August 14, 2017, https://www.washingtonpost.com/news/food/wp/2017/08/14/charlottesville-white-nationalist-demonstrator-fired-from-libertarian-hot-dog-shop/.

"More Nazis Are Getting Identified And Fired After Charlottesville," *Huff Post*, August 16, 2017, https://www.huffpost.com/entry/more-nazis-are-getting-identified-and-fired-after-charlottesville_b_599477dbe-4b0eef7ad2c0318.

Doe v. XYC Corp., 887 A.2d 1156 (N.J. Super. Ct. App. Div. 2005).

The Boeing Company, 365 NLRB No. 154 (Dec. 14, 2017).

Garcetti v. Ceballos, 547 U.S. 410 (2006).

Curran v. Cousins, 509 F.3d 36 (1st Cir. 2007).

40: CONFEDERATES

Storey v. Burns International Security Services, 390 F.3d 760, 761 (3rd Cir. 2004).

Swartzentruber v. Gunite Corp., 99 F. Supp. 2d 976 (N.D. Ind. 2000).

See also *Chaplin v. Du Pont Advance Fiber Sys.*, 293 F.Supp.2d 622, 628 (E.D.Va.2003) (finding "Confederate-American" not a protected class under Title VII); *Williams v. Frank*, 757 F.Supp. 112 (D.Mass.1991) ("Southernness is not a protected trait"). The EEOC case mentioned is *Dawson v. Donahoe*, EEOC, Appeal No. 0120114186 (February 8, 2012), https://www.eeoc.gov/decisions/0120114186.txt. The Alabama case is *Carter v. Daehan Solutions Alabama LLC*, Case No. 2:07-CV-988-WKW [WO](M.D. Ala., February 1, 2010). Rex Duke's case is *Duke v. Hamil*, 2014 WL 414222 (N.D.Ga. February 4, 2014).

"General Lee From 'Dukes of Hazzard' Losing Its Confederate Flag," *Yahoo News*, June 23, 2015, https://www.yahoo.com/news/general-lee-from-dukes-of-hazzard-losing-its-122294326432.html.

"NASCAR announces ban on Confederate flags from all races, events and properties," *USA Today*, June 10, 2020, https://www.usatoday.com/story/sports/nascar/2020/06/10/nascar-bans-confederate-flag-all-races-events-and-properties/5337579002/.

41: SECRET RECORDING

See *Bodoy v. North Arundel Hospital* 945 F. Supp. 890 (D. Md. 1996); *Hernandez v. McDonald's Corp.*975 F. Supp. 1418 (D. Kan. 1997).

See also *Heller v. Champion International Corp.*, 891 F.2d 432 (2d Cir. 1989) (recording alleged proof of age discrimination). See, e.g., *Coulter v. Bank of America*, 28 Cal. App. 4th 923, 33 Cal.Rptr.2d 766 (1994) (In employee's sexual harassment case, in which he relied on 100 secretly-recorded conversations with his co-workers, the co-workers and the employer prevailed on their counterclaims for common law invasion of privacy and violation of California's privacy law in the total amount of $132,000).

Federal wiretap law is found in Title III of the Omnibus Crime Control and Safe Streets Act of 1968, amended by the Electronic Communications Privacy Act of 1986 (ECPA), which makes it unlawful for an individual to intentionally intercept or disclose any "wire, oral or electronic communication." 18 U.S.C. §§ 2510 et seq. Prior consent by one of the parties to the communication is an allowed exception. 18 U.S.C. § 2511(2)(c). Most states have wiretapping laws modeled on federal law. Most states are "one-party" consent states, meaning that an individual can record—even surreptitiously—a conversation to which they are a party. A few states—California, Connecticut, Florida, Illinois, Maryland, Massachusetts, Montana, New Hampshire, Pennsylvania, and Washington—are "two-party" consent states, meaning, in most cases, all parties to a conversation must consent. Employers should check with legal counsel and a Human Resources professional before adopting a policy prohibiting recording. The National Labor Relations Board, in the past, has condoned an employee secretly tape recording meetings with managers in which the employee reasonably believes discipline may result unless the employer has a policy against tape recording in compliance with federal and state law. *Hawaii Tribune-Herald*, 356 N.L.R.B. No. 63 (2011), affirmed 2012 U.S. App. LEXIS 7999 (D.C. Cir. April 20, 2012).

42: POLYGRAPH

The Employee Polygraph Protection Act is found at 29 U.S.C. §§ 2001 et seq.

43: ELECTRONIC MONITORING

See 2007 Electronic Monitoring & Surveillance Survey from American Management Association (AMA) and The ePolicy Institute at https://www.amanet.org/articles/the-latest-on-workplace-monitoring-and-surveillance/.

"This Call May Be Monitored for Tone and Emotion," *Wired*, March 19, 2018, https://www.wired.com/story/this-call-may-be-monitored-for-tone-and-emotion/.

See, e.g., Smyth v. Pillsbury Co., 914 F. Supp. 97 (E.D. Pa. 1996) (Employer fired employee for sending offensive messages on company e-mail system. Employee's invasion of privacy claim failed, even though employer's policy stated that e-mail communications would remain private and confidential, since employee should not have had reasonable expectation of privacy in company's e-mail system.).

Federal wiretap law is found at 18 U.S.C. §§ 2510 et seq. The federal Omnibus Crime Control and Safe Streets Act of 1968 currently provides that it is unlawful to "intentionally intercept . . . any wire, oral or electronic communication." The penalties for violating the federal wiretap law are substantial, including up to 5 years in prison, and up to $250,000 in fines for individuals or $500,000 for organizations. An aggrieved employee also has a private civil cause of action in which damages are at least the greater of $100 per day or $10,000, plus attorneys' fees. Each state has its own wiretap law which may vary from federal law. Many state laws have exceptions, like federal law, that allow for monitoring of phone conversations.

Deal v. Spears, 780 F. Supp. 618 (W.D. Ark. 1991), *aff'd*, 980 F.2d 1153 (8th Cir. 1992).

Smith v. Devers, 2002 WL 75803 (M.D. Ala., Jan. 17, 2002).

44: HIDDEN CAMERAS

Walker v. City of Pocatello, Case No. 4:15-cv-00498-BLW (D. Id. January 31, 2018).

A case involving the need for narrowly tailored video surveillance of employees is *Hernandez v. Hillsides, Inc.*, No. S147522, 2009 Cal. LEXIS 7804 (Cal. S. Ct., August 3, 2009). An employer intruded on an employee's "zone of privacy" by videoing inside his office but did not invade the employee's privacy by focusing a hidden camera on his computer workstation only. The California Supreme Court recommended that employers should notify employees of the prospect of video surveillance on the premises, including offices, to reduce the risk of invasion of privacy.

See *Colgate Palmolive Co*, 323 NLRB 82 (1997) (employer installed hidden cameras to deter employee theft and vandalism on the premises; National Labor Relations Board upheld the union's unfair labor practice charge that the use of hidden cameras was a mandatory subject of collective bargaining). See also *Anheuser-Busch, Inc.*, 342 NLRB 49 (2004).

45: FMLA

See FMLA Regulations, 29 C.F.R. 825.113. *Bellanger v. H&E Healthcare, LLC*, No. 10-0667-BAJ-DLD (M.D.La., September 19, 2012).

Made in the USA
Las Vegas, NV
18 January 2022

41733786R00185